THE MORIAD;

OR,

End of the Jewish State.

BY

BEN ASAPH,

A CHRISTIAN JEW OF THE THIRD CENTURY.

TRANSLATED FROM THE SYRIAC HEBREW,

BY

ANSELM KORLSTOFF.

NASHVILLE, TENN.:
PRINTED BY A. A. STITT.
1857.

The Translator to the Editor.

DAMASCUS, (Syria,) March, 1853.

DEAR SIR:

According to promise, I send you my translation of the first Book of the MORIAD, or End of the Jewish State; an Epic Poem, by BEN ASAPH, a Christian Jew of the third century.

I have met with more difficulties than I expected, when I made my engagement with you; and unless you can bring out the work to advantage, my share of the profits will not compensate me for my labor and the many difficulties I have had to surmount. For,

In the first place, my good friend, Abdallah, although a Moslem, is also a real antiquary, and somewhat jealous; so that it took all the strength of the old man's friendship for me, and not a little coaxing, to obtain the original for the length of time that will be necessary to make the translation. Nothing but the service which I had rendered him, which brought on our acquaintance, of which I told you before, and which procured me the first sight of the MORIAD, could have overcome his repugnance to letting me take, from his old *box*, the manuscript to my office. But the good old Moslem really loves me —so I succeeded.

Again, as I informed you, the work is written in the Syriac Hebrew; and though I yield to none in my knowledge of that language, yet the handwriting is far from being good; and many letters, and even words, are wanting. Indeed, it is my opinion, that the author has never copied or corrected his poem; and that the original, now before me, remained in the bureau of the poet till Damascus was taken by the Saracens; and after lying there for centuries, finally came, as an heir-loom, into the possession of my friend Abdallah. But, worse still, many parts are worn off, or obliterated by time, leaving chasms; in which cases, instead of leaving a *hiatus*, I have supplied the deficiency by guess, (as you Yankees say,) as well as I could. In these places, I suspect I have failed most. Though, no doubt, take it as a whole, my version is very imperfect; for in addition to all the above-mentioned difficulties, I am (as you well know) agent for the house of the Rothschilds, in this part of the world; so that I can truly plead want of time, as an excuse for the many imperfections you may detect in the copy I send you.

Thus far, as relates to myself, and errors as translator: of the merit or demerit of the poem, or poet, I have little to say. You and the world must judge of them. But I will observe, that the Syriac Hebrew is not a language well suited to poetry. It is rather harsh, and laconic; so that, short and abrupt as my version appears, it has more amplitude than the text! It is only in the more perfect languages you will find the best poets or poems.

The time in which Ben Asaph wrote, and the subject he chose, rendered it impossible for him to make the MORIAD a great Epic Poem. History, and the theology of the day, confined him! They gave him no *Epic* hero—nor could he dare to make one. The outlines of the *Destruction* of Jerusalem were matter of history, and well known. Titus, though a great prince and good general, was no *Epic* hero; nor would the knowledge of the day let him be made one. Simon and John were tyrants—mere Rolands and Robespierres; nor could they be made any-thing else. Phineas, Lysander, and Salathiel, on the other side; and Sempronius, Manlius, and Maxus, on the other, were all brave warriors, but could not be made *Epic* heroes! Milton made Messiah do some wonders in heaven, but he could not make him his hero! Indeed, he has none. Satan comes the nearest; for he went through much, suffered much, fought well, planned well, and finally succeeded—but Paradise Lost is without a hero; yet lives in glory! The MORIAD, also, is without a Hero; but whether it will live at all, is another thing.

Ben Asaph was equally circumscribed by the theology of his day, as to Elevating *Machines*. Homer was cumbered with them; he had the gods, big and little, lying round him like tools; and no one can now say him nay; for it was the faith of his time! Milton could have Messiah raging through heaven on his chariot, and good and bad angels fighting under spear and shield, in the guise of tremendous giants, and this without offence to good taste; for his action is laid at a time when there was nobody else to fight. Now, for all this, our poet has "fallen on evil days!" He did not dare (who would, under the history and theology of the day?) make good angels attack and devils defend Jerusalem; or bring Messiah forward, under dreadful panoply, in gigantic form, hewing down the Jews as Achilles did the Trojans! History, and the *then* faith, would not permit this; and he wisely forbore. Witchcraft and demon-possession was all the machinery time had left him; and of them, I am sorry to say, he has made but a very timid use! I think he might have worked them to more purpose! Hence the MORIAD is too historic—it is not daring and unbounded enough for a great Epic, even if it had not other faults. But considering the *action* of his poem, and the time in which he wrote, Ben Asaph could not, perhaps, have safely sailed in higher latitudes. He could not take Homeric or Miltonic liberties; for he did not stand on their *unknown* grounds.

I would advise you to publish in numbers, half a book each, which, on an average, will contain about 550 verses, fifteen or sixteen of which number will comprise the work. Should it ever be thought worth while to give the numbers a volume shape, I will add a preface, giving all the account I can gather of the author, his birth, death, and whether he left any other works beside the MORIAD.

You will, for your own advantage, try and bring out the poem by subscription, notices, &c., as well as you can. I shall send the second Book the first opportunity. In the mean time, I remain yours, &c.,

Very respectfully,

ANSELM KORLSTOFF.

BOOK I.

The Decree.

Caius, walking in his Palace, and stimulated by Byblus, decrees to have divine honors paid him—The Gentiles receive it well—The Jews are thrown into consternation—The Golden Eagle is displayed on the porch of the Temple—The Jews assemble in sedition—Judeas harangues them—The Golden Eagle is cut down—The Jews dispersed by the Roman guard, in Antonia—The acts of Phineas—Ten of the Jews who cut down the Eagle taken, and sentenced to the cross next day—The Chiefs of Jerusalem meet by night in council—Their debate and sundry arguments—Judeas cuts it short by stating that the war was commenced already; how that the Romans had attacked Salathiel, Prince of Napthalia, in his own house, who defeated them, and then went and surprised Massada—They resolve to storm Antonia—The attack—Dreadful conflict under the walls—The combatants parted by a storm of wind and rain—The Romans agree to release their prisoners and retire to Cestus—The Jews exult, and hold a great feast to the Lord—The Zealots in private council doom the peace-party to death, as friends of Rome—This, and their dances and social sins, offensive to heaven.

The wrath Divine, which sunk the Jewish state,
And Salem piled in heaps, O muse, relate.
That burning wrath, which o'er Moriah spread,
And choked the Kidron with th' untimely dead!
And O! thou Spirit pure, th' Inspiring One,
Which rapt in vision the beloved John,
Who, on the Lord's day, in his exiled home,
Showed him things present, past, and things to come!

Be thou my muse! For thou canst deeds unfold,
Though hid by ages, over ages roll'd:
Say who the agent; how that war began,
Which poured such vengeance on offending man.

'Twas Rome's vain Emperor; for as Caius strode
His palace hall, (magnificent abode,)
In which a thousand lamps, profusely fed
With oil perfumed, a mellow radiance shed,
While gorgeous hangings, rich with Tyrian dye
And Egypt's azure, rivalling the sky;
Festooned with crimson, gold, and diamonds bright,
Added new radiance, and more sparkling light—
As through this dome, in his rich purple robe,
(Which in soft folds down to the carpet flow'd,)
He walked—then stood—his heart beat high with pride,
"And this, and all the world is mine," he cried.
"East, West, and North, and Afric's burning sky,
Beholds my triumphs, sees my eagles fly!
Mars, worshipped as the dreadful God of War,
Excels me not, when on my splendid car
I dash through hosts: Apollo's form divine,
Though beauteous, is surpassed, I think, by mine;
And for sweet music, from the sounding lyre,
Notes swelled to war, or soft with sweet desire,
Though he's the God of song, I well might dare
To claim like honors, and with him compare.
Why should I not, then, 'mongst the Gods be placed?
With worship, and with equal honors graced?"

While thus the tyrant spoke, or would have spoke,
His proud, vain musings by his slave were broke;
Byblus, a freedman from the Isle of Crete,
Of mean appearance—great in smooth deceit—

(By many wiles, with sycophantic art,
He gained at last th' imperial tyrant's heart;)
Entering with bows, he took th' accustomed stand;
Then said, "Great Cæsar, lo! at thy command,
Thy slave has come—and now would prostrate fall,
And worship thee, as sovereign of all!
Honors should to thee as a God be paid,
And offerings duly on thy altars laid!"
Urged by some demon, thus his fulsome words
Chimed in, and seemed an echo of his lord's.

The tyrant smiled, and aped a Jove-like nod,
And cried, "Byblus, you're right: I'll be a God!
Soon shall the splendid, rich Diana's fane,
The world's seventh wonder, on the Asian plain,
Receive my statue: in famed Delphos, too,
I'll place my altars, and have worship due:
In great Minerva's Temple soon I'll stand,
Beside the Goddess, in her Attic land!
My ensigns (1) soon shall blaze on the proud porch
Of every temple and of every church.
The Judean Temple, on Moriah's top,
Called, by those bigots, Earth's most holy spot,
There their strange God, invisible, alone,
No more shall hold an undivided throne:
Within their Sanctum shall the world behold
My image, godlike, glittering with gold!
This is decreed—so with to-morrow's sun,
Command our governors that the work be done."

Fame soon this fiat through the empire sent,
And all the Gentile nations seemed content;
But when this mandate, from imperial Rome,
(Sad harbinger of many woes to come,)

Fame spread through Judea, with each passing gale,
Spread o'er her mountains, and swept down each vale,
Like the Simoom—when its hot sultry breath
Comes tainted from the distant fields of death
And withers crowds—so, mentally o'erthrown,
Israel sent forth one universal groan!
But most the Zealots wailed the threatened crime,
And profanation of their sacred shrine!
Thus night fell down on Judea's troubled coast,
A factious people, fated to be lost.

But when the rising sun, with orient light,
Drove down to western seas the yielding night,
When o'er Asphaltes shot his slanting rays,
And wrapt Moriah in a golden blaze,
Vast crowds of Jews filled all her sacred courts,
Enraged all gazing on the Temple's porch,
Where the Imperial eagle's wings, spread wide,
Five cubits' length, displayed on either side;
The ruffled arching neck, and fiery eye,
Seemed in the act of stooping from on high
On dangerous prey!—Murmurs from man to man,
With lightning speed, through all the concourse ran.
At length Judeas, of the Asmonean line,
(A hero zealous of the law divine,)
Arose majestic, and with bearing proud
Waved round his arm, and thus addressed the crowd:

"Ye sons of Jacob, lo! the day has come,
Big with the fate of Israel, or Rome.
Yon heathen ensign on God's Temple spread,
But—-but precedes pollution still more dread!
Our Holiest of *all Holies* soon must hold
The tyrant's image bright with heathen gold.

His altars soon will smoke with flesh abhorred,
Placed by the sacred altar of the Lord!"
A smothered groan of rage ran through the throng,
Checked by their fears.—The hero then went on:

"Was 't not enough?—ye priests and princes, say!
Ten years we 've been the proud oppressor's prey;
Our priests and rulers into exile driven,
Our fruitful vales to heathen pillage given:
From Lebanon, whence Jordan's founts flow down,
And lofty Hermon, with his snow-capped crown;
From hills and vales, whence sacred Jordan flows,
Down to the awful lake of sin and woes;
From Bashan's pastures, filled with lowing herds,
To Sharon's flowery vales and singing-birds,
Israel lies crushed!—The Roman sword we see
Wave o'er Napthalia—over Galilee!
Through all this once blest land, our fathers' boast,
Our nation's rights are trampled down and lost!
All this (for sake of peace) long time we 've bore;
But shall we suffer on—still suffer more?
Stand trembling by, and see before our face,
Yon sacred Temple covered with disgrace?
The Sanctum of I AM (all gods above)
Defiled by yon rapacious bird of Jove?
The holy law, to our forefathers given,
Midst lightning's flash, and thunder-peals from heaven,
From Sinai's towering top, midst fire and smoke,
Whose basis trembled as Jehovah spoke;
While Moses, God's own friend, who Israel led
Through parching deserts, quaked with holy dread—
Shall we forsake this law, thus given from heaven,
And be, like slaves, to bestial worship driven?

And all for what?—for coward fear of death!
'Tis glorious in such cause to yield our breath.
Brethren, then rise at once, and rend away
Yon ([2]) impious image of the bird of prey!"

Loud shouts succeed the fiery Zealot's speech,
And soon the Temple's roof six heroes reach.
As when from the high cliffs of Thula's isle,
Round which the Northern oceans rage and boil,
The hardy isles-men's rope suspended swings;
Down to the region of the sea-fowl's wings,
With staff in hand, by gentle bounds they move,
Gathering the nestlings which their children love,
Though deep below them raging whirlpools roar,
And surging billows lash the sounding shore!
So from the Temple's roof, with axe in hand,
Three youths descended, of that daring band:
Loud sounds the axe, and axe to axe replies,
And lo! the wing in glittering fragments flies!
Next the fierce head, and ample golden bust,
Torn from their fastenings, sparkle in the dust.
As the demolished ensign struck the ground,
"Glory to God on high!" was echoed round and round.

But now the Roman guard, aroused at last,
(A scout informed the chief of all that passed,)
Quick round Antonia's massive towers they stood,
All ready armed, for deeds of death and blood:
Their chief, Severus, high above the rest,
Stood on a mound, and thus his men addressed:

"Romans! that ensign, which, wherever spread
O'er Rome's brave legions, still to victory led—
That Eagle, in its most resplendent form,
By bigot hands is from yon Temple torn!

The banner of great Cæsar, Rome's chief trust,
Lies, by barbarians trampled in the dust!
Shall we bear this, and let a Jewish mob
Defy our Emperor, for their unseen God?
No! down on all! Let those who did the deed
Be put in bonds—to-morrow they shall bleed!
Should the low groundlings to their coverts fly,
Pursue them not; but let resisters die."

On this the cohort (midst a cloud of spears)
Rushed on the mob, unarmed, and struck with panic fears!
As in a grove, or lawn, strewed thick with leaves,
All seared and dry, the harvest of the trees,
Should a fierce blast rush from the western sky,
The light, dry leaves in wild confusion fly,
To right and left, light whirling on before,
To different points the scattered foliage pour;
So from the Roman shields, and gleaming arms,
Dispersed the Jewish crowd, in wild alarms:
Without defensive arms, to stay was vain,
And to resist was only to be slain.

Yet some old warriors but receded slow,
With step oblique, oft turning to the foe;
As when a hunted boar, in some wild glen,
Close pressed by clamorous hounds and armèd men,
Sidelong retreats; his tusks embossed with foam;
Darts on his foes, then seeks his mountain home;
So Phineas, of the Aaronic line,
Of power superior and of form divine,
Who with reluctance made his slow retreat,
Towards a narrow, unfrequented street,
Pressed by a decade—(Nisus led them on)—
Seized from the side-way a huge craggy stone:

The vain Descurian, with his ported spear,
(His shield was down, he saw no arms to fear,)
Received the shock, and thundered to the ground,
Front, face, and eyes, one undistinguished wound;
To sieze his sword, his weighty spear and shield,
Which with a clang bestrewed that narrow field,
Was with the victor but a moment's feat;
And then as quick and sudden his retreat,
To the small opening of the narrow street.

Now fierce the pursuit; but the Roman's spear
Transfixed the foremost in his hot career;
The sword then gleamed; and him the next before
Fell headless, both parts streaming forth hot gore;
A third, a fourth, a fifth, then quick succeeds;
Third, fourth, and fifth in quick succession bleeds!
There stayed the rest, and fearful drew their breath,
Nor dared to further trace that lane of death;
All but their chief, whose rage and high disdain
Urged him to where a street received the lane:
There loud he cried, "Turn, murderous Jew, and try
Your arm with mine, nor like a coward fly.
By force or magic, you've six Romans slain;
Their corpses bleeding lie in yon dark lane:
If as a warrior you these deeds have done,
Meet me in combat, and I'll call you one.
In me you'll find a foe you'll scarcely kill—
One that will call forth all your strength and skill.
From the great Julian line I trace my birth—
A mighty name, that fills the spacious earth:
Though but the leader of an hundred spears,
Yet mightiest warriors rank me with their peers!
If thou art noble, scorning coming aid,
We'll meet, and one sinks to the Stygian shade."

To whom thus Phineas, (frowning as he spoke:)
"Roman, I'm one who scorns the Roman yoke:
Further, if thou wouldst learn my noble line,
Attend and know, it far transcendeth thine.
From Aaron, first high-priest, (ordained of God,)
Who stood by Moses, when the Nilean flood
Was changed from limpid sweetness into blood;
From him through Phineas, (whose great name I bear,)
Who, through the adulteress, sent the atoning spear.
For the dire plague, for Heaven-forbidden lust,
Strewed crowds on crowds, pale, withering in the dust.
As by the Simoom's blast for this vile sin,
Our fathers fell, all black and withering!
This foul commingling with the Midian fair,
Devised [3] by Balaam, Syria's famous seer,
Brought down this plague, and proved a deadly snare!
With zeal enraged, my sire impetuous went
Where Zimri lay enraptured in his tent,
And through the fulsome pair his javelin sent;
On which the plague was stayed—and would to God
I too might save my country by your blood!
If not—but know I waste no further words;
Our fates must now be settled by our swords."

Here ended parle—and quick each falchion gleams,
And flashes back the sun's retiring beams;
Blow, following blow, from either arm descends;
But the strong shield each warrior's life defends:
At length the Roman's glance an opening spied,
And plunged his weapon through the Hebrew's side.
The strong arched rib turned the sword's point athwart,
Which else had pierced the valiant warrior's heart!
Enraged, in quick return, between the joint
Of helm and cuirass, Phineas drove the point

Of his keen sword: the neck receives the wound,
And the brave Roman thunders to the ground.
That instant Phineas saw new foes in sight,
And knew his life was staked on rapid flight.
This he effected: all the streets were known
To him, and twilight saw him safe at home;
While the centurion, by his sorrowing band,
Was kindly borne to the chirurgeon's hand.
Meantime, ten Jews of the dispersed were caught,
Chief actors, and before the Tribune brought,
Who sentenced them that night to pass in chains,
And next day suffer crucifixion's pains!

The sun had now sunk to the western main,
And peaceful ebon night commenced his reign:
O'er towers and trees he spread his raven wings,
And hid in darkness all terrestrial things;
Fit time to reïllume the light within,
And paint more vivid all the eyes had seen;
A time when mortals, not oppressed with woes,
Sink down to rest in slumberous repose.
But Salem, on that night, slept not profound;
A mental earthquake shook the city round:
Their brethren chained, who, through their zeal for God,
Lay doomed, next morn to stain the cross with blood!
This dread event had through Jerusalem ran,
From house to house, and caught from man to man,
As when a shop, combustible and dry,
Bursts out in flames, and no assistance nigh:
Should strong west winds drive it upon the town,
Fast roll the flames, and blazing showers come down
On half their houses, till, in wild amaze,
They see their town one universal blaze;

So spread the dreadful news from one to all;
And priests and people felt th' instinctive call,
To meet instanter in the Council Hall.

From all parts of the city, vast and great;
From Zion's towers to the Damascus gate;
From the west suburbs to the sacred fane;
From every part, Zealots and warriors came.
For Salem's chief alone, for every tribe,
From Jordan's springs to Carmel's flowery side;
From Mamre's oak, where God with Abram stood,
To Dan's cool fountains, source of Jordan's flood,
Were many chiefs, whom business or fate
Had brought to the metropolis of the State
At this sad juncture: they with equal zeal
Pressed forward to consult the public weal.
Silence obtained, Annas, the great High Priest,
Slowly arose, and thus the crowd addressed:

"Brethren and Princes, fathers of the State,
What calls us here is needless to relate:
Ten of our brethren, chained, are doomed to death,
In lingering pains to pant away their breath!
It seems to me that dreadful day draws near,
Foretold, long since, by many a holy seer:
A sad alternative is more than nigh,
When we must bow as slaves, or freemen die!
But how we may avert the captive's fate,
Is now the point—of that we now debate.
There only are two ways—there are no more:
One, is to sue for mercy, beg, implore—
Or rise in arms with all Jerusalem's power,
And scale the ramparts of Antonia's tower.
What 's the best, let some advise."—Then Jeptha rose,
Around his hand and fiery glance he throws;

So large his ample chest, so dark his frown,
It seemed to cast portentous darkness round.
He came from where the Jor, swift rolling on,
Receives the Dan, and thus unites in one;
Whence, over rocks, the mingled billows break,
And roll impetuous down to Merom's lake:
"I rise," he cried, "to say, if ruled by me,
To Rome's proud power no Jew shall bend the knee;
No prayer be offered; no atonement made;
First let Jerusalem be in ashes laid!
What then! Why, rise to war—war to the knife,
And save our brethren—or each lose his life!
Soon as the morning sun salutes the skies,
Let all Jerusalem's noble warriors rise
In arms of death; and should they dare deny
To yield their captives up to liberty,
Tear down the tower, or undermine its walls,
And slay the tyrants, as the turret falls!
Does any fear to take this noble course,
Made cowards thinking of the heathen's force?
Does any think I am too bold in words?
This arm shall make them good, midst clashing swords;
This sword, which, when Vespasian's robber host
Swept over Ashur and Napthalia's coast,
Was often drenched in gore, and thinned the ranks
Of the marauders, on swift Jabbok's banks!
Nor deem that singly I this ardor feel;
Thousands on thousands burn with equal zeal;
Let but this battle-cry be flung abroad,—
'Our nation's freedom, and the Sword of God;'
Let but the Judean banner float on high,
And 'Victory, or death!' will thousands cry;
While signal-signs will show that aid from Heaven
Shall to the asserters of the law be given!

I am for force—for war! You have my mind;
Now let us hear how others are inclined."
Deep murmurs of approval, fierce and loud,
Like air disturbed, soon circled round the crowd.

Then Socius spoke, (he dwelt on Zion's hill,)
A lawyer rich and learned, though honest still:
"Elders and Chiefs," he said, "I feel no less
The nation's danger and our deep distress,
Than those whose cry is war; nor is my hate
Less fixed against the oppressors of the State;
Nor will the minions of rapacious Rome
More spare my coffers, or respect my home,
Than any present. But to rush to war,
I deem the work of madness and despair!
Have those whose zeal would urge us to that course
Thought of their legions—that o'erpowering force
Which Rome's dread tyrant at his pleasure wields—
Those towering helmets and those brazen shields
Which still have triumphed o'er a hundred fields?
On Danube's frozen plains and rushing flood,
What tribe or nation have their power withstood?
The valiant Gauls, who nobly stood their ground,
Are slain, or mourn their land in bondage bound.
The giant Germans stopped not their career,
But sunk beneath the brazen shield and spear;
Nor North alone, but Afric's burning sands,
Where Hannibal once issued forth commands,
With conquered Nile, the broad Euphrates yields,
And Tigris shoots through subjugated fields;
In fact, from where the Euxine darkly roars,
Westward unto the great Atlantic's shores,
All nations are subjected to the will
Of Rome—and Roman arms subject them still!

Say you 'twas fortune, or a timid foe?
A thousand fields of blood will answer No;
'Twas by discipline, skilful, stern, and rough,
And powerful arms, wielded in armor proof.
I've seen their legions, and with awe admired
How all the mass was with one soul inspired:
They marched, they wheeled, evolved, re-marched again,
Exact as heaven's host o'er the ethereal plain—
All armed complete: their helmets and broad shields,
When joined, strong-roofed their wide embattled fields,
From which, beneath the sun's reflecting rays,
Streamed forth a wide and sight-subduing blaze;
And as they marched across th' extended plain,
They seemed a moving continent of flame!

Such are their arms and training; nor no less,
The wealth and plundering power this race possess.
What temple midst surrounding nations stands,
Not pillaged by their sacrilegious hands?
The votive offerings, and most holy things,
The people's tribute, and the gift of kings;
Our sacred fane, where God's Shekinah shone,
Old Crassus pillaged for himself or Rome:
All, all were swept, and the vast coffer fills
Of earth's proud Empress, on her seven-fold hills!
Nor less their engines of o'erwhelming war,
Their catapults, death-dealing from afar,
And battering-rams, before whose impulse powers,
To their foundations shake the strongest towers;
Hurled by a thousand men, rock walls are vain;
The walls soon totter, and bestrew the plain!
Against such veteran troops, such wealth, such arms,—
A power that shakes all nations with alarms,—

Alas! my brethren, how can we contend!
Say what our means, and what the final end?
And first our means:—Some hunters, (brave, no doubt,)
Shepherds, vine dressers, and a mixed-up rout
Of citizens and factious robbers, sent
To lead us, spell-bound, to our punishment:
Men more disposed to trample on all laws,
Than fight as patriots in their country's cause!
By troops like these, half-armed, unpaid, untrained,
Can victory and freedom be obtained?
With such a force, can we, with hope, oppose
The mighty power of such unconquered foes?
Fathers, believe it not—nor yet believe
That supernatural power we shall receive:
So deep our nation's sins, (all unforgiven,)
Forbids vain hopes of miracles from Heaven!
What, then, the end? Your city overthrown,
And desolation wide still marching on,
You then will see whole streets enwrapt in fire,
And smoke and flames from all your domes aspire!
Then will you hear your dying fathers' sighs,
Your ravished maidens' and your matrons' cries;
You'll see our Temple, and its sacred floor,
Hemmed round with heaps of slain and streams of gore;
And worse, ah! worse—yon glorious fabric burns—
Flames up to heaven, then down to ashes turns!
Such is the end—unless from war you cease,
Bow to the yoke, and safety seek in peace."
Tears streaming from his eyes, he then sat down
Midst smothered sobs and sighs responsive round.

Then Phineas slowly rose: his wounded side
Induced much weaknes, as he thus replied:

"The arguments, I own, have power and weight,
Which Socius deems it duty thus to state.
The power of Rome is great, we all must know,
And Israel's weak, compared with such a foe,
And dreadful our defeat.—But we are brave.
Hebrews will fight before an opening grave;
When roused to arms by wrongs, although untrained,
Their rush by veterans cannot be sustained:
Each individual reckless of his life,
Still comes off victor in the single strife.
But the last evening, six proud slaves of Rome,
I, in succession, sent to their long home;
Nor do I doubt that many thousands are
My match in prowess—as devoid of fear!
'Tis discord, 'tis disunion, that I dread;
That baleful pest, through all the nation spread;
Some fierce for war, and some to peace inclined,
Cursed with a timid, base, life-loving mind;
And half of those who such bold patriots seem,
Care not for country, but of plunder dream.
Should this disunion last, with grief I own
All hopes of victory and of freedom's gone!
Would Israel rise, from Beersheba to Dan,—
In union rise, united as one man,—
The largest army Rome so far could send,
In blood and carnage soon would meet its end!
The heathen nations, all together joined,
Would fly before us, if we were combined.
Firm and united Israel's sons might stand,
A wall of fire around our holy land!
Nor do I think our sins, though unforgiven,
Would turn aside the saving arm of Heaven:
As Abram's seed, (although we feel the rod,)
We heir the promises of Abram's God.

'I'll be a God to thee and to thy seed,'
Has been made good in times of deepest need.
See yon Assyrian camp, without your town,
Where nine score thousand foes, in health, lay down:
Heaven's angel waved his sword, and furious drove
Myriads of death-tipped arrows from above—
Invisible the wounds, but instant death
With corpses filled the camp: none drew a second breath!
Was Judah sinless then? Yet God heard prayer,
And saved our fathers in their last despair!
More instances there are. But I am weak—
My late wound bleeds afresh—let others speak,
Rome grants no pardon to such men as me:
My fate is sealed, unless Jerusalem's free."
The sinking chief by friends was kindly borne,
And safely couched in his desired home.

Meanwhile the question, in the Council Hall,
Of peace or war, deep pressed the minds of all;
When Eldad, from the plains of Jericho,
Gravely arose, deliberate and slow:
"I come," he said, "from where this aid from Heaven,
In ancient times, was to our fathers given.
The heaps of rubbish on our fertile plains
Of Jericho, (the lingering last remains,)
Points out the scene, where, at the trumpet's sound,
Her massive walls lay level with the ground.
Our God did this—Nay, more: I've wondering stood,
And viewed the high spring-tide of Jordan's flood;
With veneration marked that sacred ford,
Where God's bare will, like a dissevering sword,
Cut off the waters; and the floods below
Throbbed down to Sodom's silent sea of woe,

While those above, walled up by heavenly force,
Rolled gently back, refluent to their source;
And thus the ransomed tribes, dry-shod, passed o'er,
And pitched their tents on Canaan's promised shore.
'Tis said we are too few; by factions rent;
So wicked, aid from Heaven will not be sent.
Thus thought Elijah once, and raised his prayer
As if in vengeance half, and half despair:
'They've dug thy altars down, thy prophets slain;
Of all, O Lord! I, only I remain.'
But what said God? 'I have reserved to me
Seven thousand men, who never bent the knee
To Baal.' And for this little faithful band,
God spread his ægis o'er the apostate land!
Seven times seven thousand, in this town alone,
Are found, who never bowed to Baal, or Rome!
Then trust in God; for holy men of old,
Prophets of God, have glorious days foretold,
When great Messiah, that all-conquering One,
The son of David, shall ascend his throne,
Subdue the nations, all our foes disperse,
And reign the Sovereign of the universe!
About this time, 'tis said, he will appear,
And well I trust that grand event draws near,
Perhaps Heaven's hour is at our utmost need,(4)
And Israel first must for transgression bleed.
Now, should Rome's legions round our ramparts lay,
Our faces pale with famine and dismay
When he appears—Oh! what a glorious sight!
His vengeance flaming, and his foes in flight;
His saints pursuing: blood pours down in rills,
And corpses load the valleys and the hills:
His conquering arm will soon all welfare end,
And God's blest kingdom o'er the world extend!"

Great was the applause of those who did believe;
But some the prophecy could not receive.
Of these was Jairus, (from the fertile plains,)
Where lay in heaps proud Corazin's remains. [5]
He was an Essene, virtuous and good,
Averse to war, and all the works of blood.

"Brethren," he said, "I call you to reflect:
God never did a factious race protect.
I pray you also, now, to call to mind,
('Twill make you to your burdens more resigned,)
Our fathers, more than one-third of the time
That Judah's throne was filled by David's line,
By gifts and tribute bought the nation's peace;
And while they did so, saw their wealth increase.
But Zedekiah, when he seized the crown,
By Babylon's aid, and cast his brother down,
He took an oath, by all the powers above,
He would a faithful tributary prove;
Yet (through false prophets) perjured did rebel;
And soon our city and the nation fell!
Pale famine strewed their streets with dead, and moans
Of starving children echoed through their homes!
Did Heaven then save them? No! their prayer it spurns;
Their walls lay levelled, and their Temple burns!
The wretched monarch drags a captive's chain,
And sees before his eyes his children slain:
His last sad sight was that of kindred gore—
The fiend then plucked his eyes—he saw no more!
Shall we not warning take from such deep woes,
Nor madly make a mightier power our foes?
Some prophesy Messiah sóon will come,
And as chaff scatter all the power of Rome!

I speak with trembling, but I've often thought
He's come already, but we know him not.
Jesus of Nazareth, whom you crucified,
Claimed to be Christ; and for that claim he died.
When I look back to that majestic face,
So full of wisdom, dignity, and grace;
With what vast, humble power, he walked this clod,
And worked as with the finger of a God;
When I remember, dead and dying men
His word, or touch, restored to health again;
And at his death (procured by perjured crimes)
What awful wonders! what tremendous signs!—
Dead saints arose, and through the city went;
The Temple's vail from top to bottom rent;
While the earth shook, as if in dread affright,
And the sun's radiance darkened into night!—
When I remember this, I'm forced to fear
He'll come in vengeance, should he now appear!
His choice disciples, the far-famed Eleven,
Who testify they saw him rise to heaven,
Also declare, he had pronounced this doom,—
That of the Temple's buildings, not a stone
Should on another lie, that's not cast down;
While want and war should desolate your town;
And more: that some of the then listening mass
Should live, till all those judgemnts came to pass!
If this be true, we may be well assured [6]
Messiah's arm will wield the Roman sword!"
The Council audience gave, though vexed: at last,
His words their worn-out patience all surpassed.
"Turn out that Christian dog!" some raging said;
Others called loudly, "Cleave th' apostate's head!"
But Elam Judas, of majestic size,
Fearless in combat and in council wise,

Raised high his voice:—"Brethren, I think, with you,
He ought to die, with all his treacherous crew,
Who whines for peace—yet this when time shall fit—
But now, why should this Council longer sit,
Spending our precious time, debating thus
On peace or war? War has determined us!
Our morning's outbreak, and th' heroic deed
Of Phineas' arm, by which six heathen bleed,
Brings vengeance on us in the shape of war,
Or executions—answering every prayer!
But more:—Last evening, late, I did receive
News glorious and authentic, I believe:
So wonderful, if true, its wide alarms
Will force both nations instantly to arms.
Do you wish to know? My post these tidings brings:
That Massada, the pride of mighty kings,
And deemed impregnable, but three days since
Was stormed and taken by Napthalia's prince!
His tribe's brave flag now waves o'er Herod's towers,
And calls around him all the neighboring powers!
My courier did from first to last relate
This glorious action. I can only state
The cause (for want of time) and the event,
Which seems to say, Supernal power was lent!
Informed by spies, or dreams, we know not which,
Cestus believed the brave Salathiel rich;
And that he had with other leaders planned
To rise in arms, and free his native land.
On this he sent a hundred chosen men,
To reach by night the chieftain's lovely glen;
His house thus, under darkness, to surround,
Break, seize his wealth, and bring the owner bound.
Part Milo did with skill, and laid in wait
His troops. Then thundered at the castle gate:

The answer was, the trumpet's signal-blast,
That all who heard should arm and come in haste,
Armed as they might, with bludgeon, spear or sword,
To save the castle and defend their lord.
Meantime the chieftain, midst these wild alarms,
With his brave son, assumed their ready arms;
Then rushed impetuous to the castle gate,
Inflamed by danger and vindictive hate;
Demanded their demands; which quick were told
By the centurion; cool, collected, bold,
The hero thus replied: "You say I must
Bring forth my treasures, yield them to your trust;
Then have my hands bound—yes, behind my back!
If restive, tightly; but if humble, slack;
Then mount a led-horse, and submissive come
To Cestus—dread procurator of Rome!
And should I his high mandate treat with scorn,
You'll burst my gates, and take my house by storm!
I open then the gate—let who will come,
And take my answer to Imperial Rome.
My arm's still free, and deeply will I write,
In blood, my answer to your lord this night."
Two foremost pressed: one feels Salathiel's sword,
The other's breast Lysander's spear has gored!
The slaughter swells, where'er the heroes stood,
And falling corpses swelled the streams of blood.
The household servants now in aid appear,
Armed as they might, with shovel, club, and spear;
But still the Romans through the gateway pour,
And press the warriors to the mansion door:
By effort toiled, their swords more lightly fell—
When from the mountain rose a mingled yell;
Screams and fierce shouts, and loud triumphant cries,
Roll round the castle, and invade the skies!

Down from the mountains, armed with club and spear,
Three hundred men rushed on the robber's rear;
Then heads fell crushed beneath the bludgeon's blow,
And boar-spears thrust the foemen through and through.
In twenty minutes, (save a few that fled,)
The Roman cohort and their chief lay dead.

Salathiel saw at once the die was cast,
The crisis come, he knew would come at last.
His household sent to a safe friendly glen,
He chose from out his tribe five hundred men,
Then silently marched south, till, the third night,
From a deep vale, they gazed Massada's height;
Then slowly climbed the narrow serpent path,
Like a long line of silent, moving death;
Scaled the first wall, by means I cannot state,
And safely stood before the second gate:
A battering-ram (as placed by heavenly power)
Gave war's first signal to the sleeping tower:
Hurled by two hundred men, its iron head
The solid door in shivered fragments spread:
Bolts, hinges, bars, in all directions fly,
And hissing sing beneath the midnight sky!
The garrison, by those dread sounds alarmed,
To combat poured, all frightened, and half armed:
Then came the infuriate strife, night's pall beneath:
Each party felt 'twas victory or death.
Deep gored Napthalia's boar-spears; and the sound
Of helms and mountain axes echoed round.
Lysander and the prince led on the tide;
Their dreadful sword-strokes fell on every side,
And through the cohorts made a passage wide.
The Roman chief (a demi-giant) cries:
"Yield not the ground to such base enemies;

Mind that your sires were conquerors of the world,
And from their thrones the mightiest monarchs hurled!
Romans, I'll stop those demons which you fear!"
And, bounding forward, raised his sword in air
Above Salathiel's head—but arm and steel,
In death-pain's grip, the following moment fell!
Lysander's arm, and keen Damascus blade,
Thus maimed the chief, who, faint, for mercy prayed;
'Twas granted on surrender—and unarmed,
To go where'er they pleased, safe and unharmed.

And now the conqueror strode to Floraus' room:
His heart was vengeance, and his eyes were gloom:
He found the wretch helpless, through wine and fear,
With only strength to pour a coward's prayer.
"O! do not slay me! spare my life!" he cried.
"What! pity you?" the indignant chief replied:
"What!—you? The vilest wretch that yet has come
From that detested nest of tyrants, Rome!
A human fiend, whose thirst for blood and gold
Was by no pity, by no laws controlled!
A tyrant, red all o'er with tortured blood—
For you, you wretch, a sudden death 's too good;
It were but just, those tortures you did use
Should their keen pains through all your limbs diffuse;
But I forbear." With that the falchion sped,
And clove down to the chin the trembling head!

I've said this much of this thrice-glorious deed,
To prove we are at war, and should proceed
By force of arms, and have our brethren freed.
By acclamation let the vote be given,
And all dissentients to perdition driven.

The word is war—now give it long and loud!
And War! War! War! rose from the excited crowd!

Then Annas, rising, thus: "To-morrow morn,
'Tis now decreed, Antonia's Tower we'll storm.
Death lies before the Jew who does not come,
Whether through cowardice, or love of Rome."

The Council then dissolved, and all sought rest,
Some high in hopes, and some with fears distressed,

When meek-eyed morning looked from Eastern bowers,
And shed Heaven's smiles o'er fields, and flocks, and flowers,
Night's dew-drops, pendant from each flower and spray,
Like diamonds glanced beneath the rising ray;
Then trumpet-blasts announced that Salem's powers
Were gathering to surround Antonia's towers.
As when the populace of Rome pours forth,
When victors triumph, from the north or south,
The various clumps press through each street and lane,
All to one centre, all intents the same;
Till, met from all points, none can further pass,
But form a dense, extended, moving mass:
So came the Hebrew warriors from all parts
Of their vast city, with like vengeful hearts;
The Judean banner, waving o'er them high,
Gold, scarlet, blue, tints of the Egyptian sky;
Till on Moriah's top the squadrons meet,
Crowding the extensive square and neighboring street.

The Roman cohort on the ramparts stood,
And with emotion viewed the living flood;
Their general, with raised arm and accents loud,
Stood forth to gain the attention of the crowd:
Then cried: "Ye princes of Jerusalem,
Why this sedition? Why this host of men?

What do you want, and what is your design?
Let some chief speak, for precious is the time."

The Roman thus—and thus the high-priest replied:
"Release those youths you would have crucified;
Then leave this tower, unharming and unharmed,
With all your stores, in panoply and armed.
Should you, through pride, these easy terms refuse,
Then dread the vengeance of infuriate Jews!
No mercy will be shown, should you oppose
The power resistless which your walls enclose."

To anger moved, the indignant Roman chief
Thus sternly answered, and in acccents brief:
"The slaves you seek, and deem so great a loss,
You soon may find, exalted on the cross:
And should you not disperse and hide at home,
Round every cross a hundred more shall groan,
And all your city hear a general moan!"

Thus the parle ended, and the reverend priest
Passed to the holy Temple, deep distressed.
This was the sign—and clouds of arrows fled
From bows drawn double to the barbed head.
As when from the deep-wooded Taurian Hills,
Whence rapid Tigris draws his thousand rills,
Dense clouds of pigeons, greedy, seeking food,
Whirl o'er a village, to a distant wood;
So clouds of missiles, in successive showers,
Swept o'er the arena of Antonia's towers.
The Romans drop, as when the autumnal blast
Shakes from the oak, o'er rocks, the rattling mast.
Thus from the battlements the unguarded foe,
Fell headlong, crushed upon the rocks below!

Surprised, unarmed, so swift the missiles flew,
Decades were slain, before the rest withdrew.
At length, behind their works, with rage intense,
From their machines fierce vengeance they dispense;
Their catapults and cross-bows, slanting down,
Sent storms of missiles hissing towards the town.
From all their engines on the masses pour
Rocks, spears, and javelins, with heart-sinking roar.
The thundering rocks wide lanes of horror made,
While naked breasts the whizzing darts invade.
The carnage swells around: in vain they pour
Their darts and arrows, in continuous shower;
Safe under covert the disciplined foe
Sent death in storms on all the crowd below.
"Retreat, retreat," the Jewish leaders call;
"Retreat behind the Temple's lofty wall,
Or other safeguard; nor thus vainly die,
Slain by a dastard, hidden enemy!"

This soon was done; but midst the Hebrews slain,
Malchus of Shechem rose, then fell again;
On one sound limb (the other crushed in blood)
The second time he rose, and staggering stood;
This saw a Roman of great pride and power,
And rushed to drag him to Antonia's tower.
The helpless chief he grasped, and would have led
Him, dragged and mangled, o'er the scatter'd dead;
But Judas saw, and with a furious bound
(As lioness bereaved on pilfering hound)
Rushed on the Roman, and with hurried blow
Hurled his gay helmet on the dust below.
The next stroke had been death, but his thick hair
Obliqued the sword, which, with averted share,
Hewed from the hero's head his dexter ear!

His friends perceived, and, like brave friends and true,
Five of his decade to the rescue flew;
Then twice that number of the Hebrews fly
To aid their friends: their shouts invade the sky!
As when the headmost branch of the vast Sinde
Pours down his mountain slopes, south plains to find,
He gathers aids by his commanding roar,
And streams from every side successive pour;
Rivers, not rills, at length roll down their force,
Till wild it spreads, resistless in its course;
So to the combat aid succeeded aid,
Till either host their utmost power displayed.
The Romans durst not their huge engines use;
'Twould slaughter Romans, as it slaughtered Jews!
Forced thus to combat 'gainst such mighty odds,
They roused their courage, and invoked the Gods.
Completely armed, with helmet, shield, and spear,
Their strokes were death: blood streamed through their career.
The infuriate struggle raged and spread around
Antonia's tower, and all the holy ground.
All lack of arms defensive was supplied
By Jewish vengeance and fanatic pride.
As bounding tigers, in their rage secure,
Heedless of spears, at Roman throats they pour:
The foremost as a sheath receives the sword;
The next drags down to earth its hapless lord,
And, in a moment, out his heart's-blood poured!
Thus on both wings, in wild infuriate strife,
The Jews rushed on, regardless of their life:
Wounded or slain, the masses pressed on still,
And died to give their friends a chance to kill!
The two first chiefs that issued to the plain,
And led this conflict, chanced to meet again:

"You circumcised dog!" the Roman cries,
"In a wished hour, again you meet my eyes."
"You heathen wretch!" Judeas cries, "accursed!
Of all idolaters, the basest, worst;
Who meanly pounced upon a wounded man,
But when you felt me, screamed for aid and ran!
To dark Gehenna's pit, now, now descend,
Where worms die not, and fires shall have no end!"
The furious clash of arms succeeds to words;
In fearful circles sweep their weighty swords:
The Hebrew's arm receives a half-spent blow,
Almost the instant that against the foe
He drove his sword's point; but the firm cuirass
Withstood the thrust, that hurled him on the grass.
Upon the chief, prostrate, (as if Heaven smote,)
Judeas plunged; (his sword to splinters broke;)
They rolled, they rose, they fell; but nature's arms
Stopped short of death, or great external harms.
As when two mastiffs, urged by men or boys,
To throttling rush, with snarls, and snaps, and noise;
They grapple, rear, then tumble on the ground,
With stifled growls, and suffocating sound:
Thus they. At length the Hebrew caught his knife,
And ope'd the fountain of the Roman's life:
Raging with pain, he rolled upon his side;
Grasping the dust, he cursed the Jew and died!

Thus raged the mob-like war on every side,
And death wide revelled in the crimson tide.
But when at length the fervid Syrian sun
Had more than half his heavenly circuit run,
The horrid conflict faltered, paused, then ceased;
For dense gloomed clouds rolled wildly from the East,

In deep, dark masses, heaped above the town,
And black Egyptian darkness settled down!
From pole to pole the zigzag lightning sprung,
And peals of thunder bid the tempest come.
As if in signs from heaven of pending woes,
Moriah's mount shook with convulsive throes!
Spires, towers, and Temple, tremble with the shock,
And from the mountains hurls the impending rock!
The aërial giants through the concave roar,
Rend the dark clouds, and bid the torrents pour.
Prone to the earth descends the copious flood,
And corpses float, commingled with their blood.
As when grim bull-dogs, with ferocious heart,
Hold fast their grips, and can't be torn apart;
Should a full tub of water sluice them o'er,
They part—they fly; nor think of combat more;
So the wild tempest and full floods of rain
Drove the unconquered parties from the plain!
The Roman cohorts gained Antonia's gates,
Breathless, yet glad t' escape the impending fates.
The Jewish crowd, each struggling, sought their homes;
Some to low huts, and some to princely domes.

Now, when the dreadful tempest had swept by,
And Sol smiled peaceful from the western sky,
A flag of truce the Jewish council sends,
That both the hosts might save their wounded friends,
And sad inhume their dead! Then, if mild peace
Should not descend, and bid the slaughter cease,
The rising sun should end the short accord,
And recommit the event to the sword.

The truce was granted, ('twas each foeman's wish,)
And to the blood-field weeping kindred rush—

Matrons now childless, and betrothed maids,
And hoary sires, fast sinking to the shades;
Brothers and sisters, all those sacred ties,
With smothered grief their mournful office plies;
The slain consigned to tombs, and every wound
Of mangled patriots with affection bound.
Nor less the Romans like attention paid;
Care for the living—honor to the dead.
Thus war's red banner was in sorrow furled,
And night's deep darkness canopied the world.

Now when, next morn, majestic seemed to rise
The shining ruler of terrestrial skies,
As up heaven's path his flaming orb he rolled,
And all his planetary worlds controlled,
The Jewish leaders called forth all their bands,
Renewed their courage, and re-armed their hands;
Yet from death's engines at safe distance stood,
As fearful of that recent field of blood,
Safe in the Temple; and around the tower,
They placed a strong and overwhelming power;
Resolved by famine to subdue the foe,
As the best method, though it should be slow.

Meanwhile the skilful Roman general saw
Post after post around their fortress draw.
He knew the intent, and instant gave the call
For all his chiefs to meet in council-hall.

"Friends—Officers of Rome!" he thus began—
"Man cannot act beyond the powers of man.
Our ranks are thinned by that dire hour of blood,
Stopped only by a preternatural flood.
Hemmed in by numerous hosts of desperate men,
The infuriate dregs of all Jerusalem,

With not five days' subsistence—say, then, say,
Which is the better and the wisest way?
Yield to their terms?—Or brave their plain designs?
This council's called to ascertain your minds."

On this the bold centurion, Manlius, rose,
And fiercely cried; "All yielding I oppose.
Can Rome's brave cohorts bear to have it said,
For fear of danger, you submission made?
You who, beneath Rome's eagle and your shields,
Have triumphed o'er a hundred bloody fields;
Who, from the rapid Tigris to the Rhine,
Have conquerors marched o'er famine, foes, and clime;
Shall we Rome's brilliant glories now lay down,
And leave as fugitives, the accursed town,
For fear of famine? Why, ere ten days run,
Brave Cestus will to our deliverance come,
And well avenge the deeds those Jews have done.
You have my council—honor loudly calls
Here to remain and guard Antonia's walls."

To whom thus Scarus, second in command,
(Who studied war in the Italian band:)
"I have for Roman fame as much regard,
And hold myself as well for death prepared
As any here; but yet feel bound to say,
'Tis wisdom now to give sedition way.
If Cestus, with his powers, can storm yon gate
In time to save us from impending fate,
Sure, with our aid, he soon may do the same,
And Rome instate in all her power again;
Save waste of blood, and on the rebel Jews,
At fitting time, give vengeance all its dues.

Bravery, though good, is not so great a good
As prudence, which avoids a waste of blood."

In this opinion all the council joined,
And to the Hebrews soon revealed their mind.
The Jewish chiefs, true to their former word,
Exchanged right hands, to bind the firm accord.

As night fell down, the Romans took their march,
And passed beneath the wide Damascus arch:
That night the full-orbed moon, bright, beauteous, fair,
Filled with wild radiance all the Syrian air;
As splendid through heaven's arch sublime she rode,
Her glorious train enveloped half the globe.
The placid seas gleamed bright; and every stream,
Like stripes of silver, gloried in her beam.
As under flaming torches a long train
Of silent mourners leave a sacred fane,
Where, with deep sorrow, they've interred their Lord,
Made sacred by his goodness and his sword;
So Rome's battalia, 'neath those splendid skies,
Marched, breathing vengeance and indignant sighs.
With banners furled, in silent, armed array,
Adown Bethoron's vale they took their way,
And gained their general's camp the following day.

Not thus the Hebrews viewed the lovely light:
All hearts were joyful, and all faces bright.
Through the vast city songs and cymbals rung,
And gratulations flowed from every tongue.
Praise to their chiefs and Heaven resounded loud,
And long hosannas burst from all the crowd.

The high-priest then proclaimed by trumpet's sound
(Whose tones re-echoed from the mountains round,)

A common feast—a solemn sacrifice
To Israel's God, ruler of earth and skies;
That all should come—the greatest with the least—
And hold, next day, the glad fraternal feast
For the release and safety of their friends,
And the great victory which secured those ends.
Then Salem's crowds, though deep in sins immersed,
With shouts and vain presumptuous hopes dispersed.

The trumpet's joyful sound awoke the morn,
Whose opening flush the towers and hills adorn;
A glorious sun, with its ascending rays,
Shrouded the temple in a silvery blaze;
Like a white mountain worthy of a God,
The holy fane in all its glory stood:
When Salem's multitudes with joy arose,
That primal city, (first that history knows,)
Zion's fair daughters, gay in festive dress,
Flower-crowned, with songs to God's high altar press.
Young men and blooming youths, in vestments grand;
Gray sires and chiefs, the guardians of the land;
All to Moriah's Temple held the road,
To sacrifice and feast before the Lord!
Great was the congregation; and sublime
That sight of splendor round the holy shrine!
Then came the chief musicians, with their train,
In grand procession; and their joyous strain
Filled all the air above that sea of heads—
Charms every heart, and round the temple spreads.

Next came the Pontiff Annas, great high priest,
In the rich vestments of his office dressed.
Th' Aaronic mitre on his head was placed,
And "HOLINESS TO GOD" the frontlet graced.

Twelve onyx stones, deep with the names impressed
Of Israel's tribes, hung sparkling on his breast.
Scarlet and blue, his sacerdotal gown,
All rich embroidered, gracefully fell down;
While round the pontiff, of his tribe and blood,
The inferior priesthood in their orders stood.

At trumpet-sound the gathering music ceased,
And to the crowd thus spoke the reverend priest:
"Now let a song of praise rise to the Lord,
And let it rise with loud and full accord:
Let that rapt strain which holy David sung,
Now roll in harmony from every tongue."

On this, the chief musician Shaphan's voice (7)
Was heard, sweet-toned: "Let Israel now rejoice!
Praise ye the Lord, his people—praise your king,
And let high praises round his temple ring!
Let all creation praise him—earth, air, flame,
Sun, moon and stars, give glory to his name!
Let all earth's almoners, that feebly creep,
And all the rolling monsters of the deep;
Let Lebanon, with its tall cedars, join,
And Herman, snow-capped, towering and sublime;
Let the quick lightning, fierce volcanic blaze,
And rolling thunder, sound their Maker's praise:
Let all created things, with one accord,
Loud praises sing—hosannas to the Lord!"
Ten thousand voices the sweet concert raise,
And through Jerusalem send this song of praise;
Which fills the temple, loads each passing gale,
And sinks melodious down fair Cedron's vale.

But now from every point were victims led,
With offerers' hands on every victim's head;

The appropriate priests, to take the bowls of blood,
And sprinkle round the altar, ready stood:
The dexterous flamen then proceed to kill,
And sever all the parts with nicest skill.
The brazen altar, twenty cubits square,
Soon sent its savory odors through the air;
The glowing coals beneath rich morsels burn;
Above the coals, the priests each fragment turn;
The sacred salt from canisters they pour,
And with sweet spices strew the offerings o'er.
But the great altar would not now suffice
For such a wide-extended sacrifice—
Two thousand bullocks and two thousand rams,
A thousand goats, and fifteen hundred lambs;
Hence scores of altars soon were flaming round,
(For all Moriah's mount was hallowed ground;) (8)
Nor less in rich meat-offerings was the toil;
Fine flour, mingled with sweet wine and oil,
Baked in unnumbered pans, with spices dressed,
Which still more savory made the sacred feast.
Meanwhile fit servitors continual went,
Bringing the banquet round to every tent;
The chosen shoulder and substantial chine,
With baked meat-offerings and inspiring wine!
Through all the city, o'er the sacred mound,
Joy went on singing carols round and round;
Excitement wild attuned to songs the crowd,
While incense-vapor spread a spacious cloud!
In vain the songs and odors sought the skies:
A firmament of sins forbade their rise—
Murders, adultery, theft, and every vice,
Polluted all their Psalms and sacrifice!

These sad indictions of a dying State,
Forerunners of inexorable fate,

Were seen that night in Salem—a dark set
Of furious zealots and fell murderers met:
Simon of Gorias village led them on,
And that arch-hypocrite, Gischalias John!
There, in dark conclave, they with oaths decreed
War to the Sacri should at once proceed,
And all peace-pleaders by the poignard bleed.
They strove for glorious freedom and God's law,
Through crimes, the blackest nations ever saw!
The end they seemed to seek was noble, just;
Their means, deeds dark, with cruelty and lust.
Soon through the land their power and edicts spread,
And struck the friends of peace with awe and dread—
A strong minority, who mourning felt
Their bondage a just punishment of guilt.

Nor tyrant cabals through that night alone
Were to all-seeing eye of Heaven made known:
Numbers of leading youths, in splendor gay,
To various saloons took their destined way;
Each with their band, dark pleasures their design;
Each flown with insolence, and lust, and wine. (9)
The appointed domes displayed, when opened wide,
Voluptuous beauties, dressed in radiant pride;
In numbers equal those whose steps invade
The House—as if by assignation made!
Blazing with light, flashed wide the Cupid dome
Where sin-flushed beauties in full dresses shone.
Bracelets of finest gold clasped every arm,
And broidered stomachers concealed no charm;
Jewels, and crisping-pins, and diamonds bright,
Pendent in earrings, glanced commingled light.
Their veils and wimples all were cast aside,
As down the dance with wanton steps they glide.

Their glancing feet, with golden anklets bound,
Gave forth sweet music, with a tinkling sound
From smallest silver bells, which at each move
Seemed serenading higher zones of love.
All was enchanting. As each amorous pair
Paused in the dance, as others did their share,
Words understood still thrilled the fair one's ear.
For near the bottom of this splendid hall
A door stood veiled—and yet well known to all:
Through this screened passage, ever and anon,
A pair, and then another pair, was gone;
And then another—As from that dread steep,
The Gangean falls, drift after drift-woods leap;
So, in succession, partners glide away
To lower chambers, where entranced they lay,
Laying up wrath against the avenging day.
And thus their festal day in sins went down,
And guilt and darkness canopied the town.

BOOK II.

The Advent.

God, in the midst of assembled angels, discloses his dealings with the human family—Tells Christ that the time has come for him to descend, and end the Mosaic *Institution*, and make way for the Gospel—Cestus, with the Roman army, attacks Jerusalem—When he has almost taken it, he suddenly retreats—The cause—He explains it to his army—The approach of Salathiel's band from Massada—Cestus retreats towards Bethhoron—Hard fighting through the day—Salathiel comes up and rallies the flying Jews—Furious combat—The Romans hold their ground—Night separates the parties—Cestus encamps near the gorge of Bethhoron, and Salathiel at some distance in his rear—The Roman army continue their march down the valley—The Jews attack them on both sides from the cliff, and press them in their rear—The Romans endeavor to make battle, but the cliffs are too high for their javelins to kill, or their horsemen to ascend—They march under conjoined shields—The Jews break their cover by rolling large rocks from the cliffs—Their great distress—Salathiel calls upon Cestus to surrender—He refuses—God sends a storm by which the Romans gain a respite—The main body escape, leaving four hundred to disguise their retreat, who are all slain—The single combat of Maxus and Salathiel, and of Manlius and Jephtha—Salathiel is stabbed by a pretended prophet while at supper—Lysander conveys him to Massada—The great rejoicing of the Jews, and their immense spoils.

While thus on earth, in the third heavens above,
Those blissful climes of rectitude and love,
The great I AM—the first, the emphatic ONE—
From vast infinitude, stepped to his throne;

His infinite, his sovereign will compressed
To a majestic form in radiance dressed.
A mount of condensed glory formed the throne,
Round which Heaven's rainbow, arched and fulgent, shone;
The bow of promise to the patriarch given,
Of every hue, dipped in the dyes of heaven.
The throne assumed, from thence the Almighty spoke;
His gracious voice new joys in heaven awoke:

"Ye Cherubs four, your silver trumpets sound,
And let their tones reach heaven's remotest bound,
That summons loud to the four winds be given,
Which calls around my throne the sons of heaven."

He said, and soon the deep-toned message flies
Round the ethereal plain and heavenly skies,
To the remotest tents and emerald towers
Of dominations, princedoms, virtues, powers:
Angels, archangels, through their various grades,
All hear that summons, which all heaven pervades;
And soon from all the wide extended coast
Was seen swift marching the celestial host:
From diamond palaces and glittering domes,
Of hierarchs and powers the happy homes;
O'er heaven's soft pavement, spread with living green,
And flowers sun-bright, studded like stars between;
The empyrean plain, as angels stooped to admire,
Seemed like a sea of glass mingled with fire!
Midst trees of Paradise festooned with flowers,
And odorous gales from amaranthine bowers;
With ensigns floating o'er their ranks above,
Blazoned memorials of their zeal and love,
And different degrees of glory given,
With songs moved on the dignities of heaven!

All on the way, along the heavenly road,
Hung cates ambrosial, and rich nectar flowed!
Nor were heaven's luxuries by heaven's sons forsook;
The angelic bands with love and zest partook.
How vain are those who deem the ethereal hosts
Are airy nothings—shadowy, gaseous ghosts,
Devoid of appetence and sentient joy,
And abstract love and praise their whole employ!
No: they are beings gifted with desire,
Like mortals made, only a little higher:
By full probation rectified, refined,
They rose to heaven through rectitude of mind.
As conquerors over sin and mortal strife,
God judged them worthy of eternal life,
And called them up from worlds, (perhaps like this,)
To walk with him high in the climes of bliss.
By resurrection-power, (so God arranged,)
Their glory was to higher glory changed;
All their capacities enlarged to taste
The full fruition of continual feast.
Nor sensitive alone: their mental powers
Walk wide through nature's intellectual bowers;
Charmed by sweet music of the heavenly kind,
And eloquence, the music of the mind—
Of that celestial kind unknown on earth,
And which to heavenly raptures owes its birth.
Such their angelic nature and employ,
And such the fountains of celestial joy.

And now, from all those sweet, those boundless bowers,
Before Heaven's throne arrive the summoned powers;
Orb within orb, the great hierarchies shone,
And filled their golden seats around the throne;

And next the Deity the holy *Seven,*
God's first-born sons, and great Viceroys of heaven.
The Everlasting Father then thus spoke,
And to assembled heaven his purpose broke:

"O Branch! thou first-born of the Primal Seven,
(To whose high sway my vast Creation's given,)
Within thy rule rolls on yon globe, the earth,
Where late you stooped to be of mortal birth;
Where the new Institution, and thy reign,
To stiff-necked Jews you preached, and preached in vain:
Though signs and wonders proved you came from God,
They raged the more, and clamored for thy blood!
Thy voice then warned them of their fearful doom,
And fiery vengeance that would shortly come;
And now that day, fixed by my firm decree,
(That day unknown, even, O Branch, to thee,)
That day of blood, pale famine and dismay,
When Israel's crimes shall Israel sweep away.
The wide abound of guilt and social sin
Shows that man's lesson third should now begin.
Go, then; descend and work our righteous will,
And all your prophecies on earth fulfil:
All hindrance to the Gospel now remove,
And introduce the reign of peace and love.
But you, my faithful family above,
Still happy in my wide diffusive love,
In social converse 'tis my will to show
My dealings with frail, erring man below.
For confidence and interchange of souls,
The conduit forms through which heaven's pleasure rolls;
'Tis for this purpose we disclose our plan
Of training for the skies our creature man.

"Now, the first lesson Wisdom could impart,
And deep imprint and fix in every heart,
Was this: that they were made, formed from earth's clod,
And must believe in a creating God;
And laws I gave, to teach them to obey
And know that Power that form'd them out of clay;
But all those laws they broke through lust and pride,
And sin rolled like a river deep and wide;
To punish which, and give a proof sublime
A God had made them who would punish crime,
We poured a flood of waters, deep, profound,
O'er all the earth, and every soul was drowned,
Save Noah and his house, that they again
Might people earth with a new race of men.
But though to wickedness men still were prone,
The Deluge and sunk Sodom wide made known
The ruling power of Heaven; and God, or gods,
All nations worshipped through the wide abodes.

"Thus, the first lesson being learned by man,
The second follows, (such was Wisdom's plan,)
And that was only fully to make known
That God was *Spirit*, and there was but one;
To have a nation of the Abrah'mic line,
To spread through all the earth this creed divine.
Hence Moses to the Hebrew nation came,
Proclaimed his mission and my awful name;
By signs and mighty wonders brought the tribes
To that good land where Judah's power resides.
But to you, sons of Heaven, I need not tell
How oft to idols foul the nation fell—
To vile idolatry—both great and small,
Base worshippers of Ashtaroth and Baal,

And blood-stained Moloch, and heaven's starry host,
With all the bestial gods around their coast!
A thousand blessings and a thousand woes,
The galling yoke of despicable foes,
Could not from idol-worship them restrain—
Nine hundred years I bore with them in vain.
At length the final, conquering stroke was given,
And the whole race to heathen bondage driven!
This, like the withering blow Death's angel gave,
Which Egypt changed to a continuous grave,
Effectual proved; for since I took them home,
Worship of idols is a crime unknown.
But murder, robbery, hearts depraved within,
Have sunk the nation deep in social sin;
So deep, it shows the law by Moses given
Is impotent to fit one soul for heaven.
Hence, Institution Second must give place
To Institution Third, the reign of Grace.
To all the world this lesson shall extend,
Wonders lead on, and glory crown the end.
The world must all be taught, that they may win
Eternal life, if purified from sin;
And that an entrance to the realms above
Is only gained by purity and love.
For this my Son, the *Branch*, sojourned on earth
As a mere mortal, and of humble birth;
Midst persecutions still dispensing good,
Love's reign he preached, then sealed it with his blood!
High on the cross the great Exemplar hung:
Night shrouded earth, and mute each heavenly tongue;
By his death groans the temple's veil was rent,
And all earth trembled at the dire event!
Thus the new Institution, by this scene
Of dying love, all-powerful to redeem,
And make the earth like heaven, was ushered in!

'Tis thus, ye angels, we unfold to you
Those mysteries you desire to look into.

"And now, O Branch, (on earth called Christ,) descend,
And bring the Second Institution to an end.
Sweep from the land the wretched Jewish State,
Their temple burn, and yield them to their fate.
To spirit-baptism they will not aspire,
So let Jerusalem be baptized with fire!"

Thus spoke the great I AM, and smiling, shed
Love's kindling glories o'er each happy head;
Fraternal love rolled round from breast to breast,
Seraphic love, the blessings of the blest.
Then rose the songs of heaven in sweetest strains,
Harmonious o'er the wide celestial plains;
The Fountain of all life and bliss they sung:
His praise resounded loud from every tongue:
So sweet the ecstatic tones, so soft, so clear,
Even God, delighted, smiling stooped to hear.
Nor were those harmonies of heaven alone,
Dances, joy-moved, sprang round th' eternal throne;
With banquets high the festal day was closed,
And all heaven's powers in perfect bliss reposed.

While thus above bliss rolls on without end,
The Muse, reluctant, must to earth descend:
There fierce Bellona thunders wide alarms,
And calls the Jews and Roman world to arms.
The expelled cohort from Antonia's tower
Soon met Rome's legions marching in full power,
By Cestus led, from Cesarea's plain,
Proud in their power, and now their hearts on flame
At Jewish insolence, and vowed to take
Vengeance in full—a dread example make

Of the seditious; so that nations round
Should hear the tale, and tremble at the sound.
Three legions thus soon camped on Scopas Hill,
Their vow of rage and vengeance to fulfil.

Nor were Jerusalem's zealot powers asleep:
Their rage for freedom was intense and deep:
Their late outrages and their late success,
The fear of punishment, and sore distress,
Had made them dominant; so Salem stood,
Beneath their rule, resolved on war and blood!
Under six leaders, thirty thousand men
Manned the strong walls around Jerusalem;
All men of war, well used to death's alarms,
When Galilee was swept by Roman arms.
First of these heroes, Judeas, great in fight,
With dauntless soul, and arm of dreadful might:
Fired with a love of freedom and her cause,
A patriotic sword the Zealot draws,
To vindicate the nation's rights and laws.
Next Phineas, just recovered from his wound;
With Baruch, skilful, and of thought profound;
Judas, from near Idumea's desert land,
Once the fierce leader of a robber band;
Now an enthusiast, with ambition vain,
He dreamed that Heaven would shortly him proclaim
As the Messiah, and support his reign!
The sixth was Simon Gorias, (name accursed,)
Of tyrants—all but John—the basest, worst:
Fearless of danger, and in battle brave,
A bloody, faithless, bold, ambitious knave.
These led the Jewish host, drawn out to oppose
The martial power of their besieging foes;

While thousands more stood ready at a call
To rush to combat, and defend the wall.

But now Night with her raven wings came down,
And wrapped in darkness camps, and towers, and town.
Devoted thousands, sleeping, breathed that breath,
Soon, soon to pass on the cold wings of death!
But when the rising sun, with kindling ray,
Flamed up the front of heaven, and gave the day,
The whole precinct was filled with war's alarms;
The opposing powers advanced with flashing arms.
All round the walls the Judean host appears,
With catapults, and slings, and darts, and spears:
From their broad walls they pour incessant down
(On those brave foes who durst approach the town)
A furious storm of missiles, stones and darts,
While arrows, engine-driven, pierced shields and hearts.
Gibeas Ehud, and a chosen band
Of slingers, trained to use the dexter hand—
Their round, smooth stones, sent with resistless force,
Undeviating held their destined course.
An eye or ear was all the mark they wished:
At ninety steps, their mark they never missed.
Like that dread hail in Egypt's evil hour,
The smooth rocks flew in one continuous shower.
But from the Roman shields and armor proof,
Like hail-stones from an adamantine roof,
The rocky storm rebounds; and few were slain,
Excepting those who, of their courage vain,
Their foreheads showed, and dropped upon the plain.

Then Publius spoke—the second in command,
Both brave and wise, and raised aloft his hand:

"O, Cestus, see where stands yon vaunting foe,
Pouring their missiles on our ranks below:
The only point our veterans can attain
Is simply this—to keep from being slain.
They have to bear their shields with nicest care,
To avert the sling-stones and descending spear;
While every dart their nervous arms let fly
Labors in vain against the foe on high.
Let us withdraw beyond the missiles' flight,
And with more potent arms renew the fight;
Our engines and our catapults can throw
The storm of war much farther than the foe.
Safe at due distance, we may stand and see
The abortive efforts of the enemy—
See while our engines sweep their boasted wall,
Their week artillery innocently fall."

The angry Cestus heard, approved, and then
Marshalled anew his engines and his men.
Soon from strong engines flew a slaughtering shower;
In storms their catapults and blaistia pour;
Rocks and barbed arrows hissing through the air,
And death rode widely on their wild career:
As when from famed Tigrita's clear, smooth brow,
The drift-wood plunges to the gulf below,
Torn from a hundred hills, with hideous sound,
The Tigris hurls them to the deep profound;
So from the parapets and outer wall,
The warring Hebrews in succession fall;
With shrieks and groans the hideous ruin meet,
All crushed and mangled on the rocky street!
What could they do? They took the only course,
And left the wall to such o'erwhelming force.
The Romans, masters of the bloody plain,
Slaughter the wounded and despoil the slain:

Conquerors without the wall, their camp they sought,
To boast their victory, though 'twas dearly bought.

But now, when morning, in the vales of peace,
Called forth the swains to plough, or clip the fleece;
As birds from fragrant bowers sent forth heaven's tune,
And bees were busy sipping Sharon's bloom;
Within, without the city, rolled afar
The sounds tumultuous of infuriate war.
Cestus around him called his bold compeers,
And thus the purpose of his mind declares:
"Yon gate must now be burst, or wall o'erthrown,
And yield us entrance to the accursed town;
Then let our strongest engine be brought forth,
And driven against the gate which fronts the north,
If that don't yield, then burst the adjoining wall,
And storm the breach as they in ruins fall."

Forthwith the cohorts, with contending haste,
Their mightiest engine in due order placed;
Its iron front, formed like the bold ram's head,
Had various gates and towers in ruin spread.
Placed on strong wheels, the lifeless monster lay,
But on each side the cohorts wide display
Two living lines, to give it life to play.
As when a ram, enraged against a foe,
Draws back to give more impulse to the blow,
So the engine recedes, more power to gain,
Then rushed with gathering speed across the plain.
It struck the strong-barred gate—the crashing sound,
Like sharp-toned thunder, echoed far around.
The blow was vain, but, aided by recoil,
Drew back and struck in quick successive toil;

As when strong woodmen, on some mountain brow,
Strive to hurl down into the vale below
A giant pine—long time the keen axe sounds;
Long time the mountain monarch bears the wounds;
Weakened at length, a final blow is given—
It falls—and the loud crash resounds to heaven!
So by the mighty engine's iron head,
Blows following blows, with growing impulse sped,
The gate at length gives way, and shivered lies,
And through the arch lets in the outer skies!

Now Salem's warriors, while the clangor rung,
Stood grim as death, though mute was every tongue;
All ready armed, the breach they boldly face,
To see what heroes dared to fill the space.
There fierce Hilkias, there bold Ammon stood;
While zealot Judeas, all athirst for blood,
And brave Elkanan, with the chieftains join,
And Hazor, of the famed Asmonean line.
Nor stood they long, before a column, led
By Manlius and great Flavius at their head;
A brazen column, which, with step elate,
Marched to the opening of the prostrate gate.
Then war began: blood-thirsty javelins fly,
And hostile shoutings drown the dying cry;
The strong held spear, the breast through cuirass gores,
And wide the heart's-blood on the pavement pours!
Loud sounds the voice of Manlius o'er the throng—
"Come, Publius and Septimes! rush along:
Come, all Rome's heroes! let your weapons shine,
And hew your way through yon seditious line."
As loud the voice of the fierce Zealots rung—
"Stand fast, ye Hebrews! let the heathen come:
Great is the cause for which our swords we draw,
Our nation's freedom and God's holy law."

Then raged the conflict—vanguard, right and left,
And helms and heads by swords and axes cleft.
Arms clashed on arms: incessant was the din,
As decades after decades still rushed in.
Maxus, a demi-giant, born in Thrace,
Who led them on, armed only with a mace,
Saw where Baniah's sword fierce waved around,
Felled Roman after Roman to the ground.
Such havoc to withstand, swift was his stride,
And friends and foes drew back on every side.
The Hebrew saw, but yet he would not fly:
His heart throbbed nobly, "I had rather die."
On this his javelin flew, and whizzing held
Its course beneath the Thracian's brazen shield;
Pierced through the cuirass, but did little more—
Shallow the wound, and small the trickling gore.
Not such the Thracian's blow; not such the wound:
It dashed the Hebrew hero to the ground,
Mangled and bathed in blood: nor stopped he there,
But rushed upon the thickest press of war.
Terror before him marched: on either side
His blows, death-dealing, sweep a passage wide;
Publius, Lucullus, and Ventides join,
And death walks conquering all along the line!
In vain the Judean heroes struggle still—
All, all give way to Roman power and skill:
As when a timorous herd of grazing deer
Hear German stag-hounds yelping in the rear,
They trembling fly, the well known pass to gain,
Though in such pass oft fated to be slain;
So fled the Jews, in crowds, to gain the gate,
And rest delivered from impending fate;
So general the rout, so swift the flight,
Most found asylum with their friends at night.

The victors in the quarter won remain,
Houses to spoil, and give the spoiled to flame:
Blaze after blaze flared dreadful to the sight,
And banished darkness through the hours of night.

Meanwhile the Zealots, sunk in deep despair,
Fled to their towers and quit the hopeless war:
Their power, as thunder-struck, did instant cease,
And passed at once to the mild friends of peace.
Annas and Socius, and a host of men,
The wise, the wealthy of Jerusalem,
Who sought to save their Temple and their town,
Nor on their heads bring Cæsar's vengeance down,
On full assurance given, set open wide
The brazen gates that fenced the northern side,
And let the Romans, at a signal's fall,
Pass from Bezetha through the second wall.

The city now seemed taken; but the Tower
Antonia still was in the Zealots' power.
To take this fortress, and thus end this war,
Five hundred miners to the tower repair.
Secured by shields conjoined from darts above,
To excavation quick the workmen move;
The loosened clods in massive piles appear,
And soon the deep foundation rocks lie bare.
As when the Burrampootra's mighty stream
Strikes some high bank, impetuous and unseen,
While, thoughtless, waving high o'er many a rod,
The grand magnolia and huge walnut nod;
The boiling current mines away the land,
And heaps in bars below the drifting sand;
So round the angles of the tower are thrown
The upturned earth, rubbish, and loosened stone;

And as that bank must soon, thus forest-crowned,
Rush to the flood with crash and splashing sound,
So in some hours had strong Antonia's wall,
With throes convulsive, thundered to its fall:
But while the friends of peace in hope beheld
The stronghold taken, and sedition quelled,
While the fierce Zealots, authors of the war,
Looked on their situation with despair,
Behold a wonder, (though no sign was given,)
So strange, it seemed to be the work of heaven!
At least so thought both parties, when they saw
The Roman eagles from the tower withdraw.
An order to the conquering cohorts came,
Quick to retreat back to their camp again!
An almost taken city thus to leave,
Their foes to triumph, and their friends to grieve,
Was almost worse than death; but Roman sway
Arose from troops disciplined to obey.
So, while all hearts with indignation burn,
They counter-march, and towards the camp return.
But they returned not peaceably and slow:
Behind, in storms, pursued the vengeful foe.
The Zealots from Antonia rushed in arms,
And roused the city with their fierce alarms;
They death denounced, and desolating woe,
On all who armed not and pursued the foe.
Phineas, Judas, and Hilchias proud,
Blazing in arms, led the tumultuous crowd:
Their voice above the battle's roar was sent—
"Ye sons of Israel, seize this strange event!
Lo! Jacob's God from heaven asserts our cause,
And calls on you to vindicate his laws.
Let not these wretches safe their camp regain,
Without due vengeance for our brothers slain.

A bloody token let each arm bestow,
And death, or cureless wounds, attend each blow;
That when, though weak, each boastful shows his scar,
Their sons may tremble at a Judean war!"

Excited thus, the undisciplined throng
With shouts and clamorous threat'nings rushed along;
Arrows, and stones, and darts, across the fields
Stream through the air and ring upon the shields.
Still on the Roman ranks, in urged retreat,
Charge after charge they furiously repeat.
Nor were their undisciplined onsets vain:
Blood marked the struggling scene across the plain:
The legions, not expecting such a storm,
Were not completely in retreating form.
Thus every breach or opening let in death,
And sent some Romans to the world beneath;
While all the stragglers instantly were tore
Down to the earth, and mangled in their gore.
But when they turned in phalanx form to face
The wild infuriates who pursued the chase,
The yelling rout dispersed, as baying hound
And huntsman at the wounded lion bound;
Yet soon, as flies brushed from the foaming pail,
They quick return and constantly assail.
Thus rolled the conflict on, till shades of night
And Roman patience closed the lingering fight.
The legions gained their camp: the Jews, elate
With this new triumph, passed their prostrate gate.

But in the Roman camp deep discontent
Filled every breast, and murmured in each tent.
This strange retreat, when conquest seemed secure,
Even Roman discipline could scarce endure.

This Cestus knew, and called, by summons brief,
To council hall each legionary chief.
The general (when all seated) thus began:
"Around this board there does not sit a man
Who feels for Rome's high glories more than I,
Or feels more grieved to see her standards fly.
Think you the order which has brought us here
Sprang from strange madness or a coward's fear?
No—by great Cæsar! 'Twas to save the host
From being o'erwhelmed—surrounded—lost!
Sure spies informed me that a rebel chief
Was hastening to Jerusalem's relief,
The dread Salathiel, from Massada's towers,
With his Naphtalian band and added powers!
Ten thousand furious Zealots, by him led,
To pour upon our rear, is cause for dread:
By morning light their shouts will stun our ears,
Our eyes behold their savage mountain spears.
'Tis for this cause,—lest they should us surround,
Pent in the city, hemmed on hostile ground,—
That I reversed our late victorious course,
And ordered back to camp our conquering force;
That we in safety may consult what more
Can now be done, the army to secure.
You have my reasons for this blamed retreat."—
Thus said, the general bowed and took his seat.

Then Manlius rose; his reputation stood
High for bold daring and the public good:
"O General," he cried, "our leader brave,
You've given us reasons weighty and most grave
For our return to camp; but I must own,
Had I been you, we had not left the town.

The friends of peace are many, and with joy
Would aid our arms, those tyrants to destroy.
Antonia ours, we could have held the place
Till Cæsar's marching powers had conquered peace.
But that is past: what now should be our plan,
I cannot say: let him declare who can."

Septimes, rising, said: "I can but state,
Whatever course we take, our danger's great.
The Zealots now wield all Jerusalem's force:
Who dares resist is doomed to death of course.
To re-attack the sapped, half-taken tower,
Would be to fight their full united power;
While close behind us, as our general hears,
To bar retreat, would glance ten thousand spears.
But some may say, safe in this camp remain,
And these barbarian mobs may rage in vain.
I tell you, bold compeers, when joined *en masse*,
Those mobs will raging o'er your ramparts pass;
Placed by yourselves from whence you cannot fly,
Assailed by myriads, you but fight to die.
Then down Bethhoron's valley to the plain,
(Between the mountains and the western main,)
By my advice, our army quick descends,
Soon as the morning from the east ascends."

He ceased; and, none dissenting, Cestus thus:
"I deem the opinion good just given us;
And silence shows the council's all agreed;
Then on that plan we forthwith will proceed.
Beneath the ægis of the gods of Rome,
We fear not numbers, two or three to one;
Then, soon as morning light salutes the sky,
Above our legions let the eagle fly;

Sheathed in bright arms let every decade shine,
And form a long impenetrable line;
Prepared to wheel, and to that phalanx spread,
Whose brazen front still strikes the world with dread!"
All parted satisfied with what was done,
Little expecting deeper woes to come.

At length the morning rose, which spreads such grace
O'er Nature's uncontaminated face;
But man's fell passions desolate her charms;
For now both armies rung with war's alarms.
The Jews beheld the cohorts march away,
Their armor flashing back Sol's rising ray;
And instantly the western gates unbar,
And through them roll the fierce pursuing war.
Upon the Roman's rear-guard, and each wing,
The sounding darts and barbed arrows ring;
But as the cohorts turn, and strive to join
In combat, still the Jews the fight decline.
As nursery ganders, guardians of their home,
Pursue a mastiff bearing off a bone;
With outstretched necks they scream with hissing breath,
And gàbbling seem to vow his instant death;
But should the cur at length, vexed by the rout,
Sudden with snaps and fierce barks wheel about,
With flapping wings the threatening boasters run,
Then turn and chatter of the feats they've done:
So, when the vexed cohorts wheel and pursue
In turn, in wide dispersion fled each Jew.
Yet, as true hounds driven by a baited boar,
They quick return, more furious than before;
But when the sun rolled high, the Jewish rage,
Bile-stirred, turned furious: naught could it assuage

But Roman blood. Hence, cautious now no more,
On phalanx spears the infuriate masses pour;
Like famished wolves by scent of blood impelled,
They dashed aside the impenetrable shield;
Then with short poignards sought for Roman hearts,
And death alone each separate struggle parts!
All round the lines thus raged the dire debate,
And mutual wounds were dealt with mutual hate.
The brave Elkanan and Hilkias led
The furious onset o'er the prostrate dead;
And like a rushing river 'gainst its banks,
Seemed bursting through the yielding Roman ranks.
This Manlius saw, and called on Maxus loud—
(His voice was heard above the warring crowd,)
"Come, mighty Thracian! to the rescue haste,
Or else this morning's march will prove our last!
Why should we with great heroes be renowned,
Stand high in office, and with glory crowned,
Unless midst death Rome's eagles we defend?"—
Brave Maxus heard, and hastened to his friend.

From his strong arm swift flew the lengthened spear,
And pierced Hilkias deep beneath the ear:
The warrior prostrate fell; supine he lies;
And struck with terror wild, each follower flies—
All but Elkanan: he an instant stood,
And o'er his friend poured out a tide of blood;
But quickly saw he could not guard the slain,
And all resistance to the charge was vain:
He slowly then forsook the unequal fight,
And with reluctance joined the common flight.

The foe dispersed, the cohorts now again
Marched in quick time across the bleeding plain:

They wished to gain, if possible, some hours
On stern Salathiel's fast approaching powers.
Fond hopes and vain!—the dreaded ram-horns sound—
Naphtalia's trumpet fills the air around:
Their tribe's proud banner, streaming high in air,
Told that the approaching storm of war was near.
From dead Asphaltes' cliffs, ten thousand men
On Olivet looked o'er Jerusalem;
Then northward wheeled her walls, and o'er the plain
Pursued the Romans toward the western main.
The routed Jews, when they this aid beheld,
Naphtalia's ensigns waving o'er the field,
Resumed their courage, and to battle wheeled.
Where deep Bethhoron's vale engulfs the plain,
(Along whose sides extends a mountain chain,)
The gorge was wide: there wheeled the Roman force,
Shining in arms the phalanx and the horse.
Naphtalia's heroes, with their banners spread,
Charged with their spears, by fierce Salathiel led:
Lysander, and brave Ezra by his side,
(Of Zebulon the hero and the pride;)
Dire was the conflict, when, with shouts and cheers,
They charged that brazen wall of ported spears.
At Manlius' breast Lysander's javelin flew:
It hissing erred—but brave Lucullus slew:
Deep in his throat the quivering weapon stood,
And the centurion fell midst streams of blood!
Against Ventides' helm Ezra's strong spear
Was driven impetuous, forceful its career;
Though the firm brass repelled the flying wound,
The impetus hurled Ventides to the ground.
Salathiel's weapon found a weaker part,
And pierced the gallant Gaulus to the heart.

Abner, a zealot from sweet Modin's dell,
By Manlius' arm in furious combat fell:
The spear gored through his groin a ghastly wound —
Groaning with pain, he doubles to the ground;
Convulsed, his arms extend and grasp the dust around.

Mean time, upon the right like deeds were done:
There fought those Hebrews who so lately run,
The rallied warriors of Jerusalem,
A body of full twenty thousand men.
Judeas, Phineas, Ehud led the van,
And where they moved, the blood in torrents ran!
Maxus, and Tankard, from the rapid Rhone,
And Scipio, second thunderbolt of Rome,
Headed the legions to withstand their force:
Two led the footmen and one charged on horse.
Then rose the battle's roar: loud was the din,
As charge on charge, repulsed, still charged again;
The tortoise roof of twenty thousand shields
From their discipline general safety yields,
As moved th' unbroken phalanx o'er the fields.
Sempronius with his thundering squadron came—
Two thousand horsemen dashed into the plain;
The sun's rays, flashing from their hovering shields
Of fulgent brass, illumined all the fields.
Upon Jerusalem's broken ranks they pour:
Their dreadful course is marked with streams of gore.
High in their stirrups the mailed warriors rise;
Their swords, like meteors glancing from the skies,
With power descend on arms, and helms, and heads,
And wide around the growing slaughter spreads!
This saw Lysander, this Salathiel saw,
And with their powers quick to the rescue draw;

The nimble huntsman and strong mountaineer
Were wheeled to charge Sempronius in the rear.
The Roman saw, and drew his slaughtering corps
Back to the station which they held before;
Thus that dread squadron their retreat made good,
Their swords and coursers' fetlocks dyed in blood.

But soon this sore, this long-continued fight
Was closed by the dark raven wing of night.
Salathiel's trumpet sounded a retreat,
And in mid-plain the Hebrew armies meet.
The troops encamped; and as deep darkness falls,
Naphtalia's prince to hasty council calls
The Jewish chiefs; when, leaning on his spear,
He spoke and said: "Fathers and friends, give ear.
Well have you fought this day: yon setting sun
Has seen great deeds, and lasting glory won;
But much of labor and of toil remain,
Before our tribes their ancient freedom gain.
I trust to-morrow's sun shall see the foe
Crushed in yon vale ([1]) through which they're forced to go.
But now let bullocks, wine, and bread be sought,
And from your city full provisions brought;
For courage comes from strength, and strength from food
And generous wine, which fires the languid blood.
Let this be done; and if you all incline
To let me lead your powers as well as mine,
The next day's sun shall see the imperial host,
Pursued by vengeance, overwhelmed and lost.
Soon, if united, shall our conquering hands
Sweep off these tyrants and their plundering bands."

Propped, on his sword, to this Judeas said:
"Prince of Naphtalia, timely was your aid;

The conqueror of Massada's unta'en towers
May justly claim the leading of our powers.
I speak for all our chiefs—they all would choose
You led the embattled army of the Jews."

The prince replied: "Then let us rest to-night,
And take refreshment; but with morning light
Let every Hebrew shine in armor bright.
Soon as Sol's rays flame on yon mountain's head,
Let light-armed bands along their tops be led:
Myself and veteran band their flight will urge,
And press the Romans down the fatal gorge.
Should that great Thracian hero, Maxus, dare
To vaunting stay behind to guard the rear,
Or Manlius, boasted as the sword of Rome,
Linger and say, 'Let proud Salathiel come;'
Then shall this spear with fury demonstrate
Whose arm weighs heaviest in the scales of fate.
O! would to Heaven that now I felt as sure
Our nation and God's Temple should endure
While time shall last, as that yon heathen host
To-morrow's sun shall see o'erwhelmed and lost!
Wide shall Bethhoron's vale with groans resound,
And Roman carnage load the rugged ground!"

Applauses loud the listening chiefs expressed,
And both the armies sought repast and rest.
The city forces found their homes again;
Naphtalia's warriors camped upon the plain;
The Roman legions near the gorge remain.
Sure sentinels were placed at every post
By either side, to guard the sleeping host.
Soon a long line of flames, a mile apart,
Fronting each host, from darkness seemed to start;

Wide flaring round, they glanced on armor bright,
And darker made the deep surrounding night—
So dark that from the camp-fires gazing back,
Air seemed a solid wall of painted black.
As when the forest sons, intent on game,
Around dry prairies draw a circling flame;
While smoke and flame roll upward to the skies,
The light within betrays the wild deer's eyes;
Then from the outer darkness, (Egypt's night,)
The whizzing arrows dart through blazing light
Across the isthmus left for their retreat,
And slaughtered antlers crown the smooth deceit;
While to all eyes within deep shades seem furled,
And ebon darkness wrapped around the world.

Soon as from eastern climes the unwearied sun
Had his diurnal through the heavens begun,
What time the ploughman plods his weary way,
To draw subsistence from his kindred clay,
The Roman army, after needful food,
Formed in close column, down the vale pursued:
By brave Sempronius was the vanguard led,
With Quintus Sextus aiding at their head.
The general held the centre, best to hear
What should take place in column front and rear.
The rearguard, as the point the most exposed,
Was of a chosen veteran band composed;
Manlius to lead them, none could feel dismayed,
With Maxus and Septimes to his aid.
Thus marched they on; but soon from either chain
Of beetling cliffs that overlooked the plain,
The Jewish war descends—the dart and spear,
With showering rocks, drove downward through the air.

Loud sounds the missiles on the shields below,
The brazen roof of their disciplined foe.
Judeas ruled the right, and on the left
Fell Simon poured the storm from every cleft;
While brave Lysander thundered on their rear,
With fierce Naphtalia's band and mountain spear.
Thus marched the Roman column, not in flight,
Enduring slaughter, though they could not fight;
For often as their nervous arms let fly
Their darts and javelins, slanting towards the sky,
Against the foe, they found the hills too high;
And those which did surmount, so spent the blow,
Blood-guiltless fell upon the plain below!
At every opening pass, the horsemen strove
To scale the mount and charge the foe above;
But soon they found the bold attempt was vain—
Forced to recoil, some rolling to the plain,
While those surmounting instantly were slain.

Long as the sun rolled to its height in heaven,
The legionaries down the pass were driven;
Sore pressed on every side, yet the strong roof
Of conjoined shields were 'gainst light missiles proof.
This Jordan saw, a chief of ready mind,
Nursed where the great and lesser Jordan joined;
A land of fruits, and flowers, and flocks, and grain,
Where vines and oranges perfumed the plain.
For worship he had left those lovely lands,
But left that worship in the priesthood's hands,
To pour down vengeance on the Roman bands.
On a broad cliff he stood, and called aloud
To the tumultuous Jewish mountain crowd,
"Bring hither larger rocks, compact and round—
Numbers of every size may quick be found.

By strength conjoined those mountain missiles bear,
Or roll the ponderous bolts of vengeance here:
Soon shall you see yon moving brazen dome
Crushed as it moves by each successive stone.
The impetuous rocks, whirled thundering down the banks,
Will burst their tortoise-shell, and plough their ranks."
They heard, and quickly from the cliff's high ledge,
Rock after rock with furious bounds they urge.
The shields conjoined no more protect each head,
But, crushed, lie ground beneath the incumbent dead.
Fierce o'er their arms, the wounded and the slain,
The ponderous boulders dashed across the plain:
The solid phalanx to wild fragments thrown,
And all the glen one universal groan!
For all along, from either mountain's brow,
This storm of death poured to the vale below:
Joram's fierce war from every point they play,
And death comes pouring all the dolorous way.
Those struck down in the van lie gashed with wounds,
Nor can the rearguard heed these mournful sounds:
"O! help me, friend—some water! just a drop!"—
The soulless monster can't a moment stop!
The shattered column, wide disordered, spread,
Marched for their lives o'er dying and the dead;
The whirling rocks, from all the hills on high,
Came like Heaven's vengeance volleying from the sky!
As on the day of power, when Canaan's kings,
Combined, fought Joshua near Mount Hebron's springs;
Discomfited, they down this valley fled,
God's wrath still driving hailstones o'er their head—
Heaven's whole artillery, tempest, fire and hail,
Till blood and carnage filled the horrid vale;
So now the legions of imperial Rome
Fled, terror-struck at their impending doom.

Those troops which, in fair fight beneath their shields,
Could march victorious o'er a hundred fields—
The veteran legions of all-conquering Rome—
Seemed crushed by fate, by powers above o'erthrown.

The sufferers now, almost of hope bereft,
Their beasts of burden killed, their engines left,
Hastening their march, the greater speed they used—
Worse their distress, confusion worse confused.
Haste broke their ranks, while slanting from above,
Through every gap, the downward javelins drove
With such augmented force, armor was vain,
And blood and death still followed in their train.
Even those unwounded, raging in despair,
With [2] yells and lamentations filled the air!
Thus pressed they on in agonizing rage,
To die by foes they saw, but could not them engage.

Midst this distress, the general turned his eyes
Up towards the heavens, and thus obtests the skies:
"O mighty Jove, and all ye gods of Rome,
Who claim the Eternal City as your own;
Our hecatombs have at your altar bled,
Our richest incense through your temples spread;
Then, O ye heavenly powers! look down and see
Our deep distress and helpless misery!
Behold our legions in this doleful glen,
Crushed and beat down like wild beasts in a den,
By these vile atheists of Jerusalem;
While all your altars send up to the skies
Rome's sacred incense and rich sacrifice!
Then give us instant aid, ye gracious powers;
Abridge this dreadful day—cut short the hours—
Roll down deep darkness—hide us from the foe,
And give us time to leave this vale of woe."

But ah! their idol gods no power possessed
To save their votaries when by fate oppressed;
Unlike to Joshua's God, (3) at whose command
The Syrian sun on Gibeon took his stand;
Till down this vale, the sad Bethhoron road,
He as God's besom swept the accursed of God.
They prayed to idols void of power to save
Their bleeding ranks from sinking to the grave!

Salathiel, who, upon his foaming horse,
Led on the Jews in their destroying course,
Now on the wings, then thundering in the rear,
With battle-axe or with his mountain spear,
Driving the Romans down their sad career—
Salathiel saw, and the stern hero's breast
Felt for brave warriors thus by fate oppressed;
Upon the cliff he over Cestus stood,
His sword and right arm crimsoned deep with blood;
Pitying he saw, and raised the flag of peace,
And for a moment bade the warfare cease.
Then thus aloud: "O Cestus Gaulus, why,
Why, valiant Romans, will you choose to die?
You cannot fight; why then resist in vain,
And add more carnage to that bloody plain?
Surrender, and we'll give you our right hand
That all, brave Gaulus, under your command,
Shall safely pass to your proud city Rome,
And see once more your families and home,
On a pledged promise, which must sacred stand,
Never again to tread this holy land."
Thus he; but after consultation had,
Cestus replied in accents firm, though sad:
"I know, great prince, we're in a desperate case,
Hemmed and crushed down in this disastrous place;

And I must own—for it is really true—
Your offer's generous for a barbarous Jew;
Yet with the proffered terms we can't comply:
Romans cannot surrender, but can die!
But still we hope to force our dangerous way,
And live, this wide destruction to repay."

On this the white flag fell, and war again
Began to pour its missiles to the plain;
But heaven's great Governor, the one true God,
Who used the Romans ([4]) as his chastening rod,
With pity viewed their lamentable case,
And willed to give them further time and space.
He willed—and instant o'er that vale of flight
Rolled a black tempest, dark as Egypt's night:
The embodied darkness, bursting as it passed,
Sent o'er the mountain tops the impetuous blast.
Fierce streams of lightning, like a serpent's tongue,
From peak to peak across the valley sprung,
Shivering the cliffs, while, midst the whirlwind's sound,
A trembling earthquake shook the mountain round.
From this wild storm of wind, and rain, and fire,
The Hebrew hosts tumultuously retire.
As when from summer thunder-showers the bees,
Toiling midst blooming meads and flowering trees,
By rapid wing avoid the coming storm,
And round their waxen home tumultuous swarm,
So fled the Jews, struck with an awe profound,
And soon found shelter in the valleys round;
For all untouched the adjacent country stood,
The storm swept only round the vale of blood,
Relieving thus the legions in their flight,
Who made good use of the heaven-sent respite,
And gained some miles by fall of natural night;

Till on a lengthened mount, midst all their woes,
They found some time for food and short repose.

When morning rose, it rose with war's alarms,
The Hebrew host assembling fierce in arms;
The Romans on their lengthy ridge appeared,
Drawn up as if for final strife prepared.
No signs of flight their daring aspect shows,
But death or victory o'er their coming foes.
The imperial eagle, flaunting in the air,
Proclaimed that Cestus and his chiefs were there,
As ordering and directing: at the sight,
The Jewish squadrons rushed to instant fight;
The furious charge was made on every side,
Front, flank, and rear, and shouts to shouts replied.
The missiles flew in clouds; fierce raged the strife;
The Romans fought as prodigal of life.
Salathiel and his compeers fondly thought
That all Rome's legions to a stand were brought,
And a great final battle would be fought;
But as upon the cohorts down they bore,
Before the van, marking their path with gore,
Surprised they saw that each side of their square,
Whom they supposed engaged in distant war,
Struggling upon the mountain and the glen,
In combat with full fifteen thousand men,—
Surprised they met their friends, a mighty tide,
Closing around the foe on every side;
And now so near, so straitened was the space,
Four hundred Roman (5) warriors filled the place;
Who, facing outward, in bold combat stood
'Gainst thirty thousand thirsting for their blood.
Then rose the battle's rage: Salathiel's wrath,
At this finesse, with slaughter strewed his path;

He raged with fury, that some sleeping hours
Should save the legions in Bethhoron's towers.
Nor less Lysander, Phineas, Judas, Saul,
Indignant saw their towering prospects fall;
This edged their swords, this sharpened every spear,
Made their charge furious, their revenge severe.
No generous feeling stayed the uplifted hand,
In admiration of that patriot band,
Who at the post of death devoted stood,
And for their country thus poured out their blood.
But yet that band gave not their lives for naught;
Full dearly was the Jewish vengeance bought:
As round their lines they fell, man after man,
Their square grew less, but still the crimson ran;
And still they fought—and when o'erpowered they fell,
Each sent some Jews before him down to hell.
Like to the Spartan band renowned of old,
At a full price in blood their lives they sold.
Of the four hundred, still two chiefs remained;
Maxus and Manlius still the fight sustained:
Before an arching rock themselves they placed,
And grim as death the conquering army faced.

The stern Salathiel then some pity felt:
He deemed such bravery might atone their guilt:
"Brave chiefs," he cried, "desist from further strife;
Receive my right hand and the gift of life.
Brave men should honor brave men, and still show
Compassion for a gallant, helpless foe."

To whom thus Manlius: "Valiant prince, we own,
At this late moment, you've some feeling shown;
But know, thus placed, we Romans dare not live,
And bear a life that you have power to give.

Now hear me, while I ask a nobler course:
Choose two best champions of your mighty force,
And, man to man, we two with them will try
The fate of arms, and nobly live or die!
For we propose, and trust you will accord,
That if your champions fall beneath our sword,
If one or both of us the victory gain,
Such victor then shall liberty obtain
To leave in haste this melancholy plain.
In asking this, great prince, we lean alone
On that proud chivalry for which you're known,
And our distress. Should mercy send us home,
The very dogs would bay us out of Rome.
The last live Spartan from Thermopylæ fled,
And endless shame has settled on his head;
His former course of glory could not save
That man from filling a dishonored grave.
Bethhoron's vale has seen four hundred die,
(Except us two—if we should basely fly,)
Still more devoted, yielding their last breath
To save our army from the jaws of death!
To leave the martyrs, then, of this sad day,
We can't surrender, just to run away.
We beg for combat; then, should one remain,
He 'll face Rome's noblest warriors without shame."

On this Salathiel called each Hebrew chief,
To hold short council. It was stern and brief.
"Brethren," he said, "you've heard these men's appeal:
What 's best for glory and our country's weal?
On those two chiefs to pour a thousand spears,
Would sink us down to infamy for years.
They won't surrender—then on yonder plain
Let 's add them to the thousands we have slain.

Myself will the great Thracian's arm abide:
Who will meet Manlius, with his Roman pride?"
He looked around, and instant, at the word,
Sprang to his side Mount Gilead's youthful lord:
"I claim that post," he said, "and well I trust
To strike that smooth-tongued orator to dust.
Let none oppose me, for I long to gain,
By his expiring groans, beginning fame."
"Then give the combat," all the council cried,
And swift the troops drew back on every side.

Now on the little plain the chiefs appear,
All armed with cuirass, helmet, sword, and spear;
Separate each combat, separate the event,
No counsel should be given, no aid lent.

First in importance, greatest far in might,
Naphtalia's chief and Maxus met in fight.
The Thracian warrior whirled his ponderous spear;
Salathiel marked its furious career,
And swerving let it hiss along the air;
Then sent his mountain spear—its tempered point
Pierced though the cuirass at an opening joint,
With such resistless strength and force impelled,
Its course through flesh and bones the weapon held,
Till by back armor 'twas at length repelled.
The staggering hero looked amazed around,
Then arms and body thundered to the ground:
The conqueror sternly o'er the hero stood,
Drew forth the spear and gazed the gushing blood;
Then—"Lie there, Maxus! let not shame alarm:
Your death was glorious, dying by my arm.
Such honored deaths, I trust, shall shortly come,
To grace all tyrants from detested Rome."

To this the dying chief: "Boast as you may,
The day will come—I see the dreadful day—
Dreadful to Jewry, but to conquering Rome
The day of vengeance, and your final doom;
A day when your strong towers and boasted wall
Shall shake, then totter, and to rubbish fall;
When your proud Temple, with its bigot fame
And wide-spread glories, shall ascend in flame:
Before its bloody porch your head shall bow,
And groaning die, as I am dying now!"
He ceased: no more could he inhale heaven's breath,
And his eyes closed beneath the hand of death.

Meanwhile great Manlius and bold Jephtha stood,
With lance in hand, and both athirst for blood:
From Jephtha's arm the lance flew, not in vain;
Blood from his foe's left arm gushed to the plain,
Whose right repaid it with a ghastly wound,
Which bent the groaning Jephtha to the ground:
Deep in his groin stood fixed the thrilling dart,
And soul and body seemed in act to part.
Manlius drew near, and waved his glittering sword;
Then turning round, cried: "Great Naphtalia's lord,
Am I not victor in this deadly strife,
Although I spare this wounded hero's life?"
"You are," Salathiel said: "no Roman now
Dare stain the laurels that adorn your brow:
Then haste, brave Manlius, hasten to your friends,
Before our army on their tower descends,
And your own engine their strong bulwark rends."
Round Jephtha throng his friends, with many a tear,
And bear him homeward on a hasty bier.

But now the Syrian sun was sinking down
Behind Bethhoron's hills and crowded town;

Loud shouts and songs, wide echoing o'er the plain,
The Jews' great victory and their joy proclaim!
Nine thousand Romans slain, and the rest driven,
Like fiends accursed, before the wrath of Heaven!
They lauded loud the captains of their host,
But great Salathiel and Lysander most;
While to the God of armies, grander still,
The loud hosannas rang from hill to hill,
Filled all the air, as their joint accents rose
In thanks for their great victory o'er their foes!
Meantime refreshments for the troops were sought,
And joyful multitudes free offerings brought:
The army feasted, while Salathiel sent
For all his chiefs to sup within his tent;
Rich soldier's fare the rude-formed tables load,
With loaves and wine from servitors bestowed.

As thus they feasted high in victory's joy,
Crowds mixed with servants, busied in employ:
Amongst them one, as if by Heaven inspired,
His voice and eyes seemed with strange vision fired,
Wild was his visage. Loud he thus began,
(Expectant silence round the audience ran:)
"Glory to Israel's God! the odious yoke
Of heathen bondage his right hand has broke!
Glory to God on high! sing, Jacob, sing!
Lo! Judah's Lion roars—behold your King!
The great Messiah, long by seers foretold,
Fills David's throne—behold, behold, behold!
Then laid his left hand on Salathiel's head,
Raising his right, fiercer he yelling said:
"His glorious reign, see, thus I consecrate,
And seal his mission with the hand of fate!"

While different thoughts and wonders filled each breast,
(And brave Salathiel's far above the rest,)
Deep plunged behind the Zealot's hidden knife,
Straight toward the fountain of the hero's life.
Though deep the wound, it missed the vital part,
Passing between the arteroid and heart:
Forth gushed the blood in a continuous stream,
Thus favoring life—the wound bled not within.
The miscreant fled, but fierce Lysander's sword
Flew swifter still, and through his carcass gored—
A fatal thrust, for with the assassin died
All chance of knowing the real [6] homicide.

Around the wounded chief his mourning friends
In wild confusion hurriedly attend;
To whom the hero: "Fear not for my life,
But bear me to my children and my wife,
For now I cannot aid in freedom's strife.
To you, Judeas, Phineas, and the rest,
I yield the guiding power I late possessed;
Be wise, be bold, and join in firm accord,
And fight with zeal the battles of the Lord.
Save, save, O princes, save that glorious fane
Which bears through all the world His sacred name!"
With sighs and groans the crowding concourse hears,
And the hard Jewish chieftains melt in tears.
Then to Lysander, "Quick, my son," he said,
(In feebler tones,) "let me be now conveyed
Upon a litter to Massada's towers—
This can be done during cool evening's hours;
Thence may Naphtalia's sons each seek his home,
Prepared for still more dreadful days to come!"
All this Lysander's filial care performed,
And round Salathiel soon his wife and children mourned.

Meantime the Roman legions, 'scaped from fight,
To Antipatris held their rapid flight;
There, full of shame and rage, within its towers
They wait great Titus and his gathering powers.

Unbounded was the glorying—vast the spoil
The Hebrews took in recompense of toil:
Rich robes of costliest kind, crimson and blue,
And green and gold, most dazzling to the view;
Raiment of every form, and heaps of gold,
And shields and shining helms of various mould;
With jewelled glittering swords of costly frame,
Scattered around amongst the mangled slain.
Immense the spoil, for all along the roads,
Wain after wain groaned with successive loads.
Skipping and dancing, with loud songs and shouts,
They entered Salem's gates by various routes.
Vast multitudes the conquering host attend,
And all Jerusalem to the show descends:
Myriads of voices, tuneful, bold, and clear,
With loud hosannas filled the upper air:
"We've burst the heathen chain—we're free, we're free!"
Was the loud burden of their jubilee.
Glory to God was heard in every song,
And victory, victory echoed through the throng;
But fate's dark wing their city overspreads,
And Heaven's just judgment lowered above their heads.

BOOK III.

Jerusalem Encompassed.

MESSIAH sends Stephen to the Church in Jerusalem, to tell them to flee to the mountains—Unfolds to saints and angels the destruction of the Jews—Moses and Paul deprecate his wrath—Their speeches—Christ's reply—Justifying the ways of God—Demons and the Hadean spirits permitted to aid Jews or Romans by possession and inspiration only—Titus calls his legions—Surrounds the city—The Zealot's dominant—Pass decrees of death against Romanists—They prepare for the conflict—Their bloody executions and rapine—Salathiel is laid on his couch at Massada—His family's grief—He tells them he cannot die till he sees Christ—Narrates his conduct on the day of crucifixion—Long discourses between him, his wife, and her brother on that subject—Abihud endeavors to convert him to Christianity—Recounts the wonders wrought by Christ, which made him believe—That Miriam and Hester are also Christians—He neither blames nor approves—Declares he cannot change in body or mind, but will defend the Temple or die before it—Titus raises a bank to batter down the walls—The Jews sally out in the night to burn it and the engines—Dreadful combat at and on the bank—The fury and courage of the Jews—The valor of the Romans—The battle continues till daylight, bloody and undecided.

Now midst his angels, in the earth's first heaven,
The branch Messiah (first of the first seven)
Thus spake to Stephen: "Proto-martyr, go,
(The first that suffered in my cause below:)
Down to Jerusalem with speed descend,
And warn my followers, that they now attend

To what I said on Olivet—That, when
Strange fears and trembling shook the hearts of men;
When signs from heaven and earthquakes shook the ground,
And marching hosts compassed Jerusalem round,
That then to mountains they in haste should fly,
And know the hour of indignation nigh.
Tell them their foes' brief success is from me—
A pause in war, to give them time to flee!
Then bid them fly to Pera, and the vales
Where cedars wave, beneath famed Lebanon's gales;
To Barada's lone dells, or where, among
Projecting cliffs, Leantes foams along;
Or where, far up among his leaf-clad mounts,
The sacred Jordan draws his bubbling founts;
In those retreats tell them to make their home,
Till by deep troubles, till this day unknown,
The Temple and Jerusalem are o'erthrown!
Fire, famine, and the sword will soon come down,
And wrath, unto the uttermost, destroy the town!"

So spake Messiah; and without delay
The Christian martyr glanced adown his way;
Nor stayed his flight till, in a lone abode,
He joined a congregation of his God.
Five hundred Christians, singing songs of praise
To their great Master—but in mournful lays—
Sudden he joined; then raised an anthem high,
Whose heavenly tones roll raptures through the sky:
Much more the poor disciples felt its power;
It raised to joy the sorrows of the hour.
As sweet the anthem closed, in radiance dressed,
Heaven's messenger stood obvious and confessed.
Brethren, he said, your song contained a prayer
That Christ, our Master, quickly might appear:

By him I'm sent: to me the message's given,
To say, he has come down from highest heaven,
With all his holy angels, and now sheds
Glory, through the first heaven, above our heads!
But 'tis not for salvation he has come:
This is the day of vengeance—day of doom
On this lost city, which, enraged, withstood
His offered mercy, and then shed his blood!
I was in council when the Anointed One
Spoke Heaven's decree from his resplendent throne.

To whom the hoary bishop thus replied:
"O sainted brother, who for Jesus died,
Come sit and tell us, in the bonds of love,
Of those high wonders going on above;
Of the Messiah's advent, and his will,
And what strange wonders are impending still!"

To this the Martyr: "Brother, to tell all
That has befallen, or shortly shall befall,
Would take too much of time; but this much know:
Christ has descended to these heavens below;
Myriads of angels on the pomp attend,
And glory shines all round, as he descends.
Above Judea, from rich Shinar's plain,
To where the sun sinks in the western main;
From Araby the Blest, northward to where
The snow-capped Ararat glitters in the air,
Tents and pavilions, wide extended, shine,
(Unseen by men,) all splendid and divine:
There, seated high, heaven's host all listening round,
The Saviour spoke, in colloquy profound:
As when to multitudes, on Tabor's top,
He preached that Sermon, ne'er to be forgot;

That blessed Sermon, (to the just and pure,)
Which will be felt when time shall be no more;
So now he said, to heaven's host mild and clear,
'Whoso hath ears to hear, now let him hear!
For judgment I am come: my Father's will,
Has fixed the time, and work I now fulfil.
Jerusalem is to destruction given:
Her domes and palaces must flame to heaven:
Gaunt famine soon will moan through every street,
And spectre skeletons each other meet!
By murderous factions fearfully accursed,
(For power and gold all raging and athirst,)
Dire scenes will rise, and streams of blood must flow,
And aid the falchions of the Roman foe:
From Zion's hill, and their stained Temple's door,
Shall streams of blood down to the Kidron pour;
Their Temple, once so holy, now profaned
By every odious crime that can be named,
From its foundation to its topmost spire,
Will soon be wrapped in purifying fire;
While its proud walls shall totter from on high,
And not one stone upon another lie!
The blood of saints and martyrs cries to God;
He hears them, and has sent the avenging rod.
Even when incarnate, they poured out my blood,
While guilty myriads, mocking, round me stood:
Me they rejected—me, the Prince of Peace;
Hence must the Mosaic institution cease,
And sink in tribulations—deeper pain
Than earth has known, or e'er shall know again!'

"The Saviour ceased, and Moses slowly rose;
Down to the pavement his white vestment flows:

His native meekness his mild features grace,
And glory shone as erst o'er the great prophet's face.
'Messiah, Lord,' he said, 'to whom is given
All power in this sublunary earth and heaven,
Should not mild justice with great power unite?
Should not the Judge of all the earth do right?
I own, and much deplore, our nation's guilt:
Rapine abounds, and righteous blood is spilt;
Dark social crimes abound on every hand,
And Judah is no more the holy land;
But, Lord anointed, as for that black crime
Against thy person, and thy claims divine;
That horrid deed the sun would not behold,
Which shook the earth, as Sinai shook of old;
For that, Jerusalem's crime, O! let not loose
Vengeance divine: for it there's much excuse.
Commissioned by yourself, to Sinai's laws
Was added this strong, memorable clause:
To let no prophet live that might arise,
Who by foretelling facts should thus devise
To lead them to apostatize, or change
God's worship for new gods, or worship strange.
Hence, when you came from Galilee, unknown,
And claimed to be the Eternal Father's Son;
Nathless thy wondrous works (they raging saw,)
'Twas natural they should fall back on their law,
And say, Behold a case Moses foretold;
A man of mighty deeds, in teaching bold,
A leader to new gods: now Moses saith,
Let such great prophets all be put to death.
I think, then, by the laws you gave from heaven,
Your crucifixion stands almost forgiven!'
He ended; and the holy Paul subjoined,
'That all the prophets had as one combined,

To teach the nation that when Shiloh came,
He would come a conqueror, and extend his reign
O'er all the earth; at least we so received
What they proclaimed; and thus we all believed;
So when you came, a babe, in manger laid,
And, when grown, had not where to lay your head,
We spurned your claims, and, for the nation's weal,
Had you cut off in unbelieving zeal.
Was it not, Saviour, from the opening skies,
'Midst blazing brightness, that close sealed my eyes,
Thou badest me (prostrate thrown) to light arise?
I really thought that I was serving God,
While toiling on the hot Damascus road,
With high-priest powers, and slaughter in my mind,
To seize on all thy followers I could find,
And send them, bound, to death. Now I feel sure,
Great part of those who did thy death procure,
Like me in ignorance did it, and should find
Like grace with me, for they were also blind.
And more, great Head of princedoms, thrones, and powers,
Your wisdom knows, and thus instructed ours,
That Calvary's dread scene was willed above,
As the best medium of redeeming love:
Why then should Heaven's own agents burn and bleed,
For that fiend murder, when it was decreed?'

"Brethren, all eyes now gazed that heavenly face,
So full of wisdom, majesty, and grace.
'Angels and friends,' he said, ('I call all friends
Who on my Father's will with me attend,)
I'm not displeaséd with this strong appeal:
'Tis humbly offered, though with fervent zeal.
But know ye this, that He who rules above
Knows no vindictive hate; for God is Love;

And I in feeling am his image true:
I am in Him, and Him and I in you.
When men or nations suffer for offence,
Their sufferings only are a consequence:
'Tis God's decree, his will has fixed it so,
No power or art can separate sin and woe:
Hurl God and his Vicegerents from their thrones,
No less man's sufferings, nor less deep their groans.
'Tis sin, that serpent in the flesh, that wakes
To stinging fury its ten thousand snakes:
Achan and all the Canaanitish tribes
Heaven's consequential punishment abide;
Had God not swept them by the Hebrew sword,
Still their dark crimes destruction had insured.
When deep corruption, general and vast,
Taint pressed on taint, has through a nation passed,
Distress and ruin, certain, swift or slow,
Must sink such nation to disgrace and woe!
Hence, when the son of Nun, at my command,
Like desolation, swept throughout their land;
When maids and sucklings, youths and helpless age,
Were slaughtered wholesale, 'twas not done in rage;
All suffered less, when Heaven thus swept this stage.
So, when the old world sank so deep in crime,
They added guilt as mercy added time.
When Sodom a black mass of filth became,
And violence and sin filled all the plain,
'Twas merciful to bring to sudden end
Races depraved so low they could not mend,
Or e'er to bliss and virtue re-ascend.
So now the sinful race for whom you plead
Have sinned so deep by thought, by word and deed;
Such fierce combustibles are heaped within—
Lust, murder, robbery, every kind of sin;

So great the sufferings which from them must flow,
'Tis grace to deal the exterminating blow;
Save them from slow, self-immolating pains,
By sudden death, though found midst blood and flames;
Thus swept from an existence which could give
Nothing but woe, could they for ever live!"

"On this the much-loved brother John broke in:
'Master, though it is so with slaves of sin,
Yet thou hast many servants, righteous men,
In yon vast city of Jerusalem:
Shall they no favor, no deliverance know,
But all be plunged in the same gulf of woe?'

"To this the Saviour: 'Blessed are the dead
Who die in me, as you yourself have said.
They leave a world of sorrow, sin, and pain,
And persecution, high with us to reign.
The righteous gain by death, though the remove
Be sharp and quick, which wafts them to our love.
But I have warned them, and shall warn again,
To leave this Sodom, where their Lord was slain,
Nor longer in a place death-doomed remain.
But learn, that though no Moloch reigns above,
Though heaven's whole atmosphere is peace and love,
Yet punishments direct from us descend:
By miracles all things begin and end.
The primal institution to man given,
Ended by punishment direct from Heaven.
When deep corruption had infected all,
Death's deluge-waters circumfused the ball,
And sunk in deep destruction all the race,
To give the second institution place.
Moses, thou faithful servant of thy God,
Who o'er the sea and river stretched thy rod,

Well couldst thou tell the wonders and the signs
That showed God's finger in those darkened times;
Their rivers turned to blood; fierce hail-storms driven,
'Midst lightning's blaze, across the vault of heaven;
The nation's first-born slain; the midnight cry;
The sea to its foundations bare and dry;
The mountains lightning-clothed—trembling with awe,
All ushered in the Sinaitic law.
And now that institution must remove,
With signs that show Heaven's action from above,
And make room for the institute of love;
To show the world, that though sin armed the rod,
This deep destruction is the work of God,
And that the Mosaic institution's gone,
To give place to a new and better one,
Founded on better promises, and given
To all mankind, to train them all for heaven.'

"Thus spake the King of kings to saints above,
To vindicate his justice and his love;
Then, in his care for you, has sent me down,
To tell you all to fly this fated town.
'Tell them to fly to Pera and the vales,
Where cedars wave beneath famed Lebanon's gales;
To Barada's lone dell, or where, among
Projecting cliffs, Leantes rolls along;
Or where, far up among his upmost mounts,
The sacred Jordan draws his bubbling founts:
Tell them in those retreats to make their home,
Till by fierce vengeance, till this day unknown,
Jerusalem and her Temple are o'erthrown:
Fire, famine, and the sword will soon come down,
And wrath, unto the uttermost, engulf the town!'"

The Proto-martyr thus, his message given,
Smiled peace and love—then vanished into heaven,
Where, to the shining hosts around his throne,
Messiah further his decrees made known.

"Ye saints and angels, when I rose on high,
And captive led in chains captivity,
The powers of hell I bound, and took from them
The license to possess and torture men:
Witchcraft and oracles, and curious arts,
Tormenting bodies and depraving hearts,
I from the demons took; but now restore,
(But with the limitations known before.)
They, with the wicked dead, to work may rise,
As agents in the vengeance of the skies;
By false or true predictions, as they choose,
Side with the heathen, or the infuriate Jews;
By maniac possession, whence fierce fumes
Give seven-fold strength, like him amongst the tombs;
Or fiendish fury, when, on leave from me,
They hurl two thousand swine into the sea:
So now they may possess this guilty race,
The bloody bands and factions of the place;
The hosts without, as well as those within,
And hasten on the dread reward of sin.
Meantime, while Rome's proud eagles gather round
Those walls which soon must rubbish all the ground,
Signs in the heavens above and earth beneath
Shall light destruction on, and woe, and death."

Messiah thus; and heaven, with full accord,
Cried, "Just and righteous are thy judgments, Lord.
The blood of prophets and thy saints they've shed:
Even thee, their King, to crucifixion led!

Raging and scoffing, round thy cross they stood,
And proffered gall; but now thou givest them blood,
For they are worthy! Let thy praise be sung;"
And hallelujahs round the empyrean rung!

Thus they in heaven; but on the earth below,
O'er Israel's land impended war and woe.
The Roman ensigns, at the high command
Of Titus, marched from each adjoining land:
From Egypt, Syria, Sicily, and Rome,
The legionary powers assembling come.
With them auxiliary bands, from every clime,
Compelled, or else allured, by plunder, join:
From Lybia, Ethiopia, whence the Nile
Pours down his floods to fatten Egypt's soil:
From Araby's wide deserts, parched with heat,
To where north storms o'er the Caucasians beat;
From Dacia and Albania, Greece and Gaul,
They hear war's trumpet, and attend the call.
Though variant in color, language, dress,
One thirst for rapine all these hordes possess.
They come like eagles, scenting from afar
The spoils and plunder of destructive war.
As on a summer's eve, in fervid skies,
Low thunder-tones bid clouds on clouds arise;
Round the horizon masses dark roll up,
With thunder-caps, like towering rocks atop:
The day turns night as the black storm draws nigh,
And men and beasts and birds to covert fly;
So marched compassing armies; and so lowers
The storm of war 'round Salem's land and towers;
Bethhoron's slaughter, where ten thousand died,
Cestus enraged, and stung the Roman pride.

'Twas *Cannae* and *Carraė* acted o'er;
Such the entrapment, such the streams of gore!
Even princely Titus felt the common rage—
Titus, the young Ulysses of the age;
Fearless in action, self-possessed, and brave;
Yet at the council-board wise, thoughtful, grave!
No fare too hard for him when sheathed in arms,
Yet none more gay 'midst feasts and beauty's charms.
Though not of height majestic, yet the breadth
Of his square form showed prodigies of strength:
Above his fine-formed shoulders, amply spread,
A well-nerved neck bore up a princely head:
A face of sunshine lighted up an eye
Which, when wrath-clouded, let the lightnings fly!
Such was the warlike chief, whose voice led on
The veteran legions of imperial Rome.

Nor less the Jewish Zealots marked the times:
Great was their energy, as great their crimes.
The Christians, warned, were seized with timely dread,
And noiseless to th' appointed refuge fled:
The Jews' great victory left a passage wide,
And swelled to arrogance the nation's pride:
"Freedom or death" burst from each Zealot's tongue,
And songs of triumph though the city rung:
No friend of peace durst for submission speak;
Fear ruled the wisest, and enslaved the weak:
All forced to join the cry or hold their breath,
The Patriot's cry of "Liberty or death!"
This to sustain, the Zealots spread alarms,
And forced the town and nation into arms.
The factions, headed by the tyrant John
And bloody Simon, drove the masses on:

Councils of State they formed, and soon decreed
That all suspected Romanists should bleed:
Tribunals of enthusiastic men
Filled all the quarters of Jerusalem,
Which doomed to death all prisoners, as they came,
And seized their goods in the Republic's name;
While domiciliary bands and spies
Hunted out victims for the sacrifice;
Or, when they deemed it for the public good,
With sicrii (knife) to pour suspected blood!
Nor in Jerusalem was this alone:
Through all the land fierce bands of Zealots roam;
By mock tribunals, or a murderous hand,
Pillage and death spread terror through the land.
As when through Ashur's land, in ancient days,
The torch of freedom rose with reddening blaze,
And tyrant armies, host succeeding host,
Like a dire storm, hung threatening round their coast;
The demagogues set Nineveh on flame,
Tore down the throne, and bid wild terror reign!
To be suspected of a love for kings,
Sweep the suspected from terrestrial things:
Factious tribunals, formed by bloody men,
Emptied vast prisons—quickly filled again.
There rolled death's freighted cars, and yonder stood
The crimsoned axe, and scaffold pouring blood!
Nor was this in the Capitol alone:
Thousands rolled down the Tigris and Narbonne;
Thousands of prisoners, ta'en for loyal words,
Fast bound, were slain by unresisted swords;
Compassed in streets, or squares, in each great town,
The volleying arrows swept the captives down!
Nothing but shouts for liberty could save
From banishment, or an untimely grave;

Nor did the authors of those cruel crimes
Escape themselves, in those terrific times;
Old parties by new parties, from high state
And fiercer zeal, were hurled to meet their fate!
The bloody Asgash felt the virgin's knife,
While zeal more fiendish took rough Balzar's life.
The Zeldads—ah! the bright enthusiast dame,
'Midst bawling harlots carted, scoffed, and slain!—
And Rabshekane, that spider-den'd, on watch,
The dark exploder of his sly, slow match,
Mangled and crushed, they poured his serpent gore
Down in the pool the wretch had formed before!
Thus, though more civilized, the Zealot band,
While spreading slaughter through their native land,
Turned fiercely on themselves, in strife for power;
John in the Temple, Simon in the Tower:
Between, for bloody strife, was soon made room,
By incendiary flames, foreshadowing of their doom!

While thus the factions their own vitals wound,
And Roman hosts were densely gathering round,
To Massada Salathiel, safe conveyed,
'Midst tears and wailings, on his couch was laid:
His Miriam, weeping, o'er the hero hung,
While thus love's language murmured from her tongue:
"O my dear husband, is it thus we meet,
Instead of songs and gratulations sweet?
After great deeds of victory and renown,
To be by a base, treacherous slave struck down!
Alas! my aching heart, how oft its throes
Seemed to forewarn us of these coming woes:
That thy undaunted soul, so void of fear,
Would drive thee hapless on some Roman spear,

Or, if in battle, (like a god in arms,)
Thy sword dispersed whole legions in alarms,
Should thou, and our Lysander, and your band
Spread victory's banner o'er this holy land;
Yet still, instead of glory, you would feel,
Aimed at your heart, some hired assassin's steel!
Alas! that love like ours, so true, so strong,
Which in heart-raptures has endured so long,
Should end thus in despair and depth of woe,
Which only souls like ours can feel or know!
Though terrible and stern, when in thy wrath,
Thou sweep'st the base and wicked from thy path,
Like justice in a storm, yet sweet at home
As zephyrs which from banks of roses come.
O! that deep love, joint fusion of our hearts!
Death soon must end me when thy life departs."

Thus mourned the lovely matron; and no less
His daughter's lamentations and distress:
She hung upon the brave Lysander's arm,
Like trembling, pillared flowers, amid the storm;
Who strove with fond caress—and hopes to cheer—
That loving heart, to him, than worlds more dear:
Nor less the sorrows of the youthful son,
Whose step towards manhood scarcely had begun:
All round the couch of the firm, tranquil chief,
Tears and deep sobs disclosed the mighty grief:
He saw and signed for silence—turned his head,
And then, though feebly, with deep feeling said:

"Forbear, dear Miriam; and, kind friends, forbear;
And you, my children, to my heart most dear,
Restrain this gush of grief! Knowing, I say,
Fate holds back death till a more dreadful day:

'Midst falling towers, fierce flames, and flashing arms,
(While Heaven with signs the guilty world alarms,)
There shall I fall, transfixed with many a wound,
With heaps of slaughtered warriors bleeding round!
How this is known by me, inquire not now,
But to Heaven's high decrees submissive bow:
Let that deep love which now sustains my heart,
Shed no more tears, but ply your healing art,
Whence is my prescience that I still shall live,
When I am stronger, I with pain may give."

These words though solemn, sad, and spoke in brief,
Gave to the mourners hope, and calmed their grief:
All that great skill and tenderest love could do,
To justify his words and prove them true,
Was hourly done; and as time rolled along,
The vital powers increased and grew more strong:
As when, from smallest sparks, the household dame
By fine dry fuel spreads the cooking flame,
When rising in the morning, 'tis her care
The laboring husband's breakfast to prepare;
So from the vital spark, by tender skill,
The flame of life rose up—then higher still:
The wounded chief soon convalescent lay,
Still gaining strength, as day succeeded day,
And love's soft fears to hope and joy gave way.

'Twas Jewish Sabbath, and the giant sun
Threw wide his orient gates, and proud begun
To triumph 'round the heavens—when, great and good,
Sweet Miriam's brother near her husband stood.
Her message brought him: bound by numerous ties,
Salathiel deemed him wisest of the wise:

Nor yet so wise as great, nor great as good;
Honored of all, and of the Asmonean blood.
Lysander led him to the Prince's bed,
And thus to him the wounded hero said:
"O son, Lysander, friend in dangers tried,
(Blest be the day that made my child your bride,)
Your dauntless valor and your filial care
Helped on my victory, and has brought me here:
But now withdraw, my son—the troops attend;
I've much to say to this dear kindred friend;
Nay, Miriam, stay; 'tis to you two alone
My long-kept secret I can now make known."

Still leaning on his couch, the wondrous man
To his attentive hearers thus began:
"Dear friends, I lately said, with painful breath,
That this deep wound would not occasion death;
That well I knew I longer must abide,
And higher swell the crimson battle's tide;
That while some fate unknown, beyond control,
Glooms o'er my face, and sickens o'er my soul,
One fact alone is stamped upon my heart,—
I must see HIM again ere I depart!
What wondrous *Him* is this? perhaps you ask:
To speak of Him is now my solemn task.

Near forty years ago, I scarce need tell
The supernatural wonders that befel:
The earth was shaken with convulsive shocks,
Rending to fragments the surrounding rocks;
At blazing noon, the sun, erewhile so bright,
Stripped of his splendors, hid in blackest night;
Dead prophets rose, 'tis said, and walked abroad,
And sought the holy city of their God;

Whilst, as by unseen lightning, noiseless sent,
Down to the floor the sacred Veil was rent:
All marked time laboring with some grand event!

Brother, perhaps you may remember, then
Business detained me in Jerusalem;
I then stood glorious in full manhood's prime,
Chief of our tribe, and of the Aaronic line;
Zeal and ambition ruled my ardent breast;
In me the nation saw their next high-priest:
That morn, by chance, I stood amidst a crowd,
Round Pilate's forum, clamorous for blood:
Their victim of high treason they accuse—
When Pilate asked, 'Art thou King of the Jews?'
He only raised his placid brow and head,
And answered mildly, ''Tis a truth you've said!'
Still to release him Pilate seemed inclined,
But our loud clamors overruled his mind:
To each remonstrance, shouting thousands cried,
'Away with him! let him be crucified!'
We wrung a sentence thus; and then arose
Scoffs, taunts, and insults, round this man of woes:
My zeal for our great Temple, and the Law,
(That shrine the 'circling nations view with awe,)
Filled me with pious rage against the name
Of Nazareth's prophet, and his growing fame,
Who claimed to be Messiah—God's own son,
And sovereign of the world, in days to come:
Hence, on that great, that strange, eventful morn,
I led the rabble, pointed every scorn:
'Twas I that bid the purple robe flow down,
And placed upon his head the thorny crown!
This right hand smote that cheek, illumed with grace,
And bid the vulgar spit upon his face!

Even when they led him forth to instant death,
My zeal and rage was breathed with every breath:
As standing near this man—alone—in woe,
I cried, You vile deceiver, march and go!
Go mount yon cross: 'tis your assumption-throne;
Your coronation-chant, a dying groan!
Nor spared this foot to urge him on the road.
He then turned round—the man seemed full of God!
While a majestic smile his face o'erspread,
With solemn, potent voice the sufferer said:
'Thou man of zeal and blood, stay till I come,
Then be prepared to hear thy final doom!'
He said no more—I heard no more—he passed:
These, his first words to me, and still the last!
That moment fixedness ran through my frame,
Never to alter, always still the same
In soul and body—till he comes again!

Such seems my doom. Dear friends, you both must know
I look as young as forty years ago!
My arm, the brave Lysander can attest,
With all its former power is still possessed!
Through the long fight untiring fall my blows,
My sword wide wasting ranks of fiercest foes!
Oft have men wondered, as time onward rolled,
(And you too, Miriam,) that I grew not old:
You know the reason now: I'm fixed by fate,
The same my powers, the same my love and hate.
My mind can know no change, my body none,
More than if God had turned them both to stone!
I'm bound to what I was before that day
Of zealous rage, dark horror and dismay!
Perhaps you'll ask, How could I, at that time,
Sink down to such profundity of crime?

I can but answer, that the mass of men,
Half-civilized, (as was our nation then,)
Unstirred, moves like some river, broad and bright,
Unruffled, clear, and lovely to the sight,
Holding to azure skies and trees a glass,
And to sweet flowerets and the bending grass;
But let it down disruptured rocks be thrown,
Its rage is stopless, and its power unknown;
Driftwood, and rocks, and trees it whirls along,
And by destruction makes its strength more strong.
So with a populace—smooth in its course,
Till by excitement roused to fearful force;
Then it draws to its vortex mightiest mind!—
To such a headlong power was I consigned:
The mob first caught me, then the mob I led;
(You know, where'er I am, I must be head:)
That man's strange fame had raised my Mosaic hate;
I deemed him juggler, dangerous to the state;
No wonder, then, when half Jerusalem cried,
'Away with him, let him be crucified!'
My voice sealed fate, and justice set aside:
Or that, midst such excitement, like a fiend,
My soul to cruel mockings could descend,
And stoop to acts I will not now defend.
I state all this, that wonders which surround
Your friend and husband may no more astound,
And make you feel assured I'll live, and lead
War's fury through mown ranks of gasping dead;
And till I see that smile and Heaven-set eye,
I'll know no change, nor can Salathiel die!"

With tears, which flowed from mingled joy and grief,
Soft Miriam heard, and weeping felt relief.

Her brother, good Abihud, greatly moved,
Thus answered mild the man he feared and loved:
"Brother, and leader of our noble tribe,
I joy to see you thus in me confide,
And to your wife and brother thus explain
That sometimes gloom which long has give us pain;
But much I grieve, and almost trembling say,
You stooped to blackest sacrilege that day:
You smote the man whom saints and angels sing,
The promised Shiloh, Heaven's anointed King!
Alas! my friend, that you, through causeless hate
And Mo'bic zeal, should meet such woeful fate!
Yet that kind smile, midst grossest insults given,
Would seem to whisper, you may be forgiven!
Three thousand of that furious mob you led,
Who yelling cried, 'His blood be on our head!'
Cut to the heart, in one great, glorious day,
Believing, were baptized, and washed their sins away!
Then why not you? Hear, brother, while I give
Some wondrous facts, which made me first believe
Jesus was very Christ:—Midst crowds, I stood
On Jordan's bank, when in the sacred flood
The Immerser John, as in a watery grave,
Buried this sufferer underneath its wave;
And lo! when from the crystal stream he rose,
I saw the heavens above his head unclose,
And energy divine, down from above
Cowered on his head, in likeness of a dove;
While from the heavens a voice, though clear, not loud,
These words addressed to the astonished crowd:
'This is my Son, beloved, with whom I am
Well pleased.'—On this John cried, 'Behold the Lamb!
The Lamb of God, whose banner, when unfurled,
Shall take all sin and sorrow from the world!'

Brother, yet more: I from that day began,
For three full years, to mark that wondrous man;
Mixed with the multitudes that round him hung,
And with them heard the marvels of his tongue;
For power to speak like him was never given
Before: it seemed as God did speak from heaven!
His sermon on the Mount, from Matthew's pen,
Is known to few, even in Jerusalem;
And that is but an outline of those powers
Which held its thousands chained for many hours:
His voice was rapturous, borne on with awe,
As kingly he proclaimed the gospel law.
Such Godlike themes, such heavenly eloquence,
None heard before, nor have we heard such since:
It seemed enough to prove, could words alone,
He was the mighty Saviour which should come,
Messiah-prince, the heir of David's throne.
But works than words gave higher witness still:
All nature seemed obedient to his will:
To aid his friends, water became choice wine;
O'er seas he walked, majestic and sublime;
The sore, diseased in body or in mind,
His sovereign mandate healed of every kind;
The blind from ebon darkness oped his eyes,
To gaze on flowery fields and shining skies;
The long-sealed ears drink in a mother's voice,
And hear all nature in loud songs rejoice.
I near him stood, when the dense crowd around
Forced friends to let the sick of palsy down
Trough the torn roof. With smiles befitting Heaven,
He said, 'My son, thy sins are all forgiven.'
On this, the attending Scribes and Pharisees
Loud murmured, like the sound of distant seas:

'Who's this,' they cried, 'who durst, by word and nod,
Usurp the high prerogative of God?
Who can forgive but Him?' 'That you may know
The Son of Man has power on earth below
To pardon sins,'—the Saviour turned and said
To the poor paralytic on his bed,
'Those envious men heed not, nor their vain talk,
But hear my words: Take up thy bed and walk!'
What was our wonder when, before our eyes,
We saw the paralytic bounding rise,
Take up his couch, and through the yielding crowd
Walk off, midst shouts and hallelujahs loud!
But who can tell all wonders by him done;
The lepers cleansed, the shoutings of the dumb;
Devils, in men possessed, crying with fear,
'Jesus, thou son of God, what dost thou here?
Art thou now come, and that before thy time,
To seal us close in hell's tormenting clime?'
His hand waved silence, while he calmly said,
'Come out of him!' They heard, and murmuring fled!
But the superior proof of his high claim
Was best displayed when, journeying into Nain,
Full at the gate we met a loaded bier;
Thousands around shed the condoling tear:
A widowed mother followed, bent with grief
Over that prop, so late her sole relief.
Six had she nursed beside: all, all were gone;
And there lay dead her last, her only son!
The Master felt compassion for her case,
And human sympathy illumed his face;
'Weep not,' he cried; then came and touched the dead:
The bearers stood, while he commanding said:
'Young man, arise!' and as from deepest sleep,
The dead sat up, and then began to speak!

He led him to his mother, who with joy
Clasped to her breast her dead, her risen boy!
Great fear fell on the crowd, yet from each tongue,
'Glory to God,' through all the circle rung;
'The Prophet has appeared—the great Messiah's come!'
Nor could I doubt it. To most Jews are known
The grave of Lazarus, and the rolled off stone;
That weeping scene—the sisters and the Jews;—
Nor friendship's tear did Christ himself refuse:
Four days and nights since the decease had run,
And putrefaction ought to have begun,
When the great Master, midst the weeping crowd,
Looked up to heaven, then kingly cried aloud,
'Lazarus, come forth!' and lo! bound in grave-clothes,
From Death's dark cave the dead to life arose!
But all his godlike wonders to detail,
Time and your wound forbid: you still are frail:
I'll only add, that after that dark day,
Which filled us all with terror and dismay,
Near that sweet lake whence Jordan rolls his flood,
I, with five hundred, round the Saviour stood;
Saw him and knew him; heard that gracious voice,
Destined to bless, and make the world rejoice,
The great Calvarian's face (godlike) was known
To me, my friend, as fully as your own:
If you believe me, on that day he rose
Triumphant over death and all his foes;
Full proof he is the Christ—he that should come,
And rule the world, sitting on David's throne:
Then, brother, friend, why not believe on him,
And find free pardon for your every sin!"

Here paused the good Abihud, while the tears
Stole down his cheeks, as if 't were unawares;

While Miriam's head sank sobbing on the breast
Of her dear husband, as his hand she pressed,
And murmured, "My dear lord, can't you believe,
And now the doctrine of the cross receive?
Would you, my love, a hero now become,
A champion of the kingdom that's to come,
Prisons, and pains, and death, I would sustain,
To see thee prince, in great Messiah's reign.
Our Hester and myself (let it not shock)
Have late been numbered with that little flock:
The Saviour bade, 'Fear not, 'midst danger hurled:
Be of good cheer; I've overcome the world!'
Would you and our Lysander with us join,
What joys were ours; our transports, how divine!
Come life, come death, would then be all the same;
For death for him is but with him to reign."

To this the chief: "Of this, my friends, no more:
Your faith I join not, nor your faith deplore.
The Nazarene's a wonder, that I feel,
And must be such, till Heaven the truth reveal.
I'm fixed as fate; but while this wound confines,
Let kindred feeling flow through all our minds:
Safe with our bands, Lysander, and these towers,
Let's give to love and peace the passing hours.
But when new vigor shall my system brace,
Yon sword shall flash in the proud Roman's face:
We'll burst their heathen yoke, their minions reign,
And from pollution free our sacred fane,
Or deep in carnage with my friends remain,
Midst falling turrets and the Temple's flame.
Before that holy place, holiest of all,
With dripping sword I'll fall, if I must fall!"

While thus the chief lay in Massada's towers,
Dark on Jerusalem marched the Roman powers.
As where slain carcasses bestrew the ground,
The slaughter-eagles quickly gather round
In circling eddies—prescient, as they soar,
Ere sword or priest's knife spouts the purple gore,
So round a million, fated to their doom,
Gathered the eagles of Imperial Rome;
For crowds of Jews from all their tribes had fled
Up to Jerusalem, as their nation's head:
Some fled to save themselves from robber bands,
Who (miscalled patriots) ravaged all the lands
In God and freedom's name. They terror spread:
The rich and peaceful quaked with fear and dread;
For all esteemed such were the same as dead.
Many came up to hold the Paschal feast—
That night, when the first-born of man and beast,
Through Egypt's coast, from Pharaoh on his throne
To the blind beggar, outcast and alone,
Fell withering beneath the midnight sword
Of the destroying angel of the Lord;
That finishing, that all-subduing stroke,
Which set their fathers free, and burst their galling yoke!
Others, through patriot zeal for freedom's cause,
Their holy Temple, and their Sinaic laws,
Heroic'ly came up to help the Lord
Against the mighty, armed with spear and sword.
As when the vital powers are deep surcharged
With bile corrupt, which cannot be discharged;
Swift to life's citadel, from each extreme,
The blood, alarmed, throbs home through every vein,
Leaving in icy cold each shaking limb,
Till, joined, they turn to fever-flames within;

So to Jerusalem (Judah's tainted heart,
Diseased with crime) rolled up from every part
The Jews in crowds—from all these causes named—
And left the land cold, desolate and drained;
But when full met, the mighty plethoric power
Brought on the raging, furious fever-hour;
Then factious fury made the mass insane,
And wrapt their domes and Temple in a flame.

Thus in a city four miles square, or less,
The fates a million souls, or more, compress:
Two hundred thousand shine in various arms,
All valiant men—some new to war's alarms;
But safe within their triple walls they boast,
And vow destruction to the Roman host.
But now suspension ceased, and long delay:
The day had come, that dread predicted day,
On Olivet, Jerusalem might behold
The Roman cubes to right and left unfold:
As on the mountain height the cohorts pass,
Their dazzling arms of gold, and steel, and brass,
Flashed back the western sun's descending rays,
Till all the mountain seemed a lengthened blaze;
To the besieged a grand but fearful sight,
So vast their numbers, and their arms so bright.

But Rome's chief force, by noble Titus led,
Wide on the north, more spacious plains o'erspread;
And soon the leaders, with experienced skill,
Marked out their camp on the broad Scopian hill;
The old Assyrian camp, the mount of death,
Where a whole army yielded up its breath;
And thousands, soon, of skilful pioneers,
Under their generals and fit overseers,

Rush to the work; and soon the hill they crown
With walls defensive, and a transient town.
Four gateways led up to a spacious square,
And Titus placed his proud pavilion there;
Magnificent and large, a council-hall,
When dangers new should for new councils call.
Upon the top a small, exalted stand,
From which the eye looked down on all the land;
Street, tower, and ravine, could keen sight explore,
From the great sea to dark Asphaltes' shore;
Mark, midst the battle's rage, how fought each host,
And where his own demanded succor most.

Thus lay the legions, all for war prepared—
But how to take the town, was still a question hard:
In council 't was the advice of one and all,
To launch their engines, and prostrate the wall;
Then, storming through the town, sweep every street,
Till the seditious fell before their feet
In death, or prayer. But, as there lay between
The camp and city a wide, deep ravine,
To raise a mighty bank must first be done,
Along whose top the impetuous ram should run!
On this the general gave a stern command,
To sweep the forests from the neighboring land:
"Fruit trees, the olive grove and spreading oak,—
Let all come down and load the creaking yoke!"
On this at once ten thousand axes sound,
And loud re-echo from the mountains round:
From towering heights and cliffs, the stately ash,
And firs and pines, rush down with hideous crash.
The forests headlong plunge, with fitful roar,
Like angry oceans on a rock-bound shore;

The mighty harvest from the hills rolls down,
And groaning wains convey it towards the town;
Five thousand cars their lumbering labors ply,
And soon the structure rises broad and high:
Cross-beams, strong-bolted, at due distance pass,
And bind together the enormous mass,
And over all a floor of rocks and clay,
To bear the mighty engine on its way,
And give the iron-headed ram full force,
When hurled, to strike with twice two hundred horse,
Well trained and powerful, fitted to the yoke,
And with swift kindling speed to strike the final stroke!

And now this great, this lengthened labor done,
Titus gave orders, with the rising sun,
Their mightiest engine should the walls essay;
While two whole legions, in war's proud array,
Should stand as guards; and when the wall fell down,
Rush through the breach, and storm th' accursed town!

On this the Jewish powers, though rent by jars,
Awhile suspended their intestine wars.
Judeas, Phineas, Simon, all accord
To join and fight the battles of the Lord:
The brave Elkanan, from Esdraelon's plain,
And Judas (would-be Christ) valiant and vain;
All, with wise Eldad, saw the coming storm,
Prepared to burst on them the following morn,
And joined in close consult, what should be done
To avert the dangers of the rising sun.

"Hear me," Judeas said, "each valiant chief,
In Salem born, or here for our relief:

All know yon rampart, reaching to the town,
Was raised our walls and towers to batter down;
That then their veterans, trained and armed complete,
Might death and slaughter spread through every street:
I counsel, then, that ere the morning light,
About the third hour of the passing night,
In force through wide-spread gates our powers descend,
Part fire the bank, and part the act defend:
Let flax, and straw, and oil, with pitch and tar,
Be gathered copious for this burning war;
Along the stationed lines, from hand to hand,
Quick pass the faggots and the flaming brand,
So that combustibles in streams may pour,
Till their bank sinks midst conflagration's roar!"
This council pleased the whole assembled crowd,
Which gave assent with acclamations loud.

Now when the waning moon, in th' eastern sky,
Noiseless proclaimed the god of day drew nigh,
That silent hour when nature sinks down deep
Poor wearied mortals in profoundest sleep,
The Hebrew host, through portals opened wide,
Poured forth in columns silent as the tide:
The front were warriors at all points prepared
To sweep away the feeble Roman guard;
Close following them, the appointed masses came,
To heap the fuel on the rising flame:
Phineas leads the van—and death's alarms
Soon called the slumbering legions to their arms.
Forth from their camp the quick-armed cohorts move:
The moon's pale beams play on their shields above;
Their falchions gleam beneath. With mutual rage,
Both armies now from right to left engage;

Arms, clashed on arms, rang fearful round the fields,
And sword-strokes clamored from ten thousand shields!
The volleying javelins and the whizzing spear,
With fire-tipped arrows, tortured all the air!
Here Issachar's and Ashur's sons rushed on,
And there the knotted spears of Zebulon.
Veterans from Gaul and Thracia them oppose,
Shouts answer shouts, and blows reply to blows.
Manlius upon the left his legion led,
With proud Ventides, boasting at their head,
And wide around the chiefs the slaughter spread!
At times the Hebrew masses seem to yield,
And shrink before the Roman spear and shield;
Again, as from a lull, the roaring storm
Comes on anew, more dreadful in its form;
So would the Jews return.—Fierce in the van,
Jehoahaz shouted, (the great chief of Dan,)
"Come on, Ventides: threats and boasts forbear:
Behold this sword of blood, and dread this spear.
I know you for a braggart 'mongst the crowd,
Distinguished for your pride where all are proud!"

To whom the Roman thus: "Thou gross in form,
Thy language grosser, shows thee vulgar born.
With scorn thy braggart words I thus defy:
Nay, answer not, but hear this javelin fly:
It loud proclaims, vile rebel, you must die!"

On this the javelin flew, but erring flew,
And Jadus, a bold, burning Zealot, slew.
Not so the Danite spear: in both hands held,
It crushed the cuirass underneath his shield,
And cast the vaunting Roman on the field.
Manlius stood o'er him, dealing deaths around,
While others bore him groaning from the ground.

Upon the right, next to the city wall,
Fiercer the conflict, there more heroes fall.
Judas led on the charge, and madly pressed;
His great strength trebled, (by a fiend possessed,)
Loudly he cries, "Ye sons of Jacob, come!
Let blood and vengeance greet the rising sun!
What Hebrew lingers on this glorious night,
This sword shall hew him down with morning light."
On this the furious mass right downwards bore,
The sword of Judas sweeping lanes before:
His maniac strength no second blow requires,
The head falls open, and the wretch expires!
Upon the left, with a resistless thrust,
Lucullus falls, and, writhing, bites the dust;
Varus and brave Lentellus next succeed,
And then bold Castor and Alcanthous bleed.
Thus as he raged along, his bands before,
They followed, and the ground was soaked with gore.
Though brave, the Roman leaders felt dismay
At the dire storm, and for a time gave way;
And wisely, for the excitement of the fiend
By wild exertion wrought its languid end!

Meanwhile Judeas on the centre led
His band of Zealots, he himself the head;
Bent on the ravine to pour down the fire,
For there the bank was more compact and higher.
Upon the Roman cohorts first he pours
Rocks, spears and javelins in incessant showers;
Then waved his sword, and on the rampart sprung,—
His dreadful voice o'er all the conflict rung:
"Brave men, come on," in thrilling tones he cried,
On which rolled up an overwhelming tide:
Swift on the Pyre the opposing parties stood;
Deadly the conflict, and profuse the blood:

Like India tigers, plundered of their young,
Fierce at the Romans' throats the Zealots sprung:
They seize—they grapple: then the Sicrii knife
Is driven with fury to the fount of life!
Discipline such mass fury can't sustain,
But forced retreats to the adjoining plain.
Then loud the hero called, "Pour on the pile
Straw, pitch, and faggots, and the unctuous oil!
Haste, bring the brands: their toil of nine long days,
Mountains and orchards stripped this bank to raise,
Shall mount to heaven in sacrificial blaze!"

On this combustibles of every kind
Poured to the front, pressed on by more behind;
Torches and flaming brands are quick applied,
And shouts and crackling flames roar loud on every side.
The Roman general saw, and called aloud,
To haste and bring and pour the quenching flood;
But distant were the pools—too feebly flow
The scanty showers to quench the flames below;
But still the troops with mutual hate engaged,
And all along the pyre the battle raged.
To drag their engines from the scorching flame,
The Romans strove, but still they strove in vain:
The Jews fast held them, nor could falling brands
Nor heated iron-plates unlock their hands:
When flames subsided, they the flames renew;
The engines rescued back on flames they threw.
But all the time deep gored the Jewish spear,
And Roman falchions sweep down through the air;
Loud shouts, with dying shrieks and battle-cry,
With imprecations, filled the morning sky;
The agony of sin—a dreadful sound,
In dolour echoing from the mountains round!

BOOK IV.

The Vale of Crosses.

At the request of Elias, a storm of wind raises the flames to fury—The Romans retreat towards their camp—The Jews pursue and attack them there—Sempronius is ordered by Titus to charge them with all his horsemen—He makes great slaughter of the Jews, but most of them fly through the gates into the city—Titus, much incensed, calls a council—Various opinions of the officers—It is determined to build a wall of circumvallation, and bring famine on the city—Great distress of the Jews—Two thousand of them taken while searching for food in the fields—Ordered for crucifixion unless the city yields—The Jews hardened by false prophets—A friend of the condemned flies to Massada to implore Salathiel's aid—The parting of Salathiel and Lysander from their wives—Salathiel calls his army from Naphtalia to relieve Jerusalem—A message from the city calls on him to come and save two thousand Jews from crucifixion—The parting of Salathiel and Miriam, and of Lysander and Hester—In the morning the crucifixion begins—The Naphtalians storm Cestus' camp on Olivet, and charge down on the Romans in the Vale of Crosses—The deeds of Judeas, Phineas, Simon, and others, who pour down from the city with the Zealots on the cohorts—Titus, with the horse, comes to aid the cohorts—His encounter with Salathiel—The Romans retreat to their camp—The prisoners released—The crosses made into a vast funeral-pile, on which the slain are consumed, and the Jews re-enter the city in triumph.

THUS warred both armies round the ensanguined bank,
And now the flames arose, and now they sank:

At times the fury of the Jews prevails,
And then disciplined valor turns the dubious scales.

At length the unwearied sun, with splendor bright,
Disclosed all round the horrors of the night:
When Heaven's Vicegerent on Mount Tabor stood,
Glorious as once in days of flesh and blood,
Around him, (though by mortal sight unseen,)
In radiance bright, shone saint and Seraphim;
But nearest him those two who, at that time,
The Saviour called to colloquy sublime:
When Peter saw his glory,—and the theme
Was his own death, the great Calvarian scene,—
His eyes retraced his pilgrimage on earth,
Back from Mount Calvary to his stabled birth;
The glittering temple and the struggling hosts,
Then lake Tiberias, and its lovely coasts;
That beauteous sea, on which serene he trod,
And winds and waves obeyed him as a God.

But now Elias his attention claims,
Crying, "O Master, see those sinking flames!
Shall heathens vile now triumph and prevail,
And Jewish valor at this crisis fail?
O thou, sole arbiter of things below,
Who still'st the tempest, or can bid it blow;
Who gave me power to quell proud Ahab's frown,
And at my prayer [1] the fires of Heaven sent down,
Consumed my sacrifice, and proved to all
That Israel's Lord was God, while priests of Baal
From morn till evening vainly on him call;
Then hear me now, and on yon smouldering pyre
Let south and west winds in joint blast conspire;

Burst on the half-burned rampart, till it rise
In one vast conflagration to the skies:
Though 'tis decreed Israel must feel God's wrath,
Yet, Lord, once more sweep heathens from their path."

Smiling, Messiah said, "Be it at thy word:
The Romans only are Jehovah's sword,
Which He can edge anew." On this down pours
The aërial blast—The crackling rampart roars;
The half-quenched unctuous fuel, heaped up high,
On bank and engines flames up to the sky!
As when a large barn, filled with stacks, hemmed round,
The farmer's toil exuberant has crowned:
If fiendish malice, aided by fierce winds,
The labors of the year to flame consigns,
The hard-earned grain rolls blazing to the sky,
And naught but ashes on the arena lie;
So, of the bank, raised by long toil and pains,
Nothing but cinders in one hour remains!

Aghast, the Romans fled: even Cæsar's frown
Appeared crushed pride in act of bending down;
Their smaller engines, wondrous bank, and all
Their thundering rams, to batter down the wall,
To swift destruction swept before their eyes,
While to the camp cohort on cohort flies;
Anxious within its walls to take new breath,
And leave that dreadful field of blood and death.

But this the Jewish chiefs, insatiate yet
Of blood and slaughter, vowed not to permit;
Band after band, they urge forth to the chase,
And life and death is staked upon the race.
The flying foe the Jews incessant goad,
And streams of blood mark all the struggling road:

Even when the camp's strong gates closed in their face,
Enraged they strove to scale and storm the place:
Like furious terriers, hissed by boys and men,
To drag a badger from his well-fenced den,
So climb, so dig, so pull the Jewish rout,
With hideous clamor and a bark-like shout!

This Titus saw, and with hot rage beheld
His troops dispersed, and flying o'er the field—
His very camp assaulted! Then aloud
He cried, "Sempronius, charge that yelling crowd!
Down on the mob with Rome's resistless horse,
And let death mark the fury of your course:
High on your stirrups stand; your swords, raised high,
Bring glancing down like lightning from the sky:
Let Jewish blood wash off this odious stain,
And vindicate the honor of our name."

On this, and at the clanging trumpet's sound,
Ten thousand horsemen shook the solid ground;
Earth trembled, as when hidden fires within
Shake guilty nations for some impious sin;
Ten thousand glittering swords illumed the air,
And fell regardless of wild shrieks and prayer!
Beneath the war-horse hoofs lie crushed and slain
The flying Jews, and cumber all the plain!
In vain the Hebrew chieftains bravely stove
To stop the rout, which to the city drove;
Often they turned to fight, and nobly fought;
Then, overpowered, the city gates they sought:
The appointed guards had opened wide each gate,
And thus saved thousands from impending fate.
All overta'en were slain, and silence held
Slaughter's dark canopy o'er all the field:

Bank, engines, flames and foes—all, all were gone,
And war, fierce war, seemed for the present done.

Now in his grand pavilion Cæsar next
A council called. The warrior's soul was vexed:
With rage he saw his mighty works o'erturned,
His legions scattered and his engines burned:
He therefore called to council every chief,
And thus addressed them, filled with rage and grief:

"Soldiers, the stains our arms received this day,
Whole years of victory will not wash away.
A mighty labor—our stupendous mound,
The sylvan spoils of all the mountains round—
Now lies in cinders, smoking on the ground,
Stormed by a Jewish rabble!—our grand pyre,
For slaughtered Romans made a funeral-fire!
Nay, more: before the flaming structure sank,
The infuriate wretches strove to storm our camp!
Thanks to our legions of resistless horse,
Their mangled bodies show their maddened course:
'Tis some atonement, but cannot efface
Our dreadful losses and our deep disgrace.
But we'll reproach no more: I've called you here
For your advice; so give it without fear.
How now to wage the war? build banks anew?
Or call pale famine on the rebel crew?
Draw walls around, and hem the wretches in,
Till their shrunk forms are wrapped in parchment skin?
Who can may speak. Speak on, we would hear all:
'Tis for free counsel that we made this call."

On this rose Varo: the subjected north,
Through Gaul and Dacia, wide proclaimed his worth:

"Hear me, great Cæsar," (thus the chief began,)
"The gods can overrule the powers of man:
Our friends who fell on yon contested mound
Should bear no shame, but be with glory crowned;
Nor should their comrades, who in terror fled,
Have ignominy heaped upon their head:
Well had they fought upon the charring wood,
And to scant water joined their streaming blood;
And still prevailed, till that strange western blast
(Sent by the gods) wide down the valley passed:
Then what could man avail? The unctuous load
Of toiling thousands, on the bank bestowed,
In one vast flame from camp to city spread,
Dispersed the living, and consumed the dead!
But well you've said, when, maddened by success,
The rebels dared upon our camp to press,
At your command, our brave Sempronius came
With his dread squadron, and wide o'er yon plain
The maddened mob lies mangled, crushed, and slain!
Rome then is not disgraced—but we have lost
Our lengthened pyre, the labor of a host,
And costly engines. What remains to do,
You've called Rome's generals to consult with you.
Say, noble Titus, can't we ladders form,
Ascend the walls, and take the town by storm?
Five thousand ladders instant might be made,
And twice five thousand form the escalade.
'Tis easier far than other banks to frame,
Destined once more, perhaps, to sink in flame."

He ceased: then Manlius, dignified, arose:
"'Tis brave, I own, what Varo does propose,"
He smiling said; "but has our valiant friend
Thought how we may come down, should we ascend?

The leaders, as the topmost round they gain,
Precipitate hurled headlong on the plain!
Or has he thought of yon long line of rocks,
And men and ladders crushed beneath their shocks?
Vast heaps of them within those towers are stored,
Which would instanter on our heads be poured!
Much then, O Titus, would my voice dissuade
The desperate issue of an escalade!
None sure will think this comes of coward fear;
None who have marked the fury of this spear;
None who have seen this sword wide wasting round,
And its red harvest gasping on the ground.
Then hear me, mighty Cæsar—hear me, all:
Build up new banks, and batter down their wall.
Say you they will again the torch apply,
And send our labors flaming to the sky?
Not so, great Titus; place me to defend,
And their mad sallies shall in slaughter end.
I, with my legion, will the works secure,
Though half Jerusalen through their gateways pour."

Vespasian's son in meditation sate,
And calmly listened while the chiefs debate;
Then raised his princely head: "To build anew
Our ruined bank, were difficult to do.
Where is the timber? For full three miles round,
The forests all lie smouldering in yon mound.
To scale their massive wall and lofty towers,
We might effect by our unconquered powers,
But fierce and dreadful were the desperate strife,
And prodigal the waste of Roman life.
Decimus said—and we agree with him—
'Tis best to close this horde of serpents in:

Already their dire fangs each other wound;
Already murder walks their streets around;
Already conflicts in their public squares
Show sure destruction from intestine wars:
The factions rage when we from war surcease,
And blood flows copious on each transient peace;
Both factions striving for the power supreme,
Pour forth the blood of neutrals in a stream.
'Tis only when Rome thunders at their gates,
Their rage for rapine and for blood abates.
John of Gischala, though a coward base,
Reigns in the Temple, and the Zealots sways:
Simon, the robber chief, holds Zion's hill,
And half Jerusalem owns the tyrant's will.
Each faction, as with fiendish malice blind,
Destroys the food which was for all designed.
One million souls, thus cooped, must shortly feel
Death's pangs by famine, worse than Roman steel.
And thus we'll conquer without deadly strife,
And save a mighty aggregate of life.
With your advice, then let us draw around
This fiendish den a wall and trench (2) profound;
Fairly divide the work in tasks, and then
The energy of fourscore thousand men
Will soon imprison all Jerusalem."

To this opinion all the board agreed,
And the whole army to the work proceed,
In emulating lots: divided fair,
The several cohorts to their tasks repair:
The mighty work goes on, day, night, and morn:
Some toil, some rest, in just successive turn;
While Manlius, with his veteran legion, waits,
To see what Jew dare issue from the gates.

At once, behold! all round the city vast,
The wall ascends as if by magic haste;
At every point alike! With anxious eyes,
The Hebrews see the enclosing structure rise.
As when a caravan, from some wide plain,
Gains the first sight of a vast mountain chain,
It seems a low, dark line; but, travelling on,
They see it rise and tower up to the sun,
Till at its base they stop, and, wondering, stand,
And gaze the impending limits of the land;
So to the observant Jews, from wall and tower,
The circling wall loomed higher every hour,
Till, with three revolutions of the sun,
The mighty work stood perfected and done.

Meantime, Messiah's wide permission given
To all the spirits which had fallen from heaven,
The demons who by guile had gained abodes
Through heathen lands, and worshipped were as gods,
Together with earth's great departed ghosts,
Which filled dim Hades' wide unbounded coasts,
That all might [3] join, as led by love or hate,
And aid the Jewish or the Roman state;
These, all unseen, did in vast numbers come,
Some friends to Jewry, some in aid of Rome:
They hold no council, nor in concert join,
Yet in God's hand they work his will divine,
Roll on the wheels of fate, and haste the day—
That hour of burning terror and dismay,
Ordained to sweep the Jewish state away!

And now, in council on the nation's state,
In full committee the Sanhedrim sate.

Of their two rival chiefs,—of bloody jars,
Intestine murders, and external wars,
They held debate—and fierce the long debate;
Midnight had come before they deemed it late:
When, lo! through the east door a man appears,
Of fierce demeanor, and advanced in years:
His hoary beard was long, uncombed, undressed,
With Maldad's (a false prophet) soul possessed.
When near the midst, he flung his arms abroad,
And cried, "Hear, earth, the burden of the Lord!
Hear ye, ye princes—hear, ye elders, hear!
Fear not the heathen's ([4]) shield or glittering spear!
The Lord through Zion soon will thunder loud:
The Lord will stamp down Rome and all the proud!
Raise high the ensigns of your God, raise high!
Jehovah in a whirlwind will pass by!
I'm sent of God—then hear his awful word:
'My jealousy is up to fury stirred
Against the heathen.' Their old lions roar
Like bulls of Bashan! What! shall they devour?
Their carrion eagles rend their own vile hearts!
Come, all ye fowls of heaven, and take your parts!
The earth shall shake, and fiery tempests pour,
And to Gehenna sink the Roman power.
Then sit not here—decree that all arise;
And those who do not join in vengeful cries,
Hew down—to God a glorious sacrifice!"
Down on the table came his clenchéd hand:
The lamp and ink-horns trembled on the stand.
With foaming lips he turned with furious haste,
And from the door down through the city passed;
Still prophesying to each gathering crowd,
With frantic gestures, dissonant and loud.

To Simon, the bold tyrant, he passed on,
And then to that worse, meaner tyrant, John.
Into the council—chiefs—indeed, the whole,
He deep infused the frenzy of his soul.
As when a dog, rabid from putrid meat,
With foaming jaws runs snapping down the street,
The white frothed poison enters at each wound,
And the dire plague is scattered all around;
So this false prophet, by a fiend possessed,
Transfused his mental poison through each breast.
The whole Sanhedrim, struck with zealous awe,
Quick passed, as Heaven's high will, his bloody law.
The tyrants, too, sent bands of hardened men
To make strict search through all Jerusalem,
For all on whom suspicion breathed its breath,
To seize their goods, and hurry them to death.
They cried, "Let all apostates feel the rod:
Spare none but friends of liberty and God."
This dread proscription passed, (a fearful sound,)
And blood, and groans, and rapine spread around;
Provision stores all plundered, burnt, destroyed,
Leaving whole districts desolate and void!

Meanwhile some prophets of a milder kind,
Nor less enthusiasts, though less blood-inclined,
Proclaimed aloud, (and claimed they spoke from heaven,)
That the Messiah to their prayers was given;
That they had seen him, though as yet concealed,
Nor till the appointed time would stand revealed;
That in some hour of deep distress he'd come,
Display his power, and re-assert his throne;
That though, like Gideon's band, there only stood
Three hundred patriots, hemmed around with blood,

Yet, as fierce lightnings dart forth from the west,
And hurl down towers and temples in the east,
"So with a sudden glory will he come,
And save his people from the power of Rome!
On Olivet, and all the Judean hills,
Shall corpses fall, and blood pour down in rills:
O'er all the land wide wave the vengeful sword,
The sword of David, and of David's Lord!
Their vast engines of war, bows, darts, and spears,
Shall Salem serve for fuel seven (5) long years;
Seven months shall scarcely serve to inter the slain,
Spread o'er the hills, the valleys, and the plain!
Then fear not, Zion—to his temple throne
The Lord, Messiah, suddenly shall come:
Even in the latest hour of deep despair,
His glorious ensigns shall in heaven appear,
And while the thrones of earth are tumbling down,
Assume his right, earth's universal crown."
These wild predictions of false prophets, ghosts,
Pervade Jerusalem and Judea's coasts;
Raise the fierce Zealots' blind presumption high,—
And "God and liberty" was all the cry!
The Romans' languor time and space affords
To turn upon themselves their factious swords;
Murder and rapine through the streets abound,
While groans of the suspected wailing round,
Joined with fierce combats, formed a fearful sound!

But now Messiah, as the hour drew nigh
When doomed Jerusalem must in ruins lie,
To attending angels hath his mandate given,
To astound the nations with dread signs from heaven.
High o'er the city, (ensign of the Lord,)
"Bathed in the heavens" blazed forth his mighty sword.

The hilt, a fiery star, first ([6]) struck the sight,
Thence slowly lengthening in a stream of white,
But changing soon to purple, then deep red,
As blazing 'cross the cope of heaven it spread.
There, night and day, the dreadful emblem hung,
Unhidden by the radiance of the sun.
Amazement seized the nations at the sight;
Some swelled with hope, some trembled with affright.
But not the sword alone, for all around,
Above the horizon, steeds and chariots bound,
On each third night: all fierce, in horrent arms,
The spectral squadrons rushed, midst war's alarms;
Round the horizon, two degrees above,
The fierce battalions to the combat move:
The furious charge, the rout can there be seen,
And seeming blood spread o'er the aërial green:
The rapid chase, the rushing horsemen's bound,
In a few minutes sweep the horizon round.
As when in the far-famed Olympic games,
The rangéd coursers champ in tightened reins;
Spectators stand upon a central mound,
To view the rapid struggle circling round;
As at the appointed sign the swift steeds spring,
All eyes gaze on them flying round the ring;
So gazed both hosts, as round the verge of heaven
The phantom squadrons seemed with fury driven!
All faces paled, and deemed some awful doom,
Or the grand crisis of the world, had come.
The Zealots hoped those wonders in the sky
Foretold the God of heaven himself drew nigh
To save his people—and would once again,
On Scopia's hill, show ninescore thousand slain.
Others, more moderate, viewed it as a sign
That Christ would come and head them in due time;

His conquering banner shortly be unfurled,
To save his Zion, and subdue the world!
The Romans to their auguries looked in vain,
Whole hecatombs of bulls and sheep were slain:
Titus, with all his priests around him, stood,
Inspecting entrails, midst a flow of blood,
Nor omen found; but, turning with a frown,
He cried, "Yon sword hangs o'er the guilty town:
Those fiery horsemen, bounding round (7) the sky,
Are phantoms of Rome's conquering cavalry:
Such are their arms, and such their helmets bright,
And such their bearing in the spectral fight.
Those rushing chariots seem so like our own,
It brings to mind the circus sights of Rome.
The omens then are good: they say that Heaven
Jerusalem has to destruction given,
And that by Roman arms! Thus would I read
Those signs, and say, the gods have so decreed.
But brave men need no signs, nor have they fear,
Though wonders should through heaven and earth appear.
His sword for glory every Roman draws:
His favorite omen is his country's cause.
Then shake not at those signs, which poltroons dread—
'Tis Roman valor has the world o'erspread!
Be Romans still, and, following this bright sword
Of victory and of glory, rest assured."
Encouraged thus, the legions gave acclaim,
And loud resounded their great general's name.

Meanwhile, pale famine had its work begun,
Still pinching keener, each revolving sun:
Upon the poor and slothful it began,
That class which seemed forsook of God and man;

And next the laboring class, who daily strove
To feed the craving objects of their love:
Who in the times of peace could scarcely gain
Enough their wives and children to sustain;
Now cut off from employ and all supplies
By war and rapine, they, with weeping eyes,
In want themselves, day after day low fed
Their pining blood, with lessening bits of bread:
The finest feelings of the human heart
Deep pierced with dolor in its tenderest part.
Nor were the wealthy in much happier case:
Bands of marauders ransacked every place,
Destroyed provisions all, or bore away;
And fell destruction seemed the order of the day.

Thus did the circumvalving wall begin
To crush the pent-up multitude within:
The furious Zealots, urged by fiends beneath,
Spread wide the cry of "Liberty or death!"
They o'er the city held despotic sway,
Still murdering those who strove to fly away—
Even those suspected!—while the Romans took
All who by flight the fated town forsook:
All who climbed o'er the walls for food or flight,
Were prisoners made, or slain as foes in fight:
Two thousand who had thus from famine fled,
Were caught while hunting food, and captives made.

Titus long mused—"What shall I do with them—
These poor, unhappy, sacrificéd men?
They say they meant not to assail my troops,
But glean some herbage, or dig up some roots;
By hunger driven—'tis hard that they should die,
Though taken as an open enemy!

I'll call my generals round me, and advise:
My generals are courageous, just, and wise."

The council called—the Cæsar rose and said,
"Our guards two thousand prisoners have made.
To keep and guard [8] them is a useless cost:
'Twould take five centuries of our valiant host.
To set them free, and all who scale the wall,
Amounts, in fact, to no blockade at all:
Doom them to death were policy severe.
Let some one speak: some council we would hear."

On this Sinctelles rose, and thus replied:
"'Tis no great question, yet we must decide.
I would advise to send them o'er their wall,
And let them to their Jewish mercy fall.
Provide them ladders: those who won't ascend,
Let them mount crosses—a befitting end.
Should friends receive them 'twill decrease their food;
And if they're slain, we're guiltless of their blood.
And thus our troops will be relieved from guard;
And either way, they'll meet a just reward."

Julian, a tribune of great power and fame,
To this replied: "'Twould blot the Roman name
To slay those wretched men. Let them go free:
They're bound to taste enough of misery.
Rome's conquering grandeur minds not petty things,
Nor cruel acts bend down her subject kings.
This city we can take, no matter where
These wretches fly from this destructive war.
I think this is the noblest, wisest way;
But still deferring to superior sway."

This council seemed to favor find with most
Of the great leaders of the Roman host;
But Vendix rose, to cruelty inclined:
The demon Moloch (late) possessed his mind.
A father and a brother, tortured, slain,
Rose to his view, and his fierce soul inflame
Against the Jewish race—"Might I," he cried,
"Have weight, the wretches should be crucified.
Why spare one of this hateful, viperous crew,
To gods so odious, venomous to you—
A nation of vile mob, deep sunk in guilt,
Who through long ages helpless blood have spilt!
When o'er this land they from the desert spread,
Behind them women, babes, and age lay dead!
Who has not heard of that vile butchery vast,
When Saul, their bloody king, through Amalek passed?
Men, maids, youths, sucklings, given to the sword,
And, as they say, by orders of their Lord!
Nor yet enough that all o'ercome must bleed,
Their torturing spirit demons can't exceed.
Their shepherd king, that champion of their law,
Placed men beneath the harrow and the saw!
The sons of Ammon, ta'en in open war,
Dragged to these tortures, keen beyond compare!
Think Romans, think—my father and his son
To pillars bound, and scourged till life was gone!
Think how the noblest Jew in these late times,
Glorious in goodness—for denouncing crimes,
Was by them taken, scourged, defamed, belied;
Nor stopped their rage, till he was crucified!
To Pilate's wish to save the just, they said,
His blood be on us [9] and our children's head!
These are the men thus doomed, whom we have caught,
And should to crucifixion's pains be brought:

Such deeds should fix deep hate on all the crew.
Where is the Roman that would spare a Jew?
Yes, where's the Roman? 'Tis not Cestus sure,
Who left Bethhoron red with Roman gore!
'Tis not the kindred of ten thousand men,
Whose bones lie bleaching in that horrid glen!
'Tis not brave Maxus' shade—last of that band
Who for their country made that desperate stand!
Salathiel, (dreadful name,) in single fight,
Sent this last victim down to endless night!
Think then of this Thermopylæ of Rome,
And spare no Jew who in our power may come:
I cry, with tortured friends, as once they cried,
'Away with them! let them be crucified!'"

This speech all mercy banished from the board,
And death's dread fiat passed with full accord:
Even Titus to the vengeance now gave way,
And though he gloomed, he nothing did gainsay;
For Cæsar, though somewhat inclined to good,
Was bred to carnage, and was nursed in blood!

While thus the Jewish pride and Roman hate
Rolled on the car of destiny and fate,
Salathiel to full health and strength arose;
Through all his frame his former vigor glows.
Early from all Naphtalia's hills and dales,
(Where orange groves and cassia load the gales,)
The prince had sent for choice ten thousand men,
To rally round his flag, and save Jerusalem.

And as down from the north he saw them come,
His heart beat high to try his strength with Rome.
He turned them round Massada to the road
That led to God's high Temple, once his bright abode.

But now before him stood, all bathed in tears,
A wild embodiment of hopes and fears.
"Great prince," he cried, "O come, O! quickly come,
And save my friends from their impending doom!
Two thousand of our brethren fettered lie,
Caught searching herbs, and two days hence must die:
Unless before that time (thus they've decreed)
Jerusalem yields, they on the cross shall bleed.
Amongst them I've a father and a son,
Whose prayers (with thousands) bid me ceaseless run,
And plead you would to their deliverance come.
For the fell tyrants will not yield or bend,
Though half Jerusalem the cross ascend!
Come, then, great hero of Bethhoron, come,
And save us once more from the rage of Rome!"
With groans and tears, the wearied man fell down,
And mournful silence filled the chamber round.
At length thus spake the chief: "Go, say we come,
And will be there with the third rising sun,
To save them, if God wills: if not, His will be done."

Now for a bold, decisive point in war,
Salathiel bids Naphtalia's sons prepare
To march at noon, next day, with all their powers,
And leave Massada for Jerusalem's towers.
But ere the prince and brave Lysander drew
Their swords for Salem, well the heroes knew
They had to pass a scene, which to sustain,
Was worse than legions charging o'er the plain:
They had to leave their loves, that made home, home,
And rush to scenes of death, and perils erst unknown!

The chieftains now were armed; their coursers stood
Pawing, impatient, in the adjoining wood.

When the Naphtalian chief his Miriam found,
(She'd seen him arming, and in tears was drowned,)
"Why thus," he cried, "my love, indulge in woe?
'Tis God's own voice from heaven that bids us go
And save the helpless from a cruel foe.
Yon sword of God, which flames athwart the heaven,
Those rushing combats round the horizon driven,
Call us, my love, to guard our sacred fane.
Where danger lowers, the foremost place we claim,
Foremost in danger as the first in fame.
The wondrous signs which through the concave shine,
Are omens good, and promise aid divine.
My life, I feel, stands charmed and guarded round
By some strange power, [10] mysterious and profound,
I feel assured midst death I'll safe remain
Till I behold that eye, that face again!
Besides, all mortals—most the brave and great—
Are wrapped around by Heaven's decree of fate.
No hostile hand can send me to the tomb,
Until the hour ordained by Heaven shall come.
Then why shun danger, in its wildest form,
When called by duty to the battle's storm—
When called by Heaven to guard that sacred fane
From Jews' pollution and from Roman flame?
Still more, dear Miriam: should we die for God,
By dark assassins, or in fields of blood,
Both of our faiths behold an opening heaven,
And crowns of glory to such martyrs given;
Then stop those tears, and let us nobly part,
As heroes should, with an undaunted heart."

On this the mournful matron raised her eyes,
And strove to rule her grief, and thus replies:

"O my dear husband, 'tis not captive chains:
(Though when you're gone, what else for us remains?)
I think not of myself, or our sad fate,
A burning temple or a ruined state;
My soul flies trembling out, and sees some plain,
Where, hemmed midst corpses, you, my lord, lie slain—
Panting perhaps for breath, mid smothering dust,
Or craving water, parched with dying thirst!
O! could I but be there to haste and bring
The cooling moisture from some living spring;
To hold it to your eager lips, and see
Your eyes beam bright to know it comes from me;
To raise your languid head, catch your last breath—
This would console me—lingering down to death.
For long I cannot live when thou art gone:
'Midst friends I'd droop, disconsolate, alone.
Yet go, my husband, meet the mighty foe;
My prayers attend you from this heart of woe.
I'm Israel's daughter, of the Asmonean line,
And feel, with you, my country's wrongs are mine."
The armèd warrior clasped her to his breast,
And with a kiss these parting words addressed:
"Like Miriam spoken; and should I, in defence
Of our God's temple, fall, then fly you hence;
Your brother dear will guide you to some glen,
Far from the scenes of war and bloody men;
There think of me, and let your thoughts be sweet,
Till in a happier world our spirits meet."

This said, the fate-fixed chief turned round and gave
The firm, mild mourner to a favorite slave.
Then left the room, and stood beside his horse,
To mount and head his army on its course;

Yet waited for Lysander. That brave chief
Was still employed to calm his Hester's grief:
She met him as he sought her: on his breast
She cast herself, enfeebled and distressed.
But when within her arms her lord she found,
Her grief burst forth in words with tremulous sound:
"Life of my life," the weeping fair began,
"O! leave me not, thou much too daring man!
From fields of blood I know you've victor come,
But can you face the embodied powers of Rome?
No, borne down by whole legions on the plain,
Thine arm grows weary, and thou must be slain!
Methinks I see thee, wounded, fainting, fall,
Or in the field, or near the Temple wall.
Was it for this you crushed the robber band,
First took my person, next my heart and hand?
Was it for this, regardless of renown,
You for my love laid all your (11) prospects down—
Your troop of Syrian warriors, armed for Rome,
Sent back disbanded to their mountain home?
Could my soft, grateful heart resist such charms,
Such love, such graces, such renown in arms?
No, since that day I've been entirely thine,
And thought thy heart was as intensely mine!
How high the bliss of that remembered hour,
When all my world entered my virgin bower!
Then, dear Lysander, let us now retreat
To the wild hills that hold your Syrian seat;
Or if the hatred of vindictive Rome
Should wrest from you your rich paternal home,
Then let us fly to some secluded vale,
Far from the scenes of blood and misery's wail!
With thee, a cave were paradise to me;
Without thee, paradise but misery!"

Tears ever flowed as the fair mourner spoke,
And sobs, and sighs, and groans her utterance broke.

To this the much-moved husband thus replied,
As tenderly he placed her by his side:
"Dear Hester, think not for a chief's renown,
Or through blind zeal, I'd aid yon fated town.
I worship one great God who rules above,
And lesser gods, his ministers of love.
To every nation some one is assigned, ([12])
To scatter wide his blessings o'er mankind.
To all of them should thanks and praise be given,
But most of all to the great King of Heaven.
For no religion would I draw my sword,
By me for creeds no human blood be poured.
Far less, my love, would I, for dying fame,
Spread death around, and triumph o'er the slain.
Far rather would I now with thee retreat
To some lone cottage, or my mountain seat;
But can I leave your sire, my noble friend,
Whose soul is fixed for freedom to contend,
And to the last Moriah's fane defend?
I cannot bear to think upon that hour,
When, near borne down by legionary power,
Your war-worn father, leaning on his spear,
Should panting say, O! was Lysander here!
Or still more helpless, bleeding on the field,
And I not there to spread my covering shield!
How often has he said, with generous pride,
'Lysander, when you're raging by my side,
I fear no danger—'midst the deep array
Of doubling ranks our swords can still make way.
Before our floating helms and blazing shields,
The mightiest warriors have forsook the fields!'

Can I forsake him when my aid he claims,
To save from lingering crucifixion's pains
Two thousand of your race? My love, say No!
And then undaunted to the field I'll go.
And should we fall, the noble Abihud,
Your uncle—not less wise than brave and good—
Will guard you safely to some friendly glen,
Far from the paths of war and bloody men.
Then bid me go, and to this lingering kiss
Let your response, my love, be, Yes—go—yes."
To his soft whisper the response was given,
Then from his arms she sank, ([13]) and knelt to Heaven.

And now each warrior at the head appears
Of full ten thousand strong Napthalian spears:
Twelve furlongs east the town they camped that night,
To rest, to feast, and sleep, and arm for fight.

At length from his bright chamber in the east
The sun stepped forth, that pompous punctual guest.
His glowing eye o'er all the landscape spread,
And smiled, rejoicing on each mountain's head:
To mist-filled vales, his levelled rays above
Sent twilight down, like the first dawn of love;
His glories mellowed by the obstructive cause,
Like beauty beaming through a float of gauze.
Such was sweet nature's face, when down the vale,
Between two mountains, formed to catch the wail
Of shrieks, and groans, and sobs, (that horrid glen,
Where demons crucified their fellow-men,)
A crowd of groaning, helpless wretches passed,
Their features famine-shrunk, ([14]) with fear aghast.
Along each side, crosses of rough-hewn wood
Lay heaped in piles, and close beside them stood

Grim men, with nails and hammers in their hands,
Waiting to catch their officers' commands.
Already had the horrid work begun,
And hundreds screaming on the crosses hung;
Dragged down, and stripped, and nailed as they came in,
Their shrieks half drowned by the loud hammers' din!
The sufferers and those awaiting fate,
Formed one joint wail, too dreadful to relate:
From cliff to cliff, loud cries and groans rebound,
And echoes answered echoes all around!

But now a sound more wild, more fierce and proud,
Burst from Mount Olivet, as thunder loud:
The ram-horn's blast, the horsemen's bounding tramp,
And fierce Napthalia, storming Cestus' camp,
Appalled the murderers in their barbarous glen,
And drowned the groanings of the suffering men.
As when a dark tornado from the south
Roars through a forest trending to the north;
The traveller, quaking, hears some space before
The whirlwind's sound, the elemental roar,
The towering pine, strong oak, and mountain ash,
Hurled in confusion with a deafening crash;
So heard the Romans the tumultuous sound
Of shouts and clashing arms, wide echoing round.
Upon the Roman camp, with axe in hand,
And ported spears, rush down Napthalia's band!
Lysander and the chiefs, Simon and Zoar,
Their plumed helms waving, thundered on before.
The gates are burst—the circumvalving walls,
Weak at this point, before their fury fall!
The guards unguarded—most had gone to see
The morning's work of death and butchery.

The few remaining either timely fled,
Or in the encampment at their posts lay dead.
Down to the vale of groans the victors came,
(The Roman camp behind them all in flame,)
Impetuous as when Heaven's whole watery store
Upon a lengthened chain of mountains pours;
The adjacent ravines roaring, tumbling on,
Till with joint fury they unite in one
Broad flood, that sweeps the whole adjoining plain
Of flocks, and herds, and stacks and standing grain.
So down the mountain the assailants poured,
So through the valley swept the united horde.

But Roman discipline and courage still
Would not give way—they formed beneath the hill.
All Cestus' legion at the camp not slain,
And one of Cæsar's, sent to guard the plain,
Embodied close: shield joining shield, they stood
With levelled spears, to meet the assailing flood.
Then raged the combat: man to man opposed,
And rank to rank with mortal fury closed.
Along the north-west slope, where smooth descends
The hill, and in the vale of horror ends,
The conflict burned!—Eliphaz on the right,
And Dothan, fiend-possessed, led on the fight.
At brave Lucullus flew the Hebrew spear:
The weapon entered deep below the ear:
Prone fell the warrior on the rocky ground,—
Groans, curses, arms, returned a mingled sound!
Siverius saw, and raging at the deed,
Sent forth his lance with fury's nervous speed;
It erred, but, whirling on its fated course,
Stuck down proud Asa from his foaming horse.

Nor less upon the left the battle bleeds,
Nor less the number of heroic deeds:
By brave Lysander and Napthalia's might,
Even Roman valor often turns to flight;
Then turns again, their broken ranks reform,
Bear down anew, and meet the coming storm.
Thus, as to ascertain some named supplies,
The merchant's trembling scales now sink, now rise,
So, as the orb of day rolled up the sky,
The furious combatants pursue, then fly;
Nor can the Romans to the plain descend,
For yet the Jews the embattled hill ascend.
At length great Cæsar heard these strange alarms,
And round him called five thousand horse to arms;
Sempronius at their head!—Was heard afar
The thunder sound, as they rushed down to war:
The Hebrews' front was broken, and disarray
Marked the fell havoc of the dubious day.

But not unseen from Salem's walls and towers
Was this long strife of the conflicting powers;
The wished-for rescue soon was seen by all
The kindred mourners hanging on the wall.
Phineas, when he beheld, to Judas cried,
"Why do we, in our fame and prowess' pride—
Why do we stand, with armèd warriors round,
And hear war in yon cursed vale resound?
Napthalia's chiefs have to the rescue come,
And now stand struggling with the powers of Rome,
For us and ours. What Jew dare longer stay?
Open the gates, and give our fury way."
He said—and soon from all parts of the town
The Jews in multitudes with shouts ran down;

Zealots and peace-men—names were all forgot:
A common furor drove them to the spot
Where bled the conflict—where the Roman shields
And glancing swords flashed dreadful o'er the fields.
Simon, the tyrant, Judas at his side,
Upon the left withstood Rome's rushing tide:
Possessed by Jehu's ghost, his natural power
Was trebled in that sanguinary hour:
Through plume and helm his quick-descending blade
Cleft open wide the bold Elexor's head.
Strabo, Decimus, and young Festus bleed:
Alfidus next; Rufus to him succeeds:
His maniac prowess no resistance found,
Till nine brave chiefs lay groaning on the ground!
Exhausted then, the furor left his breast,
And pale and languid, he drew back for rest.
But Judas still held on his fierce career,
And at Lufidon whirled his weighty spear;
The impetuous weapon err'd, but pierced the side
Of great Metellus, Padia's boast and pride:
Nor stayed his hand, but with his sword cut down
Three Roman knights of valor and renown,
And office high in rich Tavilla town.
But on the right Vespasian's son now shone,
Heir to his glory and the imperial throne:
Dreadful the slaughter that around him spread,
With twice a hundred knights, he charging at their head.

Lysander saw, and to Salathiel cried:
"O father, turn and view yon homicide;
'Tis Cæsar's self: I see his plumage wave,
Hemmed round with peers. O! let us haste to save
Our friends, fast sinking to a bloody grave!"

Salathiel heard; and as the heroes move,
Napthalia's spears, borne like a leaning grove,
Attend their course, and met the cohorts' might
In long-contested, bloody, dubious fight.
Fierce on great Titus and his waving plume
Salathiel rushed; his sweeping sword made room.
As down the cliff, to meet him, Titus came,
His courser, stumbling, dashed him on the plain;
Upon his sword-arm lay ([15]) the encumbering horse,
As near him rushed the Hebrew in mid course;
The keen spear's point above the Cæsar hung,
But came not down, though as in act to come:
"O Prince," Salathiel cried, "born to command,
'Tis God himself withholds my lifted hand:
Sure Heaven's own ægis, o'er you now unfurled,
Proclaims you destined to command the world.
But for this ransomed life—o'erpowered and slain,
When dead Salathiel lies on yonder plain,
Or by yon Temple's wall in fate's last strife,
O! yield my body to my weeping wife!"
No more was said; for, quick as levin flame,
Full twenty knights down to the rescue came;
In swift retreat the hero's safety lay,
And soon he joined the Hebrews' wild array.

But Titus, mounting now his horse again,
Restrained his cohorts from the slaughter plain.
"Return," he cries, "but in firm order turn,
Lest by a mob the imperial camp should burn.
If they pursue, then wheel, and let their gore
Down from the cliffs to yon sad valley pour."

But all the Jewish chiefs, Salathiel too,
Saw at a glance 'twas dangerous to pursue.

The hero raised his voice, and hills around,
And the long, bloody vale, returned the sound:
"Down to the crosses rush! ye Hebrews, go,"
He cried, "and save your friends from pain and woe.
The mourning sufferers from the cross take down,
And let their friends convey them back to town.
Those bound in heaps release, and bid them straight
Fly to asylum through the open gate.
And you, brave Hebrews, who have won the day,
This is no time for triumph and delay:
Haste to the crosses, pile them up on high:
In one long heap let their cursed engines lie:
Upon it lay the Israelitish dead,
The crucified, and those who for them bled;
And may the winds of heaven be freely given
To waft our brethren's spirits up to heaven."

On this ten thousand, instant at the word,
Rushed to the appointed work with full accord.
The sick and wounded, placed on many a wain
And haste-formed litters, slowly left the plain.
Others the reared-up crosses, (stained with gore,)
Raging, rent up, and to the structure bore:
With these hundreds not [16] used they quick combine
With fuel, straw, and prunings of the vine;
Fences and groves, and all the houses round,
Are brought in loads to raise the enormous mound.
Great was the lengthened pile, and o'er it spread
Were many thousands of the untimely dead:
The crucified, and those despising life,
Who to the rescue led the morning strife,
All heaped in haste, now waited but the brand,
Which soon was brought by many a willing hand.

Meantime dark clouds (such was Messiah's will)
Arched the sad valley o'er from hill to hill;
And on the appliance of the kindling flame,
Down on the pyre the northern tempest came:
No rain-drop fell, but blast succeeding blast,
Spread wide the roaring flame—impetuous—vast!
As when the Macedonian, flushed with wine
And victory—claiming a descent divine,
Led by a courtesan—applied the torch
To Persia's capitol and Magian church:
The flames, as drunk as him, roared o'er the town,
And all the glory of the East sank down
To a cinderous heap; so now, fierce flaring wide,
The wind, borne burning, flamed from side to side,
And thus the vale of slaughter purified.
Not till real night succeeds the Heaven-sent cloud,
And natural darkness spread its sable shroud,
Ceased the wide flames: by fits they glowed and burned,
Then sank: the enormous pile to ashes turned,
And night in sables o'er the Cedron mourned.

But ere that hour, the Hebrew chiefs, elate
From their great victory, sought the city gate.
Simon, the tyrant, all his armor red
From frenzied fight, his band of Zealots led:
Judeas, Phineas, Abner, and Talmud,
With other leaders from the field of blood,
Followed in train. But at another gate,
Napthalia's heroes passed in solemn state,
Sore toiled with lengthened conflict; but shouts still
In triumph rose, as they ascend the hill.
Loud acclamations greet them as they come,
And hail them as the conquerors of Rome!

But though the victory thus was hailed with joy,
'Twas mixed with moans and famine's ([17]) dread alloy.
Through all the city, though of success vain,
A sad substratum spread of woe and pain.
Gaunt Famine winged the air from home to home,
While in low hovels starving infants moan;
Mothers, with hunger stung, search round for food,
To snatch some morsel for their suffering brood;
Gaunt, famished mortals roam from street to street,
And neighbors, starving, starving neighbors meet;
While spectral skeletons, with gibbering cry,
Glide o'er their heads, then vanish in the sky.
Hopes to the highest raised for late success,
Were mixed with groans and wailings of distress:
These formed a sound to ears before unknown—
Victory's wild shouts joined with the funeral's groan!

Meanwhile to quarters passed the hostile powers:
The Jews to Zion and Antonia's towers;
Napthalia's warriors filled the huts and halls
Of owners slain and cast beyond the walls;
The Roman legions to their strong camp sped,
Bringing with them their wounded and their dead,
Which o'er the plains and mountain sides lay spread.
With stern, proud grief, not tearless, they inhume,
And vengeance vow o'er every warrior's tomb.
Nor felt they not the hateful, humbling tone
Of groaning friends and cohorts overthrown!
Thus on the fate-doomed city sunk down night,
And Scopa's hill felt glad of the respite.
Beneath night's ebon pall, o'er all things spread,
Both armies mourned the living and the dead.

BOOK V.

The Denunciation.

Great distress of the city, by plunder and famine—A Zealot bursts into Titus's tent—Informs him that a mother had set before him her roasted child—Calls upon him to take the city, and thus save the people—Josephus sent with an offer of peace—The speeches of Josephus and John—Josephus is struck down by the contrivance of Maldad, and peace prevented—Who Maldad was—A fugitive from Cœlo-Syria—His crime—Brings a band of men to aid in the defence of Jerusalem—Is demanded by the Priests of Baal—The Sanhedrim called to consult on the matter—Maldad's defence before the Sanhedrim—John makes a speech in his behalf—They refuse to deliver him up to the Priests of Baal, who had demanded him—He stirs up the Zealots—Has Josephus stricken down, and peace prevented—Jews rush on the Romans unprepared—Dreadful battle under the walls—The Roman legions give way—Titus, with a great body of cavalry, charges the Jews—All slain who cannot gain the opened gates—Silvius, Titus's dearest friend, slain—His dread denunciation on that event—The discourse of Salathiel and Lysander on the course they should take.

Now Sol's bright rays, piercing the alleys through,
Glanced down and saw the depth of Salem's woe.
His beams disclosed, low moaning, all around,
Vast crowds of famished, pining prisoners, bound;
Suspected friends of Rome, whose scanty food
Scarcely sufficed to move their stagnant blood.
In other districts deeper woes appeared;
The plundered home—the violated maid,

Wailing beside her mother. Sad she sits:
Now gleams her reason; then her reason flits;
Body and soul both crushed, she, living, dies;
And death alone can end the sacrifice!

But through more squalid walls and doleful homes,
Heaven's beams glanced down, darkened by dying groans.
There the pale mother has no tears to shed;
Her waking infants feebly cry for bread:
"Children, I've none," she, sinking down, replies;
And stupor kindly lulls her agonies.

Heaven's great Vicegerent saw, and, pity-moved,
Called round his throne his ministers above;
Then thus: "Ye thrones and dominations high,
Angels, archangels, ruling now the sky,
The days of tribulation now draw near;
Nay, Salem's groans proclaim they now are here.
Men's hearts all trembling, (1) failing them for fear:
Such days of woe, and worse, which must haste on,
Since earth's creation never have been known,
Nor ever shall be. And unless my power
Shorten those days and haste the final hour,
No flesh from the fierce vengeance could be saved,
But all the race in ruin's gulf ingraved.
But, for the elect's sake, a precious band,
Now groaning under persecution's hand,
Those days we now will shorten—bring the end,
And let the Temple in fierce flames ascend.
The Sinaic Covenant now must pass away,
And give place to the new, the Gospel day.
For this, let all those signs, through earth and heaven,
Foretold by me and ancient seers, be given;

Let mad, false prophets cry, (2) Lo! here—lo! there—
Fill nations with vain hopes and wild despair;
Let earth be shaken, meteors fill the sky,
And heaven to earth proclaim, the hour is nigh;
For this end, let the Hadean spirits come,
And demons stir the heathen powers of Rome;
While lying prophets, as in ancient days,
The Jewish factions to wild frenzy raise;
That all the nations round may see Heaven's rod,
And know that sin brings down the wrath of God!"

Thus spake Messiah; while around his head,
And through the heavens, benign his glories spread.
Then thus, to Abraham: "Father, descend,
And let thy kinsman, Lot, with thee attend.
Assume your earthly forms, as when below,
And to Massada's frowning fortress go;
There to my friends, in converse free, disclose
The vengeance coming on their cruel foes.
To good Abihud, now the family's head,
Let all you know of Heaven's high will be said;
As friends with friends, hold free and kind discourse,
And give instructions for their future course.
Tell them, midst all their sorrows, fears, and grief,
Even at the latest hour, I'll send relief."

Titus, mean time, to take Antonia's tower,
Had called around him all the Roman power;
Had raised new banks, with forests brought from far,
With orchards, houses, all the wreck of war.
In vain had the eruptive Jews once more
Essayed to burn it, as they did before;
Manlius, true to his threat, soon spread the plain
With piles of Jewish mob, cut down and slain.

Well did the carnage, round the banks that day,
The slaughter in the Crosses' Vale repay.

But Titus now in his pavilion sate,
With friends consulting on the affairs of state;
When, lo! a suppliant entered at the door,
With pallid face, his garments rent and tore.
Humbly he knelt, with dust upon his head,
His eyes suffused, and hands up heavenward spread:
"Hear me, great prince," he cried, "and chiefs of Rome:
God sent me here, or how could I have come?
For suffering thousands I am sent to say,
'Tis Heaven's high will you make no more delay.
One hundred thousand of the friends of peace
Have suffered long, and still their woes increase.
The tyrant's bandits, by rapine and blood,
Have to their stores ta'en all the people's food.
They can sustain the siege till famine sends
Down to the grave the poor, who are your friends."

"Who and what are you?" cries the Roman chief,
"And what your meaning? Let your words be brief."

"Great Cæsar," he replies, "I have been one
Of the dread followers of the tyrant John;
Head of a band, to range where we might please,
Slay the suspected, and provisions seize.
And now, (all horror-struck,) hear me disclose
The dreadful acme of this famine's woes:
As, in our search, we passed a widow's door,
(A house we plundered some short time before,)
And meant to pass it by—but a perfume
Of baked meats, rich as from a banquet-room,

Caused us to enter, [3] seize the woman fast,
And ordered her to bring that nice repast,
On pain of death. She grimly smiled, and said,
'Release my hands, and I'll the table spread.'
She did, with a white damask cloth, and soon
Brought forth a cover from an inner room,
And placed—O God!—before us a roast child,
Its baked, crisped hands across its breast! then wild
Screamed: 'Eat, ye fiends! you beasts need not be nice,
Since I, its mother, have partaken twice!
See its left side: 'twas there I chose my part;
Through that wide rent you'll find its tender heart!
Nine days of hunger, raging fierce within,
Brought on by you, has caused this horrid sin.
But eat—I've kept it for you—and may God
(If one there be above earth's wretched clod)
Let loose the fiery vengeance from his hands,
On the cursed tyrants and their hellish bands!
May all the fiends below or on earth reign,
Rage round and through them, with tormenting pain;
Long agonizing, may the wretches lie
In torturing flames, and vainly pray to die!'
Then, with a maniac scream I can't forget,
(Aghast I heard it, and I hear it yet,)
She flew forth to th' adjoining room, and fell—
In fits or death—I know not, nor can tell;
For, horror-struck—appalled—I, trembling, fled,
And, Heaven-impelled, am to your presence led—
To say, great Cæsar, 'tis the will of God,
You—whom he deigns to make his mighty rod—
That you to action your great engines call,
And batter down their last remaining wall;
Pour all your powers, and crush the robber bands,
And save the dying city from their hands."

This said, while horror held the circle round,
He left the presence with a manaic bound.

Titus a moment sate amazed; but now
He turned towards heaven his eyes and frowning brow:
"Romans," he cried, "and has this deed been done—
A crime unknown before below the sun?
This monstrous deed, this sad, soul-shocking crime,
Should bring down vengeance, human and Divine.
A city marked with this foul, fiendish stain,
No longer midst the nations should remain.
Too long for my own fame and just renown
Have we lay starving out a rebel town.
It stands not with Rome's grandeur thus to wait,
Like a court-guard before a hostile gate.
No! signs Heaven-sent and loud our honor call,
To crush the tyrants, and prostrate their wall.
But yet, before we bring our engines down,
And with dread slaughter desolate this town,
Once more the olive branch we will extend,
And bid them bring these horrors to an end.
Five hundred thousand, 'tis to us made known,—
All friends of peace, and therefore friends of Rome,—
Have, since this siege, been from their ramparts thrown;
All dead—all slain—by their infuriate strife,
By pining famine, or the assassin's knife;
And daily, still, by hundreds corpses fall,
Like carrion cast from their polluted wall.
To stop at once this wide-extended woe,
And streams of blood which otherwise must flow,
Go thou, Josephus, and to conference call
John and his Zealots, near the Temple wall:
Offer free pardon, if they will submit,
And add such reason as you may judge fit:

If they refuse, then Heaven itself says, Go,
And end this lengthened agony of woe."

Meantime, according to the Lord's command,
New signs and wonders terrified the land.
Still gleamed God's sword across the vault of heaven;
Still horse and chariots round its verge were driven,
And now bright meteors, blazing through the sky,
Impressed new terrors on each gazing eye;
Deep earthquakes Salem shook with dolorous sound,
As if destruction murmured under ground;
Strange, spectral forms through all the air were seen,
Fantastic, hovering earth and heaven between.
Still more: the Temple's beauteous eastern gate,
Of wide dimensions and of ponderous weight,
(Full twenty men were to the action put,
The folds to open and the gate to shut,)
Now, as self-moved, before their wondering eyes,
With clanging sound it shuts, then open flies.
By this, the Roman Augurs said, 'twas shown
They could instanter take the accursed town;
While through the city lying prophets rove,
Proclaiming God from the high heavens above
Was hovering o'er them with his angel-guard,
To save his Temple, and his friends reward.

But, still increasing, went that awful sound,
Which, for seven months, had walked the city round:
"Woe to Jerusalem! to Jerusalem woe!"
In voice sonorous, melancholy, slow.
Midst those dread signs which bright in heaven appeared,
Morn, noon and night, those mournful sounds were heard.
To buffetings and scourgings, all he said
Was, "To Jerusalem woe! she dies! she's dead!"[1]

As through the streets and round the walls he'd go,
He still croaked forth, "Woe to Jerusalem! (5) woe!"
This boding form was ominous and wan,
Half figuring death, and half resembling man:
He ate what any might at times bestow;
But still he cried: "Woe to Jerusalem! woe!"
From whence this wretched, wandering mortal came—
Whether Heaven-sent, or some poor wretch insane—
The moving world knew not, nor seemed to know;
But, still, his everlasting note was "Woe!"
Along the ramparts, wide, his arms he'd throw,
And scream aloud: "Woe! to Jerusalem woe!"

These signs, through heaven above and earth below—
The blazing comets, and denouncéd woe—
The flaming sword—Heaven's chivalry in arms—
And man, and matter, trembling with alarms—
Spoke loud, from heaven above to trembling earth,
Of dire events forth struggling into birth.

And now Josephus, near the temple walls,
John and the Zealots to a parley calls.
For this an olive-branch was waved on high,
And John went forth, to listen and reply.
Soon as he placed himself where he could hear,
Josephus thus addressed each listening ear:
"O, all ye Jews, with your fell tyrant, John,
Attend the message I have come upon.
I come to offer peace even at this hour,
On due submission to great Cæsar's power.
Why should you thus prolong this useless strife,
So full of woes, so prodigal of life?
Your city groans with still increasing woe,
And soon your homes must lie in ruins low.

Think of your brethren suffering famine's pains;
Think of yon holy Temple wrapped in flames;
Think of those woes, and from vain warfare cease,
And timely take the offered branch of peace.
You say, O John, you fight for freedom's cause—
For Israel's liberty and Israel's laws.
I grant, a nation free may wisely fight
Against invading powers of equal might:
Should Syria, Moab, Ammon, or the bands
Of roving Arabs, try to seize your lands,
And subjugate you, then 'twere just and wise
To fight till death, and pain and death despise;
But when, I ask you, was Judea free,
Or when had Israel sovereign liberty?
Since that vain strife, when Pompey forced your towers,
You've been subjected to the Roman powers.
Even Herod, though a king, yet nothing did,
But as Mark Antony or Cæsar bid.
You ever have been vassals since that day,
Governed by Roman chiefs and Roman sway.
You fight not then your freedom to maintain,
But strive as rebels, and you strive in vain.
Can you throw off those bonds that bind the world?
Tear down those ensigns over earth unfurled?
A single city 'gainst those mighty hosts,
Which of continued conquests justly boast?
Believe it not, but with my offer close,
And end these horrid, desolating woes;
And should your Roman Governors oppress,
Apply to Cæsar: he will give redress."

Thus he; and soon the tyrant John replied:
His oratory was his power and pride.

Mean in appearance, neither wise nor brave,
Yet cunning made him a successful knave.
He ruled by a sweet, zealous eloquence,
Which charmed the ear, and mystified the sense.
Mild was his face, though cruel as a fiend:
For blood, not Moloch's self could him transcend.
From the low mass he took his dread career;
By soft deception first, then blood and fear.
Then thus he spake: "Josephus, art thou he—
That craven chief we sent to Galilee?
That beauteous province, midst whose groves and flowers
You let Vespasian and his heathen powers
Crush their fair vintage-fields, and spread each plain
With maidens ravished, and our brethren slain?
You, who our towns in quick succession lost,
The readiest to submit of all the host?
You, who, when with your band hemmed in a cave,
Could stoop to meanness your mean life to save!
Caused all to die—those patriots led by you—
Assuring them that you would follow too;
When, lo! by trickery you remained the last,
Then o'er their bodies to your conqueror passed;
Fawned on him—told him God had bid you say
He soon should mount to the imperial sway!
You coward traitor! dare you then to plead
With noble Jews to imitate your deed?
Dare you our holy Temple now to name,
And bid us kneel to save it from the flame?
You ask us your dear starving friends to spare!—
Brethren, no doubt, and friends to Rome they are,
Who feel the pains to cowards justly due—
Or vile apostate traitors, such as you. [6]
Those who are willing thus to live mean slaves,
Can't sink too soon to their dishonored graves.

You speak to us of our great Temple's fate,
Like a vile heathen, as you've been of late.
This city and this Temple are God's own,
And he can send deliverance from his throne;
And if he wills not, let his will be done.
Go tell your master where his tent now stands,
Our God struck down the proud Assyrian bands.
Full ninescore thousand sought for rest that night,
Who lay pale corpses 'neath the morning light.
So now, in his own way and time, he'll come
And overwhelm the heathen powers of Rome.
His arm's not shortened—no; he still can save,
And with vile traitors glut the opening grave.
You have our answer, now: our mind you know,
So bear it to your master. Traitor, go!"

Incensed Josephus thus aloud replied:
"O tyrant, formed of insolence and pride,
Reproach you me for being overcome,
And made a captive by all-conquering Rome?
Do you reproach me that they spared my life,
When victory had put an end to strife?
What! you, who fled, base fugitive by night,
And left Gischala in a coward's fright?
Who broke your oath, and then, fiend-like, decoyed
Six thousand souls to fly and be destroyed?
Women and children left in wild despair,
Whose shrieks and groans convulsed (7) the desert air!
You speak of Israel's God—his mighty power
To save his people at the latest hour:
All this, O John, to us is fully known,
And has in Israel's deep distress been shown.
When hemmed by mountains on the left and right,
Behind, two hundred thousand foes in sight;

When all our fathers trembled in despair,
The sea before, ([8]) and Pharaoh in their rear,
God said, by Moses, March: at his command
The raging sea rolled back on either hand,
And paved a spacious way for Israel's host,
Through which they passed safe to the opposing coast.
Then on the hardened king and all his slaves,
Refluent poured the overwhelming waves.
But they, O John, were marching on the road
Marked out by Heaven—obedient to their God.
Is such your case? O no: with blood you've stained
His holy Temple—all his courts profaned:
Around his altar lies the murdered dead:
Not blood of lambs, but human gore you've shed.
You've robbed heaven's king—his statutes you despise;
Have stopped the ceaseless, daily sacrifice!
And can you think God will assert your cause,
While violating all his holy laws?
No! wretched people, look around with fear,
And see what signs through heaven and earth appear.
Can you forget, even on your last feast-day,
The sight you saw with wonder and dismay—
A beauteous heifer, led to sacrifice,
Brought forth a lamb, before your wondering eyes!
Do not these numerous signs, ye Jews, declare
Your fate is sealed, if still you urge this war?
Then yield, ye chiefs, and from destruction's grave,
Yourselves, your brethren, and your children save."

Thus spoke Josephus, with a flood of tears,
As if impressed with sympathetic fears;
Such tears as orators have still at hand,
When strength of multitudes they would command.

Deep feeling ran through all the Hebrew crowd,
Who called for peace with acclamation loud.
Even some Zealots seemed that way to tend;
And John, who bent to what he could not bend—
The general voice—was to accept of peace,
And, by submission, let their sufferings cease.
The attending chiefs of Judea and of Rome
Believed all obstinacy overcome;
But, as the orator came to a close,
A sudden tumult at some distance rose;
And ere he could descend, a flying stone
Was sent by some one, to the crowd unknown,
And smote the learned scribe, that spoke so well,
Who, stunned and staggering, from the rostrum fell.

Now, this sedition was a deep-laid plan:
From Cœlo-Syria late arrived a man—
A fugitive from vengeance. His dark crime
Touched human rights, and powers esteemed divine.
Bold, young and handsome, and of some estate,
But wicked, sensual, false, and profligate.
He saw a priestess of the Baalbec fane—
A bright-eyed beauty, of a spotless fame—
The spouse of Nicanor, a Syrian lord,
Renowned for wisdom and his conquering sword.
But, from the fair Apama's eye, a dart
Of lustful love inflamed the villain's heart.
He sought her presence—knelt—did much implore,
And offered presents—gold—a boundless store;
But the chaste dame, enraged, not without fright,
Banished at once the insulter from her sight.

In Baalbec's gorgeous temple lived a dame—
An ancient priestess—Sacrax was her name.

To occult wisdom she made some pretence,
And would, at times, the will of gods dispense.
To her went Maldad—such the villain's name—
Told of his burning love and hopeless flame.
He said: "Two thousand shining dinarii
I offered her, if she would once comply.
Unless, good dame, you some assistance give,
My love consumes me, and I cannot live!"
The Sibyl said: "Sir, give to me that sum,
And I'll contrive to have your pleasure done.
You, three nights hence, must in my chamber lie,
Robed as Adonis, radiant from the sky.
I will impress her that this god of love,
To enjoy her charms, will come down from above.
She will submit, and you, by me being led,
Shall, as Adonis, mount her wishing bed."

This fixed, the crone next to Apama told
How Lord Adonis did to her unfold,
"That he was smitten with your lovely charms,
And wished to clasp you in his godlike arms.
More: says, flower-decked, you in my room must lie,
And with him join in heavenly ecstasy!
Now, dear Apama, daughter of my heart,
Will not you take his message in good part?
Our fairest Syrian damsels glad would move
To an appointment with this god of love.
Even princesses, for whom charmed mortals sigh,
Would spread their arms t' embrace him from the sky.
Come then, thou loved one, by the hour of nine,
Flower-crowned, in night-dress, rich and soft and fine."
To this the enthusiast devotee replied:
"And does my lord thus call me to his side?

I'm highly honored by his love; and I,
With duteous love, will with his love comply."
But Sacrax wished passion with zeal to join:
So, next day, gave the medicated wine,
Potent with drugs of sovereign power, t' inflame
And send the glowing wish through every vein.

A plot so deeply laid, with such address,
We scarce need say, was crowned with full success.
Nor need the indignant Muse at length declare
The sumptuous bed, and flower-wreathed, blushing fair;
Suffice it only at this time to say,
The sensual villain revelled o'er his prey,
Till sated lust warned him to steal away!
As when the envenomed snake pours in the wound
His long-stored poison, with a hissing sound,
Then softly turns, and silent glides away
To clumps of fern, or walls in old decay;
There noiseless coils his folds, still as a stone;
So Maldad, thief-like, stole off to his home.

But when one passion leaves a vicious mind,
Often a worse will ready entrance find.
And thus with Maldad. Of his person vain,
He'd found his suit rejected with disdain.
Without revenge, (to him a passion sweet,)
He deemed his lustful triumph incomplete.
For this fell purpose he his victim sought,
Whom wily Sacrax to her chamber brought.
At sight of him the priestess stood amazed,
And on the intruding fiend with anger gazed.
"Madam," he said, "be calm, nor think that I
Can e'er again insult your purity:
My former passion now is, happ'ly, gone,
(But, mother, let us have some words alone.")

Then, in continuance: "You need not be told
Of my warm prayers and proffered sums of gold:
For all my prayers and gold you would not sell
What you with rapture gave! Well, that's as well:
A purchased love, love's joys will always miss,
You thought—so gave me yours, and tasted bliss!
Nay, start not, priestess, with those vain alarms:
But two nights since, I panted in your arms!"

Enraged, the helpless victim fierce replies:
"Hence, villain, hence! nor kill me with your lies.
'Tis false: it ne'er has been, nor e'er shall be,
That you obtain even a smile from me;"
And rose to go. "But stop," the ruffian cried;
"Hear out my lies, and of their truth decide.
I'll speak of things which only can be known
To you and I, (or some one else,) alone.
Do you remember, in a gorgeous room,
With mellowed light, and sweet with rich perfume,
Upon a sumptuous bed, just after nine,
You lay, flower-crowned, in night-dress soft and fine?
And as, undressed, the blooming god drew nigh,
How heaved your breast—how flushed your cheek and eye?
How, when he soft pressed in to seize your charms,
You turned, and clasped him in your glowing arms?
Say, did you not there hours, caressing, lie,
Marking each hour with a new ecstasy?
Nay, one word more, and it is only this:
Did not you, with a soft, sweet, murmuring kiss,
Say: 'Dear Adonis, how you gods above
Transcend all mortals in the joys of love!'
And on his toying finger place this thing—
A small love-token? Is it not your ring?

I played Adonis."—The wretch had said more,
To please his pride and make his vengeance sure,
But, with a scream, the wretched devotee
Rushed past the door, in wildest agony;
Nor stopped till, like a maniac possessed,
She, fainting, sunk upon a sister's breast.
The cruel monster quickly fled away,
Soon to meet vengeance, at no distant day.

For hours Apama's senses seemed to reel;
But still she lived, those horrors to reveal.
Keen was the rage of Baalbec's lordly priests—
(They held, great beauty was for temple feasts!)
The wretched Sacrax, under torture, told
All she had done for promised sums of gold;
By which she had obtained an easy death,
And quick suppression of her mortal breath.

But most 'gainst Maldad Baalbec's priesthood raged:
To take him, mountain-robbers were engaged.
The injured husband, poor Apama's lord,
No harshness used—gave no reproachful word;
He only said, even should real gods insist
For sensual love, women should gods resist!
"To this belief my judgment is inclined,
Though well I know 'tis not the general mind,
Our Syrian damsels ([10]) deem, when gods above
Demand love's joys, to yield is pious love!
Then, dear Apama, since this deed was done
By deep deception, cease to pine and moan.
I go to take full vengeance, if I can,
On this vile villain—dangerous, impious man.
If he is lurking on our Syrian ground,
I trust, ere long, the miscreant will be found."

This said, Nicanor called his valiant band,
To make strict search through all the adjoining land.

But vain was all pursuit: Maldad had fled,
And into Salem's walls some robbers led,
Through zeal for freedom's cause, (such were his boasts,)
And save the Temple of the Lord of Hosts.
And when, for sacrilege in Baalbec's towers,
He was demanded from the Jewish powers,
And the High-Priest, as by his duty taught,
The great Sanhedrim had to conference brought,
To try the point, if they should render up
This warrior chief, in whom great trust was put,
He firmly did deny the alleged offence,
And boldly stood upon his innocence!

"'Tis true, O great High-Priest," he thus began,
"At times, I own, I've been a sensual man:
Uncommon beauty always raised that fire
Which young lords feel, of amorous desire,
The beauty of this priestess is divine;
Like lightning, it inflamed this heart of mine.
I sought her presence—wooed, implored, and kneeled,
And all the fervor of my heart revealed.
With a firm, steady glance I was repelled;
And to all gifts and prayers this course she held.
But still it seemed, she never dropped one word
To stir the vengeance, or incense her lord!
This led me on to proffer, sue, complain,
Till, tired, I ceased, deeming all efforts vain.
After some time, surprised, I got a card,
Sweetly perfumed, in nicest form prepared;
And its contents!—(O, what was my delight!)
An invitation, friendly and polite,
To sup with her and some few friends that night!

I have been thought a handsome man by most,
And dressed that night without regard to cost;
And, without vanity, may safely say,
If it was ever true, 'twas true that day.
Perfumed and tasteful dressed, modest, though fine,
I made my entrance at the appointed time.
Two ladies, only, sat with us to sup:
Rich were the viands; Chian (11) filled the cup.
The bright Apama, richly robed with care,
Though always fair, bloomed more divinely fair.
I state these facts in this defence of mine,
To mitigate what I must own a crime;
That you, my judges, when you hear out all,
May see I fell where most of men would fall;
And that, in what has passed, I only am
A sorely tempted, persecuted man."

Thus, having a propitious hearing gained,
By blackest lies a slanderer ever feigned,
He thus resumed: "Discourse, trifling and light,
For some few hours consumed the wasting night.
I thought once more I would, ere my remove,
Prefer again my suit of hapless love.
Apama's friends, in usual time, retired—
A thing I dreaded much, and yet desired;
For then, I thought, she'd rise and bid adieu,
And I must leave—I nothing else could do.
She rose indeed, but said, 'Sir, ere you go,
I have a curious antique vase to show;'
And smiled: I bowed, and took her passive arm,
Entering a room perfumed, with damask warm.
The vase indeed was beauteous, so I said,
And asked (quite stammering) where it could be made.

She smiled; then said, 'Dear sir, this sweet perfume
I only keep in this, my private room.'
What further passed on that remembered night,
To this grave body I must not recite;
Nothing should meet this reverend council's ear
But what e'en angels might unblushing hear.
Whate'er you may suppose, I own is true.
Inflamed with love, alas! what could I do?
What, senators, could you?—or you?—or you?
Deeds past I now lament and deeply blame:
Men, while they sin, and after, a'n't the same.
Under temptation, I but passion felt:
Now passion's gone, it leaves the sting of guilt.
You now know all my crime, in thought, word, deed:
'Tis for this venial sin they thus proceed.
Nicanor and the priests are so enraged,
It only by my blood can be assuaged.
How what did pass was unto them made known,
Is past my knowledge: that I freely own.
Perhaps some slave, maltreated, took that way
A long black list of injuries to repay;
And from the facts I fully have disclosed,
Their false, forged accusation was composed.
Poor Sacrax had, to escape a torturing death,
To seal this forgery with her dying breath.
Yield me to them, I can no justice have;
I die by torture—the mid-air my grave!
Shield me from them, I wield a sword and spear
Oft dimmed with blood, but never yet by fear.
I wish with you to wave that dreaded sword
Fierce round the holy Temple of the Lord."

Thus glossed this dangerous but high-gifted man,
Almost spontaneous, and without a plan.

His frankness, and his boldness in defence,
Scarce left his judges reasons for suspense.
But John arose, who loved himself to hear,
(His own sweet voice was music to his ear.)
"Brethren and friends," he said, "it seems to me,
This is a case in which we 'll all agree.
And, first, why should we try to hide the shame
Of Baal's heathen priests and idol fane?
They loud denounce as sacrilegious crime
What, by Adonis done, they'd call divine!
What heathen lordling, or what Baalbec priest,
Who seeks not beauty for his private feast?
Does not this vice through all the great abound?
Scarce hid, at times it walks the nation round.
In Shushan, Corinth, (12) Babylon, and Rome,
Where pride and lust hold a divided throne,
To meet a neighbor's or a brother's wife
In secret, is the sweetest spice of life!
Though censured, fined, and stigmatized by all,
Yet, as just now, with the proud priests of Baal,
'Tis only to preserve lust's secresy;
For 'tis the theft (13) gives the sweet ecstasy.
In all the upper world, a legal wife,
Unless she swerves too, has a piteous life:
Plan sweet love-meetings, if her husband does,
And snatch the joys of interdicted loves!
Through all the higher walks of luxurious life,
Soon the old firm of husband, home, and wife
Will prove a partnership of hate and strife.
If such the winked-at course of half the race
Who seek such sins, how stands the present case?
Brave Maldad loved intense—was then decoyed
By a fair priestess, and her love enjoyed.

Those strong temptations which surrounded him—
Temptations great without, and worse within—
Might well have drawn a Joseph into sin.
But that's not all: The day draws nigh—'tis here—
Which calls round Salem every sword and spear
That owns her cause. Lo! that dread hour I see,
When Zion burns, or else Jerusalem's free.
Strange signs surround us: red above our town,
God's sword is streaming, and will soon come down,
If we prove faithful; and, in blood drenched deep,
Rome's circling host to swift destruction sweep.
Nícanor, in their camp, with Baalbec's slaves,
Is forging for us chains, and digging graves!
Shall we, to please them, yield up this brave chief,
Who nobly draws his sword for our relief?
Forbid it, common sense—forbid it, Heaven!
But to their envoy be this answer given:
'When Judah 's free, we 'll hear your idol's cause,
And do what 's right, according to our laws.' "

He had said more; but Annas, the high-priest,
By a strong sign, his eloquence suppressed.
" 'Tis needless, brother John, to spend more time—
The whole assembly's views accord with thine,
I should suppose. We 'll put the question thus:
'Those who would bow to Baal, let them say, Yes;'
So speak." But dumb as death the assembly sate,
As listening to the oracles of fate.
"Why, then, say, No." 'Twas done in loud acclaim,
And the grand chorus was Jehovah's name.

Now such the man, who, when the branch of peace
Seemed hovering round to bid destruction cease,

Instinctively the consequences felt—
That then no arts could hide his slanderous guilt.
So, as the signs of peace began t' appear,
He and his band passed round from ear to ear
Amongst the Zealots, and, with many a word,
Entreated them not to forsake the Lord;
And to put on Rome's chains, throw down the sword:
Bade them remember Florus and his guilt,
His wide-spread robberies, and the blood he spilt;
That, should they now submit, God's holy fane
Would smoke with swine's flesh on his altar slain;
That God, if they proved true, would soon draw nigh,
And save them in their worst extremity;
For prophets and bright signs from heaven proclaimed
God wouldn't let his Temple be profaned,
Or altar with abominations stained.
Thousands who heard these words did firm agree,
To die around the altar, or live free;
Then secret armed, that, when the truce was broke,
They might give Rome a bold, decisive stroke.

And now, by Maldad's orders, that small stone,
Pregnant with ruin, was unerring thrown.
Josephus, stunned, fell senseless to the ground,
While rage and clamor echoed all around.
And thus the danger of this profligate
Rolled on the will of Heaven, and Salem's fate.

As when that inland sea, by Prusias made
To sail his barge ([14]) and court in high parade,
Stopped at a pass (by three flush rivers fed)
Wide as Asphaltes o'er the country spread,
Till, by accumulated weight, the mound
Burst, and the rushing flood whole districts drowned!

So, as the Roman cohorts filed along,
Poured through the gates the infuriate Zealot throng,
In a continuous stream, till all the field,
'Tween camp and city, flamed with spear and shield.
The Roman generals saw the coming storm
Of Jewish fury, in its wildest form,
And hastened to the van, to form the square,
And bring their phalanx to the front of war—
War unexpected, of the deadliest kind,
Formed of stern fate and fiercest zeal combined.
To right and left the Zealot masses spread—
Judeas, Phineas, Joram, at their head;
With Eliezer, tyrant Simon's son,
And fell Abiram, who great fame had won.
Nor less the Roman chiefs were seen to shine,
Radiant in arms, along their forming line.
Manlius and Scipio, with Cerales brave,
Spread out their line like a long fiery wave.
As when wide grassy plains, by Sol parched dry,
Are rashly fired, and west winds rule the sky,
Comes flaring down on villages and farms;
The threatened peasants spread in answering arms,
And quick resolving, as their last defence,
Fire 'gainst the fire, and spread a wide, dark fence
Of blaze-swept ground; while each opposing fire
To conflict bends, and in joint flame expire;
So the opposing hosts, with loud alarms,
To combat flew. Wide flashed their dazzling arms,
Till, in mid space, with equal rage they met:
Shield against shield, and spear 'gainst spear was set.
Great Manlius led the van. His brazen shield,
Like Hesper rising, glanced across the field.
Him Joram saw, and, with presumptuous pride,
Advanced, and thus the Roman chief defied:

"Manlius, come on! Though wide resound thy fame,
Though great thy skill, and giant-like thy frame,
Think not to terrify or frighten one
Who from a line of mighty kings hath come.
My great ancestor, when a nameless youth,
Met far thy greater in the cause of truth.
In Elath's vale the tall blasphemer stood,
Loud cursing Israel, and defying God:
Young David met him in fair freedom's cause,
His armor—zeal for God and Israel's laws.
Before his arm the vaunting giant fell;
His huge trunk poured a blood-stream down the dell;
And I, in freedom's cause and God's, now trust
To lay your far-famed honors in the dust."

To whom thus Manlius: "Poor, young, thoughtless man,
Why haste to end that life you've scarce began?
Think, was your God such God as you pretend,
Would he from purity and heaven descend,
Your viperous generation to defend?
Your city now is black with deepest guilt:
What streams of blood have your assassins spilt!
Think you there is one God, and only one,
And he confined to your vile tribes alone?
Where 's Hercules; where 's Mars; and, far above
All minor gods, our universal Jove?
Have not his signs through earth and air been given?
His sword now flames across the vault of heaven!
This would I to your bigot nation say:
To you, young man, retire, while yet you may;
Nor, proudly boasting of your God, presume
To meet my arm in war, and seal your doom,
And force, through pride, your passage to the tomb."

To whom the Hebrew: "Scoffer as you are,
I've but one answer—'tis my flying spear;
And may the God of Israel aid this dart
To reach thy proud, blasphemous, heathen heart."

With dexterous skill, below the shield, high raised,
The weapon flew, and the left elbow grazed:
Puny the wound, yet thrilling was the pain.
Enraged, the Roman bounded from the plain,
And whirled his weighty spear with threefold force,
Crushing through shield and cuirass in its course:
Clear through the Hebrew passed the ghastly wound,
And hurled the youthful warrior to the ground.
Then, high in rage, his weighty falchion drew,
And on the common mass with fury flew,
And at each stroke some bloody Zealot slew.
Then loud he cried: "Come, Strabo—Scipio, come—
Come on, Ventides—all ye chiefs of Rome!
Strike for Vespasian's glory! Through yon mass,
Our swords shall hew a bloody, groaning pass."
Then right and left the combat raged amain,
And blood and carnage loaded all the plain.
Before the Romans, thus by Manlius led,
The Jewish crowds gave way, were slain, or fled.

But on the right, the Zealots' headlong course
Long time resisted all the cohorts' force.
There Judeas, Phineas, Simon and his son,
And the brave kinsman of the tyrant, John,
Led on the Jews, and wide the contest spread,
And thick behind them lay the gasping dead.
Their spears and missiles spent with bilious rage;
The opposing hosts in closer strife engage
'Gainst Roman courage and disciplined darts,
Hands to their throats, and poniards to their hearts.

Possessed by dead men's demons, fierce the strife:
The Roman's short-sword and the Zealot's knife
With equal fury sought the seat of life.
By Simon's arm the brave Lentillus bled;
By Phineas' spear young Cato joined the dead:
Nor less the Hebrews, by the Roman sword
And vet'ran spears, had their dark masses gored,
And blood for blood through all the conflict poured.

Thus, for some hours, as poised by equal weight,
Wavering, uncertain, hung the scales of fate:
There, Jewish fury slaughters wide around;
Here, Roman valor strews with dead the ground;
With equal wounds each adverse battle's gored,
While shouts and groans o'er all the conflict roared.
But when the sun rolled down his evening way,
To hide his glories in the western sea,
The scene was changed. Then came a distant sound,
As if a trembling earthquake shook the ground.
It came from full five thousand chargers' tread,
By Cæsar's self and bold Sempronius led;
Their riders' swords, all drawn and raised on high,
Glanced through Sol's rays like meteors from the sky.
Soon as the sound loud o'er the conflict spread,
The Zealots, terror-struck, for safety fled.
As when rapacious kites, on outspread wing,
Their lengthened shadows on the barnyard fling,
The feathery brood swift to some covert flies,
Warned by their mother's fierce, distracted cries;
With outstretched necks and pliant limbs, they rush
Swift to the shed, or some thick sheltering bush;
So fled the Jews, (though some were warned too late,)
In flight and terror, through the expanded gate.

All those who failed the asylum thus to gain,
The charging horsemen drove across the plain.
On limbs and heads keen fell the Roman sword,
And blood and brains in mingled masses poured.
Soon the whole field was swept, and all lay dead
Save those who timely through the gateway fled.

But as, with reeking blade and bounding plume,
Titus thus led the slaughtering powers of Rome;
As near the gate the wheeling squadrons drew,
From the broad walls volleys of missiles flew.
Most fell innoxious, bloodless, on the plain,
But some proved fatal; by them some were slain:
Amongst them, Silvius from his saddle bends—
The nearest, dearest of all Cæsar's friends.
From early youth to that dark hour of fate,
They seemed as one, though differing in estate;
The same their sports, their friendships, and their hate.
An arrow, engine-sent, his shield above,
Between his chin and loosened corselet drove:
The lengthened shaft with such impetus flew,
The thrilling steel pierced nerves and sinews through.
Down had the warrior fallen, in youthful charms,
Midst dust and blood, with his resounding arms;
But friends rushed in to intercept his fall,
And bore him, dying, from the hostile wall.
Titus gazed on him as he passed; then turned—
His breast with grief and indignation burned;
Then loud—his hand obtesting to the skies:
"Hear, all ye gods, ye Roman deities!
Hear, Mars, Apollo, and imperial Jove;
And thou, these wretches name all gods above—
That thou art sole—the universal God,
In whose strong hand I may be but a rod;

Hear, and record in heaven my solemn vow,
To lay Jerusalem level for the plough!
You all have seen a brother of this race,
Sent with the olive-branch of peace and grace,
Struck down midst his vocation! heard the roar
Of those barbarians through yon gateway pour,
Rush on my peaceful, unsuspecting guard—
A scanty cohort, and all unprepared.
You all can witness—you beheld the scene—
Their wild-beast fury, and the ensanguined green;
My soldiers groaning in their own blood-stream.
And, O ye gods! my friend, my heart's allied,
Struck down in death while warring by my side!
I would have saved their towns and holy fane,
As proud memorials of Vespasian's fame;
But now, all peace, all clemency, begone!
Let death and wide destruction hasten on.
I call on vengeance, fury, and despair,
And bid fell ruin, my chief guest, be there;
He, with red hand, his canopy shall spread,
And roll his chariot o'er the gasping dead.
All that resist shall sink to bloody graves;
The rest dispersed around the world as slaves."
He said, and with his red sword smote his shield,
And, breathing vengeance, left the ensanguined field.

But through the hours of that destructive day,
In Zion's towers, Napthalia's chieftain lay,
After his glorious victory in the vale,
Which stopped the mournful crucifixion-wail.
Part of his band was sent to Galilee,
The rest retained to keep Jerusalem free.
Salathiel's dreadful name and victories won,
like Heaven's voice on Simon and on John.

Courted by both, and by the weak adored,
He mitigated persecution's sword;
But when of peace conference he was told,
And that Josephus' speech had taken hold,
And brave Lysander urged, "Father, let 's go,
And our great influence with that party throw;"
He gravely answered: "Do they as they may,
In that great question I shall nothing say.
When I behold pale famine wasting round,
Women and infants gasping on the ground,
I have no heart to say, peace shall not come:
You Jews shall not bend down the slaves of Rome;
But still, far less could I my voice record
With the whole nation, should they pass the word,
'Open your gates to Rome's imperial lord.'
I'll therefore leave the issue, though 'tis great,
To destiny, or God, whose will is fate;
And should our chiefs submit to heathen powers,
I leave for ever these subjected towers.
For well I know, their altars soon will burn
With offerings vile to all their gods in turn,
Close by God's altar; and—O, deep disgrace!—
Their statues stand in the most holy place;
While their procurators, bent on rapine,
Tread down all laws, both human and divine.
I, therefore, in such case, will seek a home,
Far from lost Israel and tyrannic Rome;
With my dear friends to foreign climes I'll flee:
If this land holds me, it must hold me free.
But should this conference in nothing end,
And our brave chiefs for freedom still contend,
Then shall this sword around the temple wave,
Assure the timorous and lead on the brave;

And if I fall, my friends for me may search
Between the altar and the sacred porch.
You know, my son, that I stand fixed as fate:
I cannot die, or change my mortal state,
Till I again behold that smile—that face—
So full of awful dignity and grace:
An event that may suddenly take place.
I sometimes hope the Nazarene may come
As great Messiah, conqueror of Rome;
That, in our latest and most trying hour,
He 'll head his saints, and crush the Roman power.
Then shall this sword in his great battle shine,
And Gog and Magog feel the wrath divine!
The Cedron, now a dried-up, scanty flood,
Shall swell with corpses and their streaming blood;
Their shields, [15] their darts, their engines, bows and spears,
Shall serve as fuel seven revolving years.
But, should such thoughts prove vain, then I can die,
Or still live on, if such my destiny,
And firmly meet that fate I cannot fly.
But, as this moment we are told that war
Bursts forth again, and Judah's sword is bare,
Do thou, Lysander, leave this field of strife,
And haste to save your mother and your wife;
Convey them safe to some sequestered glen,
Far from the scenes of blood and bloody men.
Your arm can't save me, when my time is come:
Though brave and generous, you are only one.
But know you this: My life's last drop is shed
Near God's high altar, and midst heaps of dead!"

To this the brave Lysander thus replied:
"My friend and father, and Napthalia's pride,

Think not in this I can your voice obey:
I here remain, if fate commands your stay.
We 'll face together the dark front of death,
And yield together our expiring breath.
Could I before your noble spouse appear,
Sneaking to Massada, and you left here?
'Twere joy, with sword in hand, nobly to die,
Rather than meet that mild, reproaching eye.
'Where is Salathiel? Has my lord been slain?
Or have you left him?' she would faint exclaim.
Even Hester's love, to my warm bosom pressed,
Would turn to icicles while I caressed:
Her soft, sweet, rosy lips, which used to join,
With soft electric shock, in bliss with mine,
Would palely gasp, and ask, 'Can this be so?
And am I doomed to feel this humbling woe?
Where is the glory my fond heart cast round
My dear Lysander? Where can it be found?
In danger's hour he left my sire alone,
And, recreant, sought for safety at his home.
O! what a pang to love! what deep distress,
To find my husband's honor lost, or less!'
Rather than sink thus, in my Hester's eyes,
Down to a being which she must despise,
I'd rush on Cæsar in his guarded might,
And die a thousand deaths in noble fight.
My soul stands fixed, that, when fate stops my breath,
And I lie housled in the arms of death,
Each briny tear above my pale corpse shed
Shall fall upon the honorable dead.
No more, then, father: I am fixed as fate:
We side by side will meet this dire debate;
And should you sink on the contested field,
Above your head I'll hold my covering shield,

And send some foes, with your expiring breath,
To attend your steps down through the gates of death:
Or, if I 'm first, I have no doubt you 'll pour,
Hot on my feet, some streams of hostile gore!"
No more was said; but, with instinctive grasp,
The warriors' hands were locked in mutual clasp.

This on a terrace; but descending night
Soon veiled the town in darkness from their sight;—
When, lo! on gazing towards Moriah's fane,
They saw the temple filled with lambent flame;
The entire building in soft radiance shone,
Like innate splendor in the opal ([16]) stone.
No spark, no flame from its mild glories passed;
'Twas like Shechinah, only still more vast.
At length, embodying, it appeared to rise,
And lose its splendors in the upper skies.
Contending nations viewed the solemn sight—
Some in dismay, and some in wild delight.
The Zealots cried, "Behold! our God has come,
To save our nation from accursed Rome."
Others, "He 's left us! Lo! we've seen him go,
Shadowing deep darkness—emblem of our woe!"
The doubtful Romans gazed, no way assured,
But trusted to their courage and the sword.
Thus, both hosts waited the impending storm
The sun might bring, in blood, the following morn.

BOOK VI.

Nocturnal Conflict.

The patriarchs attend to Messiah's will—Visit Abihud and his Christian family—Their discourse—At Abihud's request, while overlooking the Dead Sea, they describe the country as in their days—Lot relates the catastrophe of the Cities of the Plain—Directs Abihud and family to retreat to Bethlehem, and departs—Titus batters the walls—His engine breaks—A night escalade resolved on—The Jewish guard round Antonia slain while sleeping—Dreadful conflict through the hours of darkness—Short addresses of Manlius and Salathiel to their soldiers—Maldad asks for Nicanor—Is mortally wounded by him in single combat—His band rescue him and wound Nicanor—The battle renewed with increased fury—The great deeds of Judeas and other Jewish chiefs under the power of possession—Of Manlius and other Romans—Titus at length orders a retreat—Salathiel addresses the Jewish chiefs—They agree with him—Their preparations, and those of the Romans, for the decisive contest on the following day.

WHILE thus impending hung the storms of fate
O'er Salem's towers and all the Judean state,
The patriarchs to Messiah's word attend,
And to great Herod's towers unseen descend.
From Massada's bold cliffs, eve's shadows spread
Across that sea, so fitly called the Dead;
For there dead nations lay, in ashen graves,
Covered from sight by salt sulphureous waves;
And there those waves rolled death-like—heavy, slow,
Like melted metal, over scenes of woe.

No living thing [1] its sluggish flood contains,
But death and death-like silence o'er its bosom reigns!

Now, as the western sun shot his last rays,
And tipped th' Arabian pinnacles with blaze,
The heaven-sent messengers appeared before
Good old Abihud, sitting at his door.
Kind salutations instantly took place,
And radiant smiles illumined every face.
"Come in and lodge with us," the Christian said.
"We will"—(and then each patriarch bowed his head;)
"For know, good brother, therefore are we come:
We have a message to this Christian home."
This said, they followed to a room of state,
Where Miriam, Hester, and her brother sate.
The father of the faithful caught all eyes:
They gazed with admiration and surprise.
His tall, majestic form, his radiant face,
His lofty brow, his lips so full of grace,
Struck old Abihud—it was so much like
The Nazarene, though not so glorious bright.
Then thus to them: "My lords, whence have you come,
To this our humble, half-imprisoned home?
Your presence, so august, serene, would say,
You come from Him we're striving to obey."

To whom the patriarch: "You've spoken right:
We have a message we'll disclose to-night:
'Tis from Messiah, the great King of kings—
(To-morrow we will speak of minor things.)
Know, then, as once he promised, he has come,
And in his hand wields all the power of Rome.
O'er Tabor's top he holds the court of heaven,
From whence these signs through earth and air are given.

Soon shall destruction sweep aside your foes;
In fire and blood the Jewish state must close;
Their splendid Temple tumble from on high,
And not one stone upon another lie (2)
That's not cast down; while, o'er Moriah spread,
Shall lie in heaps the dying and the dead;
The rest, not slain, be sold to foreign climes,
And expiate in bonds their heinous crimes.
I am the father of the faithful seed—
The father of all Israelites, indeed:
Of them you are; 'Then fear not, little flock,'
You're of his Church, built on his truth—the rock.
These words of his we thus bring to your mind,
By his command, that you may rest resigned,
Safe in his mighty hand, which holds all power,
Through life's fierce storms, or death's appalling hour."
The circle next of heavenly themes discourse;
Of Christian hopes, and faith, their only source.
Their words sent glowing love from breast to breast,
Till time brought on the balmy hour of rest;
Then, with a song of praise, each took their way,
And slumbered sweetly till the following day.

Now, o'er the Arabian mountains Sol's bright beams
With orient glory on Massada stream;
The opposing western cliffs, smitten by his rays,
Shone like a wall in mild artistic blaze.
Below his slanting beams, dark vapors lay
O'er all the dread Asphaltan lifeless sea.
When all the family with their heaven-guests stood
Upon a terrace o'er the solemn flood,
Then thus Abihud to the patriarchs said:
"Come, let us sit, and speak of Christ, our head.

Can he, on earth so merciful and mild,
Who healed the heathen's slave, and blessed the child—
Can he indeed in wrath and vengeance come,
And sweep Jerusalem with the sword of Rome?
Will he, the kind, the merciful, the great,
In wrath lay Zion—burning, desolate?
His works, while he sojourned with us below,
Proclaimed his heart averse to human woe."

To this the patriarch—"Vainly mortals still
Would form a god and comprehend his will:
But know ye this, I am empowered to say,
Vindictive wrath is not God's usual way.
Sin always brings down consequential wrath,
Which pains the guilty in their downward path.
But when corruption all a land o'erflows,
And God would worn-out institutions close,
Then seeming vengeance shakes all nature round,
Till e'en by infidels a God is found.
Thus, when all flesh sank in corruption's ways,
Their general, sudden end, the hand of God displays;
A mighty flood the heavens on earth outpour,
A boundless ocean, and without a shore.
All living things, whose life was in their breath,
Sank down beneath this overwhelming death;
And thus to future ages was made known
His Godhead and the terrors of his throne.
But why look back? Before us lies yon lake—
Two thousand feet below, its billows break
When storms can raise them—sixty miles in length,
And near twelve miles across, its greatest breadth.
Brother Abihud, what has Moses said?
How was that awful, solemn chasm made?"

To whom the elder—"Brethren from above,
(Sent from our God with messages of love,)
To you are known those dreadful scenes of woe,
For you then pilgrimed on this world below:
Then, while we sit, kindly to us unfold
Those wondrous changes which took place of old.
What kind of people—what was nature's face,
When you for Sodom humbly sued for grace?"

To whom the patriarch—"You no doubt have seen
The upper Jordan, and its fields of green,
And harvest-plains, with vine-clad hills between.
'Tis beauteous now, but lovelier was that land
When I from Charran came at God's command;
Or when beneath the banners of the Lord,
I Lot and Sodom rescued by my sword.
Then all was glorious: Jordan's three-fold founts
Welled forth redundant, beneath Lebanon's mounts:
Their crystal currents rolled through (3) flowery vales,
Whose odorous bloom perfumed the western gales:
Thence flowing on, receiving stream on stream,
Through orange groves and loaded vines they gleam;
Till, watering all the plains, at length they make
Their final union in broad Merom's lake.
It seemed as if the north and south combined,
And all their treasures in this region joined.
Round youths and maidens heavy harvests spread,
While fruits and flowers hung mingling o'er their head;
The oleander, rose, and eglantine
Bloomed through the myrtle groves, and round them twine
The orange and pomegranate of the south,
Mixed with the peach and apple of the north.

Its sloped position faced the southern sun,
Fenced on the north by lofty Lebanon.
This gave it its soft clime, its fruits and flowers;
Its flocks and herds, and amaranthine bowers.
All upper Jordan then, down to the sea,
Of various name, but now called Galilee,
Bloomed as a garden fresh from God's own hand,
And might, in truth, be termed a goodly land.
The lower Jordan thence wended its way,
In beauteous windings, to th' Elathian (4) Sea:
Its widest plain was at this juncture found—
A lovely plain with populous cities crowned.
But Lot, who, when our wealth made us divide,
Chose that low country, in its flowery pride,
Can best describe that Eden which he saw,
And its dread fate, which thrilled the world with awe!"

To this the younger patriarch replied:
"O Father of the faithful, Israel's pride,
I well remember all those lovely scenes,
The flower-crowned valleys and translucent streams.
The sacred Jordan, where this Dead Sea lies,
Then bright meandered through a paradise:
Yon fearful chasm, now so dread abhorred,
Bloomed then, fair as 'the Garden of the Lord.'
Thus glorious bloomed those plains and all their coasts,
When swept with ruin by th' Assyrian hosts;
All worth attention, slain or captive led:
They only left the dying and the dead.
Triumphant east they marched, with feast and song,
And drove us captives and our spoils along!
That was a glorious woe-redeeming time,
When, roused from feasting, and confused with wine,

The Hebrew warriors midst their orgies poured:
On every side glanced the Abramic sword,
While in their van fierce blazed the ægis of the Lord.
In one short hour the greater part lay dead;
The rest, dispersed, east to th' Euphrates fled.
My far-famed kinsman then, with all the spoils,
Returned triumphant from his warlike toils:
To Sodom's king he generously restored
The goods and captives rescued by his sword;
And in few years the wide-extended plain
Was blooming like a paradise again!
But ah! their prosperous state was fraught with crime:
Their only gods were lust, and wealth, and wine.
They were Egyptians—colored dingy white,
Without a priesthood or religious rite,
Except on feast-days, when he worshipped best
Who most surpassed the vilest lustful beast!
I often thought I'd leave the luxurious glen,
And seek society with mountain men;
But still detained by children and my wife,
Who loved this plain of luxury and strife,
Where shone the highest of mechanic skill,
To raise the palace, or the rich soil till:
Buildings rose glorious 'neath their forming hand,
While a new Eden crowned the flowery land.
Great was their skill in all luxurious arts,
But worse than brutes in vice—deeper depraved their hearts.
Held by these ties, I lingered midst a crowd
Of crimes that cried to heaven for vengeance loud,
And vainly strove, with eloquence from Heaven,
(For sure I am, supernal aid was given,)
To work repentance and bring on reform,
And thus avert the dread impending storm.

I am not vain, and yet I wish you'd heard
That strong appeal which I that day preferred,
When, father, you in prayer with God appeared.
But all in vain. Hisses, with groan on groan,
And scoffs and threatenings, drove me to my home.
There, as I sat at eve, before my gate (5)
Two beauteous strangers stood: 'twas growing late.
I saw their beauty marked by lustful eyes,
And knew them doomed, a beastly sacrifice;
So lured them to come in. What then befell,
Our great first prophet has described too well
For me to mend. Rescued by heavenly aid,
We stood in Zoar, trembling and afraid.
Just as the sun arose, with splendor bright,
Which gleamed, then closed in gloom, resembling night,
A tempest, down the Jordan from the north,
Rolled dark as night, and met one from the south;
While on the Arab mountains, from the east,
One still more livid met one from the west:
From every point, the zigzag lightnings' flame
Shot through the gloom, and smote the guilty plain:
The bolts Heaven sent, plunged stopless through the ground,
And fired the fuel in the abyss profound.
Like, yet unlike, that grand and startling sight
Of meteors on a calm autumnal night,
When from the concave of the heavens on high
They stream diverging down the placid sky;
While these, converging, in wild conflict rain
Heaven's fire and brimstone on the guilty plain:
The wide substratum, sulphur, spume, and coal,
Ignited, heaved, and raged without control,
All yon spread space, where those dark waters lie;
Then flamed towards heaven, and sparkled in the sky.

Three days and nights heard one continued roar;
The flames still raging while the waters pour;
For Arnon from his utmost springs rolled down,
And Jordan swelled from lofty Lebanon:
Cedron with all the streams of Galilee,
And Jordan refluent from the Elathian Sea.
For nine long days each rivulet and stream,
Down in the abyss their roaring torrents teem,
Before the fires were quenched, and yon salt flood
Rose up and hid the plains where Sodom stood.
One thousand feet (the fueled stratum gone)
The guilty plain sunk hissing, bubbling down.
From Kerak's heights this dread finale I saw,
(For we from Zoar fled, with shuddering awe.)
You, father Abram, from Mount Hebron's height,
And I from Kerak, saw that closing sight—
The whole sunk plain in billowy smoke arise,
As from a furnace rolling to the skies, ([3])
Which in time settled to this sulphurous lake,
Whose heavy billows o'er sunk nations break.
We, who gazed on, plainly discerned the Rod,
And direct judgment from the hand of God."

To this the Christian elder soft replied:
"Brethren from heaven, I now rest satisfied
That the great King of heaven and earth at times—
When he thinks fit—stoops down to punish crimes,
And show he governs all things, and to give
New laws as man new lessons can receive.
We should rejoice that Christ the Lord has come,
In fire from heaven, or with the sword of Rome,
To sweep away that persecuting race
Who him rejected and his offered grace,

And who, relentless, on his followers pour
Tortures and death, whenever they have power."

"Nor is it cruel," the great envoy said:
"Their social guilt proclaims them dying—dead!
If left alone by consequential woes,
The state in anarchy and blood would close:
Hence a swift vengeance, which to nations' eyes
Shall prove that judgment, coming from the skies,
Is best for them—a nation whose deep guilt
Was crowned by blood divine, on Calvary spilt.
With wicked hands they shed Messiah's blood,
And should in death discern the wrath of God.
More—to confirm his faith, ([6]) Christ's prophecies
Must be fulfilled in vengeance from the skies,
To plant the gospel and to give it strength
To conquer nations—and the world, at length!
And now, daughters of Israel, well I know
You wish for knowledge I cannot bestow:
Those two great heroes to your hearts so dear,
Round whom clings every hope and every fear,
Will meet their fate—but what, I cannot tell;
But this we must, before we bid farewell.
The Master says, swift to that stable go,
Where first his eyes oped on this world of woe;
There, in that sacred cavern, you will find
A family of Christians true and kind:
There wait expectant, midst the world's wide din,
And let your hearts and hopes be stayed on him,
Till Salem and Moriah's Temple rise,
Wrapped round with flames, and sparkle in the skies;
And in those days of desolating woe,
Angels shall guard, and tell you where to go."

This said, the Faithful's hands raised high above,
Thus gave his blessing; "May the God of love
And inward peace protect this little flock,
And keep it steadfast on the Church's Rock,
Midst this dire crisis and destruction's shock."

As when the Saviour stood, midst the Eleven,
(The door being shut,) ere he rose up to heaven;
So thus the envoys instant disappeared:
No door was opened, and no sound was heard;
But soon they joined the angelic throng on high,
Above Mount Tabor in the mundane sky;
And there, before the Mediator's throne,
Reported all they saw, and what was done,
And held discourse on wonders still to come!

But while heaven's great Vicegerent thus attends
The sorrows of his persecuted friends,
Still flamed his sword of wrath across the sky;
Still signs and portents spoke destruction nigh;
Still meteors glared; still shook the earth below;
And still the cry, "Woe! to Jerusalem woe!"
Maniac or prophet, none could tell or know;
But Jaled's loud, continued cry was "Woe!
Woe to Jerusalem!" Round the walls he'd go,
Stop oft, and cry, "Woe! to Jerusalem woe!"
Ceaseless as time's own wheels or waters flow,
He walked, and yelled, (7) "Woe! to Jerusalem woe!"
Full in accordance with this croaking sound,
Famine's dark wings were flapping all around;
Thousands, pining with want, for offals roam,
And proved the woe denounced had struck the town.
'Twas prophecy, alas! and history too;
Pale dead each hour proved the denouncement true.

The spectral crowds the boldest might appal;
Each glared on death, and death glared on them all!

Such horrors hung around the Jewish state,
While Titus, raging at his favorite's fate,
Brought now around him all the power of Rome,
Resolved destruction's work should quick be done.
Hurled by a thousand men, his engine swung
Burst on the walls—the walls responsive rung:
With power increased, shock fast succeeded shock;
But still unmoved remained the impassive rock.
For four long hours the ram its blows renewed,
But still the wall stood firm and unsubdued:
At length, impelled with a decisive stroke,
The iron head was into fragments broke!
Meanwhile the Roman archers scoured the walls,—
Jew after Jew in quick succession falls;
Nor unrevenged the Zealots bite the ground,
But dart return for dart, and wound for wound.
At length, their headless engine drawn away,
The assailants closed the labors of the day.

Moody and discontent, the council sate,
With Titus brooding o'er their engine's fate;
When Doris, who from near Mount Etna came,
(Whose towering top oft visits heaven in flame;
A giant beacon gleaming from afar,
Hot from the bowels of intestine war,)
Rising he spoke—"Why not, in night's dark hour,
Scale their proof wall, and seize Antonia's tower;
Slaughter their sleeping guards, (safe in success,)
Give death so quick, they cannot ban or bless,
Or sound alarm in parting life's distress?

Myself and Cassius will the danger lead,
If ten more Romans will with us proceed.
Should the gods prosper us, soon unseen flies
Rome's conquering eagle, bright through midnight skies.
Then give Rome's trumpet breath!—At that proud sound,
Let one whole legion, armed, haste to the ground;
Through postern or rent wall we 'll let them in,
And then proud victory's conflict shall begin."

Cæsar approved the plan. And now, behold,
That hero band, determinate and bold,
Ascends the shattered wall, and stands before
(The guards deep sleeping round) the outer door.
A whispered consultation, as they stood,
Prefaced the silent work of death and blood:
At once twelve spears came down, and pierced twelve hearts:
Each sleeping soul to endless sleep departs!
Death waits each Roman's step, (with moaning sound,)
And gushing blood floated the porch around!
There lay the dead, as when, from mountains cold,
Gaunt, hungry wolves invade the sleeping fold;
Quick work they make, and soon around they spread
The helpless flock in blood—dying and dead:
So lay the Jewish guard, while their fierce foes
With their tall ladders to the ramparts rose;
And soon Rome's ensign o'er Antonia's height
Was waving, ere the tenth hour of the night,
While the loud trumpet's blast was heard afar,
The appointed signal for the rush of war.
Waked by the sound, the inner guard arose,
And deemed the tower was taken by their foes;
In wild affright, over their comrades dead
They left the tower, and to the Temple fled.

Meantime the Romans, o'er the broken wall,
Poured their armed legion at the trumpet's call:
Cerales led them on, and with him came
Tribunes and heroes, great in Roman fame,
All ready armed; and now this martial power
Ranged round Antonia and possessed the tower.
But soon the Zealots, roused by these alarms,
Poured from the Temple, raging and in arms:
Judeas, Phineas, Simon led them on,
While from the porch loud cried the tyrant John:
"Ye sons of Jacob, rush upon the foe,
And lay the sacrilegious heathen low.
Moriah's sacred mount, where Abram built
God's primal altar, and where first was spilt
Expiatory blood—lo! heathen vile
Crawl o'er its summit, and pollute the soil!
See, at this hour of darkness, sly they come,
Like prowling wolves—such are the wiles of Rome:
Through ev'ry heart they hope to plunge the spear,
And show their coward murders by the glare
Of God's great Temple, flaming high in air!
Rise, then, ye sons of Israel—draw the sword
Against the mighty—rush to help the Lord!
For freedom and our God, strike down the foe,
Nor let one heathen need a second blow.
High o'er this mount, God's sword once parched the air,
But quenched in grace, by holy David's prayer:
Now fiercer flames that sword, and broader spreads
O'er Rome's idolatrous and impious heads.
They have no prayers can Israel's God evoke,
Or turn aside the wide destructive stroke.
Then march beneath the ensigns of the Lord:
Let each spear glitter: flame each Hebrew's sword;

And soon your foes, as smote by burning levin,
Shall from this mount or down to death be driven!"

His words inflamed each furious Zealot's breast,
As down upon the Roman ranks they pressed.
Simon, John's kinsman, Phineas, and the spear
Of Simon Gorias, (men unknown to fear,)
With Judas and Elmoden, chiefs of power,
Led on the Zealots that dread, darksome hour.
Fierced raged the conflict: twice five thousand men,
(Five shouting "Cæsar," five "Jerusalem,")
In combat met, beneath night's darkest shade,
With clangor dire—sword-strokes on armor brayed;
The battle-cry and clash of arms rang round
The towers and Temple, with tumultuous sound.
As when two ships, by adverse winds from heaven,
Against each other with fell force are driven;
As from opposing waves they downward dash,
Their meeting hulls shiver with hideous crash;
And wide around the splintered fragments spread,
O'er struggling seamen drowning—and the dead;
So rushed both armies from their several posts;
So met midst darkness the encountering hosts;
So, like to shivered fragments, lay supine
The dead and dying, all along the line!
Such the strange sound of shouts and wild alarms,
Of deadly sword-strokes and resounding arms!

But night's deep darkness canopied each host,
And order soon was in confusion lost;
Mixed, intermixed, no one his comrade knows;
Friends' swords are plunged in friends, mistook for foes!
As when, at some low Bacchanalian feast,
His drunken votaries, for a trifling jest

Or ancient grudge, two staggering clowns begin
A fisty fight, fools from all sides rush in:
They pull, they rend, they shout, till, fired with rage,
The whole drunk rout tumultuously engage:
Devoid of light or sense, they deal their blows,
Now on their friends, and now upon their foes;
Now rolling on the ground like dogs in strife;
Now searching for their murderous girdle-knife,
To ope the fountain of a neighbor's life:
Thus fought both armies, midst the shades of night,
Wild and tumultuous through the lengthened fight.
The Zealot bands, disordered and enraged,
Oft met as foes, and deadly combat waged:
The Romans suffered less—their watchword known,
Gave each to tell all warriors from their own.
Their strict discipline also gave them power
To keep some order in the darkest hour;
While the fierce Zealots with blind fury send
Spears through a Roman now, and now a friend!
Great deeds were done by chiefs unseen that night,
Who lost their glory for the want of light;
For dreadful was the slaughter—wide were spread,
O'er all the mount, the dying and the dead!

At length the rising monarch of the day
Bade mild Aurora wide her charms display:
O'er fields and fountains, gardens and sweet farms,
And Nature's roseate bowers, she spread her charms,
As if to lure him on; but as he rose,
His beams glanced down on war, and death, and woes!
Paused, and embodying round Antonia's towers,
(Their ensigns wavering,) stood the Roman powers;
Resolved the Temple (when full day should come)
To storm with all the veteran powers of Rome.

The Hebrew Zealots, midst their comrades slain,
Looked up to heaven for miracles in vain;
Others for human aid gazed hopeful still,
And cast expecting eyes to Zion's hill;
When lo! through the south gate, waving on high,
Napthalia's banner friends and foes descry!
Salathiel and Lysander led the van,
And welcomes loud rang round from man to man.
The chiefs had heard faint clamors of the fight,
But deemed it some small riot of the night;
But when informed that from Antonia's towers
Titus against the Temple poured his powers,
They instant armed, and called their faithful band
To meet, sword-girt, with mountain spear in hand;
Nor waited for the whole, but hastened on,
The rest to follow with their kinsman John.

Meantime the cohorts, under Manlius' care,
Moved down to end this dubious morning war.
Titus had said, "March in disciplined form;
Disperse the Zealots, and the Temple storm;"
Not knowing that Napthalia's powers drew near,
Armed with the boar-knife and rough mountain spear.
But Roman valor and their martial pride
From this new foe disdained to turn aside.
Manlius, in front, rang forth these thrilling words:
"Rome's glory rests on Roman hearts and swords!
Let not fresh foes and banners in array,
Make the world's conquerors tremble with dismay;
Though wearied with this long-continued fight,
(Involved in darkness and the shades of night,)
Yet let us still Rome's victories repeat,
And army after army still defeat!

The noble Titus from yon tower (8) looks down,
To see who best deserves the laurel crown.
Full-armed he stands, almost by force withheld
From issuing forth before you to the field.
Now let him see great deeds of glory done,
Deeds worthy you, and him, and conquering Rome;
Down to destruction this new army send,
And in their blood this tedious warfare end."

Salathiel led the Jews. Few were his words:
He pointed first to heaven, next to their swords;
Then loud his voice: "Ye sons of Abraham,
That warrior-prophet, friend of great I AM:
Remember this eventful day we draw
Our swords for freedom and God's holy law.
If we prove recreant, chains and stripes attend,
Bondage and insults, shameful without end:
This sacred mount, where faithful Abram stood,
With stretched-forth arm to shed his dearest blood;
Yon holiest place, where God's Shechinah shone
In splendor, at the prayer of Solomon,
With heathen altars will be compassed round,
And offerings vile pollute this holy ground!
Ere this I see, with sword in hand I'll fall,
Midst streams of blood, before the Temple's wall.
Then let our word be 'God and Liberty,'
And triumph glorious, or in glory die!"

On this the frowning front of war drew near;
Each adverse host, glittering with shield and spear,
Reflecting back the sun's ascending ray,
And giving double splendor to the day.
But ere the deadly strife of war began,
From out the Hebrew ranks stepped forth a man

Completely armed: "Stop! stop awhile!" he cried
To either host, (his arms expanded wide:)
"Hear, noble Titus—all ye chieftains, hear!
For a short space, this general war forbear.
There is a man who, with his ruffian band
And power superior, drove me from my land;
Who, aided by Baal's priests, with slanderous lies,
Hath me demanded for a sacrifice;
Nicanor is his name. If he lurks here,
Bid him step forth with helmet, shield, and spear.
And O! great chieftains of these raging hosts,
Restrain your armies at their several posts,
Till we decide (if forth he dare appear)
The issue of our individual war!"

The generals waved their swords, (a well-known sign,)
And still as marble stood each hostile line:
Nicanor then stepped forth, in arms arrayed,
Plumes from his helmet nodding o'er his head;
To whom thus Maldad: "Vain, proud Syrian lord,
At length we meet, 'neath helmet, spear, and sword.
With plumes you've decked your coronetted brow,
Doomed soon, I trust, to trail in dust below.
I own, your beauteous priestess I've enjoyed
In mutual love, till every sense was cloyed;
Not as a forged Adonis—no, by Jove!
'Twas only mutual, ardent, rapturous love."

More had he said, but, fired with tenfold rage,
Nicanor rushed, the braggart to engage;
Disdaining words, he as a lion sprung,
Or lioness, to avenge her injured young.
At the same instant flew each lengthened spear,
And, quivering past, along the sounding air,

Both struck one deadly blow. With mortal wound,
Maldad fell prone—his brazen arms resound:
The forceful weapon all his right side ploughed,
And wide the wound welled forth a tide of blood:
Nor did his keen spear with less fury fly—
It only soared a finger's-breadth too high;
Grazed, with slight wound, across Nicanor's head,
And wide his helm and nodding plumes lay spread.
Bare-headed, swift upon the fallen foe
The hero flew to give the final blow:
Above the dying man he furious stood,
His glittering sword raised high, athirst for blood;
But instant paused, and said, (grief in his eye,)
"Maldad, recant that horrid, slanderous lie:
Do justice, and perhaps you may not die."

He looked as if he would confess his crime,
But if he would, the slanderer had not time;
For his bold followers rushed to his relief,
Wounded the conqueror, and bore off their chief.

On this, both armies hurried to engage,
Shocked and electrified with added rage.
As when a low-hung cloud, surcharged with rain,
Darkens the mountain-tops and neighboring plain,
Unrent, till thunder through the concave roars,
Then down the riven mass in torrents pours;
So both the hosts, made furious at the sight,
Met, raging, in renewed conflicting fight!
The sound of spears rebounding from their shields,
And sword-strokes' clang, rang dreadful round the fields.
Salathiel and Lysander led the van:
"God and Napthalia!" loud behind them rang.
Where'er they charged, decades were overthrown:
They seemed to strike with powers beyond their own:

As fierce they moved, fell slaughter marched before;
Behind them, dying men, and groans, and gore!
Manlius beheld, and rushed, not without fear,
To meet the chief, and stop his blood-career:
Both plumes were waving as they nearer tend—
When on the right the prince espied a friend
Borne down by numbers, in unequal strife,
And flew to avenge him, or to save his life.
Around his fallen friend wide space he made;
Even heroes drew back from his reeking blade!
Manlius, meanwhile, released from dangerous war,
Rushed midst the Jewish ranks with sword and spear;
At his loud voice, Rome's bravest with him join,
And deadly conflict spreads along the line.
Great Manlius met mad Dathan's wild career,
And through his giant body hurled his spear:
His weighty falchion next the hero drew,
And on the common mass in vengeance flew:
Elias, Simon, Jotham, and a crowd
Of valiant Jews, lay weltering in their blood!
Like deeds of glory, on the left and right,
Marked out the heroes of this lengthened fight:
Here Phineas, burning with a priest-like zeal,
Through brave young Fabius plunged the shining steel:
There Judeas, red with slaughter, raged along,
Demon-possessed, and more than mortal strong:
He met Sempronius, and each chief addressed
His strong-urged javelin at the other's breast:
Sempronius wounded fell, and then a tide
Of John's grim Zealots spread destruction wide.
The Roman ranks those dreadful charges thin,
While still Napthalia's bands came pouring in:
The cohorts, weary, faint, half overcome,
Receded slowly—Romans could not run.

The noble Titus, from his lofty seat,
Perceived their case, and sounded a retreat:
The war-worn troops, safe in Antonia's towers,
With food and wine refreshed their wearied powers.
Nor were the Jews less pleased to drop the shield:
They 'd saved the temple, and had kept the field,
And fondly hoped, at length the time was come
When they would burst the galling chains of Rome.

Now in the porch, before the Holy Place,
Met the great leaders of the Hebrew race,
Salathiel, whose prompt aid that bloody day,
And mighty deeds, had given him boundless sway,
Resting upon his long blood-gouted sword,
Waved his right arm, and thus addressed the crowd:
"Chieftains and soldiers, to my words give ear!
The awful crisis of our state draws near.
Well have we fought this day, and Rome's proud powers
Are fain to hide in their night-stolen towers:
To follow up this victory is ours.
But ere to-morrow's sun the sky descends,
We conquerors stand, or else our nation ends!
This sacred Temple, glorious in our eyes,
Wrapped round with flames, must sparkle in the skies,
Unless our swords dissolve oppression's chain,
And spread the tyrant's cohorts round this fane!
Think not our foes will lie in yon strong tower—
Next morning sees condensed the Imperial power,
Enraged, and blazing bright in brazen form,
To die, or take this holy house by storm!
Then let me thus advise: Let every store
Be opened to our warriors and the poor;
Let all our forces, to restore their blood,
Have portions plenteous, both of wine and food:

There is no need one lingering loaf to save—
To-morrow gives us plenty or a grave!
I long to see the glorious sun arise
Bright o'er Asphaltis, rolling up the skies;
Then, girt in arms, we'll stop Rome's onward course,
And stand unmoved against their utmost force.
Even should great Manlius, decked with glory, come,
(Whom flatterers style the mighty sword of Rome,)
I'll meet the chief; and with God's aid, I trust,
My spear shall stretch their champion in the dust.
Then cast aside all fear—on Heaven rely,
And nobly die, if we are doomed to die!"

To this, Judeas instantly subjoined:
"Napthalia's prince has well expressed my mind:
Then let the starved and soldiers freely share
What food remains, and nerve their arms for war;
For generous wine and food will strength impart,
And send fresh courage through the sinking heart.
And we'll need all; for lo! the day has come
That seals our nation's fate, or humbles Rome:
Scenes will be witnessed by to-morrow's sun,
The world will shudder at till time is done!
But let us hope. Prophets and holy men
Now prophesy, through all Jerusalem,
That the sword blazing 'cross the vault of heaven,
The furious combats round the horizon driven,
Are but sure signs that God in time will come,
And step between our destiny and Rome;
That he will prove us to the latest hour,
And then display at once his heavenly power—
Once more through the Assyrian camp spread round
The vaunting foe, black, gasping on the ground!

This I believe: go, therefore, brethren, go;
Through night prepare to meet this mighty foe:
Myself and brother chiefs will lead you on
To death or freedom; and God's will be done!"

He ceased, and cheers and acclamations loud
Spoke full accordance of the list'ning crowd,
Who to their quarters went, now less oppressed,
To take refreshments, and then sink to rest.

Mean time the Roman generals round the board
Of Titus sat, with generous viands stored:
Much they discoursed of what that day had done;
Much of the issue of the day to come:
How for the dreadful conflict to prepare,
And end at once this long, this bloody war.
The noble Cæsar mused—then strode the hall—
Then paused, and said: "This area is too small
For all our host. Hear, then: I deem it best
To call the strong and bravest from the rest;
These Roman heroes in three legions form,
Completely armed, to meet the ascending morn,
Strike down the Zealots, and the Temple storm:
The rest may guard our camp, or armed here lie,
The posts of fallen warriors to supply."
Again he walked—then stopped, and raised his head;
His face gloomed solemn as he gravely said,
"Those wondrous signs which hover o'er this place,
And the mad fury of this Zealot race,
Who argue thence that their great God will come
At fate's last hour, and blast imperial Rome,
Convince me that the God, all gods above,
Has called me to a work I cannot love;
But now, my country's honors and my own,
The imperial splendor of my father's throne,

Forbid delay: to-morrow's setting sun
Must see yon Temple and this city won;
While, to supply the absence of his light,
Domes, towers, and spires shall blaze throughout the night."
Then said, "Chiefs, be prepared!"—Turned, bade adieu.
His eyes gleamed vengeance, as the chief withdrew.
Instant he sought his couch, to sink in rest,
And calm the rising anger of his breast.

Thus night sank down, and canopied each host,
With troublous dreams and spectral visions tossed;
But to all waking eyes, through all the night,
More hideous signs and wonders struck the sight:
The evil demons, from the abyss profound,
And souls of wicked dead, (now all unbound,)
Ranged through the camps, and, entering, full possessed
With fiendish passions every warrior's breast:
Red meteors, as if loosened from on high,
Slow and portentous streamed adown the sky:
Dry, stormy blasts through all the mountains roared;
Still fiercer blazed the long-suspended sword;
More fierce the combat the horizon round,
The charging horsemen, and the chariots' bound,
The rallying and the rout; while through the town
A sound till that foreboding night unknown—
The sound of raging seas; (9) for from each shore
Was heard the Asphaltan and mid-ocean's roar!
Though at great distance, yet the billowy war
Seemed nigh, and filled the stoutest hearts with fear;
While round the walls, prophetical and slow,
Jaled still cried, "Woe! to Jerusalem woe!"
Midst stripes and buffetings, still on he 'd go;
Then stop and cry, "Woe! to Jerusalem woe!"

As climax to those signs, a new one came:
The Temple's self was filled with lambent flame,
Like God's Shechinah, in the holiest, where
It first all-glorious shone at Moses' prayer!
The whole internal space and lofty dome
With supernatural radiance brightly shone!
Ere long it slowly seemed to ascend the sky;
And as it rose, wide spread the mournful cry!
As from a thousand hearts, it struck the sense:
Its burden was—"Arise, (10) let us go hence!"
Still, as towards heaven it rose in slow suspense,
The sad wail solemn rose, "Let us go hence!"
At length the sad moan died: fading light
Was lost to many a trembling gazer's sight;
The awful spectral vision all was gone,
And night in pitchy darkness filled his ebon throne.

Now morn arose, and, bright from orient climes,
O'er Olivet the sun with splendor shines;
His beams the fields and dewy grass adorn,
Empearling drops on every flower and thorn:
His slanting rays, as up the heavens he rolled,
Tipped flush the spires and Temple roof with gold;
As if the orb of day, as on he passed,
Knew of ten thousand views this was his last;
That ere o'er Sodom's sea he rose again,
That dome would sparkle with a fiercer flame,
Till all its glories sank, and one dark blank remain.

In the first heavens, where for a time abode
Heaven's great Vicegerent, Minister of God,
Around whose throne the saints and angels bend,
And to his words with reverent awe attend—
"Hear, all ye progeny of light," he said:
"That day has come, perhaps too long delayed—

That day of vengeance—when a sentence just
Says to lost sinners, Turn again to dust!
They have rejected me! God's voice from heaven
Full forty years was for repentance given;
But what the issue?—Deeper all the time
Have they been sinking down in blood and crime.
Now, almost maniac, through their city's bound,
Murder, and famine, and death-groans resound!
Judgment with mercy then leads on the day,
To sweep this nation and their fane away,
With signs that show my hand stretched from above,
To introduce the law of peace and love.
Long will it struggle with the carnal mind,
Against the powers of hell and flesh combined;
Nor gain the victory till revealed I come,
And then the work triumphant shall be done!"

He ceased; and spirits blessed, which waited round,
With hallelujahs made the heavens resound;
"Righteous and just art thou, thou King of saints,
To avenge thy martyrs and their long complaints;
Holy and just thy judgments, mighty God!
Thou givest this bloody nation to drink blood, ([11])
For they are worthy: they 've thy children slain!"
And hallelujahs rang round heaven again.

Meanwhile, below, the fierce contending hosts,
Sheathed in bright arms, were gathering to their posts.
Long time it took, and hour succeeding hour,
Ere Rome's choice legions (the assailing power)
Were formed in all their terrible array,
Their arms reflecting back the blaze of day.
Less disciplined, on moved each Jewish band,
In massive power, with shield and spear in hand;

Led on by many warriors, high in fame,
Zealous to save their temple from the flame,
(That holy place,) or round its walls lie slain:
Swift through the southern gate they constant pour,
Till all the holy ground could hold no more.

The ascending sun had now gained half his way
Up to the zenith, and gave wide the day,
When war's loud trumpet, echoing from afar,
Propelled the opposing hosts to instant war.
Most dreadful was the charge 'long all the line;
The spears lay level—high the falchions shine:
By demons either host drove to this strife;
None turned from danger—none regarded life:
Thousands of men, infuriate, all possessed
With dead men's demons raging in each breast,
To conflict rushed! Phineas on the right
Led on the Zealots, foremost in the fight:
His great ancestor's spirit, in that hour,
Urged him along with supernatural power;
An equal fury marked his bold career,
As when through Zimri rushed the altar-spear.
At great Metellus his strong javelin flew,
And pierced the Italian's shield and body through!
Prone fell the warrior midst the bleeding slain,
While Phineas rushed his weapon to regain;
Then plunged once more the bloody death-barbed dart
Through his gay corslet to proud Lausus' heart!
Whole Roman ranks before his rage gave place—
When mighty Gauldus met him face to face—
Gauldus, who ruled whole districts as his own,
In chieftain glory on the rapid Rhone.
A thousand spears the hero with him brought:
Though high in fame, he still more glory sought.

A moment gazed each chief, as they drew nigh:
Then Gauldus spoke, inquiry in his eye:
"Who and what art thou, prodigal of breath,
Who ravest thus, followed by groans and death?
Art thou a mortal man, or fiend from hell?
Nay, answer not: this flying spear shall tell."
On this both jav'lins flew, with rage intense;
Vain was the cuirass, or the shield's defence:
Phineas fell; the weighty Gallic dart
Pierced through his shield, and quivered in his heart!
Prone fell the warrior, gazing on the sky,
And smiles enthusiastic closed his zealous eye!
Nor vainly flew his spear's avenging point;
It pierced the groin, and rankled in the joint
Of the proud victor: doubling down he bends,
And grasps the dust, amongst his dying friends!
Forth from the ranks was borne each fallen chief,
In silent sorrow and unspoken grief.

Mean time, upon the left like deeds were done;
There brave Judeas led the Zealots on:
Simon, and Judas, and Alcandor shine
All bright in arms, and with the hero join.
Long time the Roman phalanx they withstood,
And doubtful held the field of death and blood.
At length, o'ercome, the common soldiers fled,
For half their comrades lay amongst the dead;
But Judas, who before had made it known
He was Messiah, and claimed David's throne,
Stood on the field alone, and loudly cried,
"I wait some Roman chief, bloated with pride,
To singly meet my arm. Say, is there one
Who dares to meet me? If so, let him come:

The issue shall to both our hosts proclaim
The war's result and the brave victor's name!"

He ceased; and Drusus, who a cohort led
Of noble warriors, worthy of their head,
Stepped forth and said: "Judas, we 've heard of you,
That arrogant and bold enthusiast Jew;
Who, though too mean to creep this earthly clod,
Assumes (fame says) to be a demi-god,
Before whose arm princes and kings shall fall,
And you, as Lord Messiah, govern all!
Your bold assumption this good spear shall try:
Now loose your vengeance—let your fury fly!"
He said, and, rising high above the field,
Whirled his long lance against the opposing shield:
Vain its defence: the long resistless dart
Pierced through the shield, and rested in his heart:
Down in his blood the bold impostor fell,
And his inflated spirit sank to hell!
His awe-struck followers in confusion fly;
Their shrieks and wailings mount the upper sky!

But from the centre shouts were heard afar—
There heavier rolled the tide of Roman war.
Great Manlius, famed in arms, led on the van;
Where'er he moved, the blood in torrents ran.
With Eneas' soul possessed, (first of his race,)
The Zealots fled the terrors of his face,
And wide before him left an empty space!
Napthalia's chief with grief and rage beheld
Even his Napthalians flying from the field;
Then to Lysander—"Turn our men from flight:
I go to meet yon chief in single fight."

Bright blazed the helmet on his towering head,
And earth resounded with the warrior's tread:
Manlius beheld him as the ranks divide,
And saw his purpose with a warrior's pride.
In mute suspension stood the warring hosts,
As if spell-bound, and gazing from their posts.
Salathiel, at due distance, paused and said,
(His right hand raised to heaven, his left spear stayed,)
"No more shall Manlius and Salathiel's spear
Turn from each other in the ranks of war.
But late we met, when a distressing sight
Called me as recreant from the proffered fight:
Again we meet; and as the fates decree,
Rome reigns triumphant, or Jerusalem's free!
But, Roman, hear—(would all the world might hear;)
'Tis not for glory that I launch my spear;
'Tis not for riches or ambition's power
That thus I war, and meet this dangerous hour:
No! 'tis for freedom—earth's most noble cause—
Yon sacred Temple, and God's holy laws.
For this, to stop your bloody course I've come,
To try conclusions with the sword of Rome;
But fair and open be our latest strife,
And let the fates decide of death or life."

To this the Roman chief sedate replied:
"Know, far-famed prince, your country's boast and pride,
That I, as you, despise all selfish ends:
'Tis for Rome's glory that my sword contends,
To crush sedition, and on every tower
Plant Cæsar's ensigns, emblems of his power.
Where is the nation, save your maniac horde,
But joys to call the great Vespasian Lord?

'Tis but to quell rebellion, then, that I
Bid my sword glitter, and my javelin fly.
But now, why longer thus, with empty boasts,
Hold awe-struck, in suspension, both our hosts;
Then to the conflict come—begin the strife!
Though fame reports you hold a charm-bound life—
That for some crime, a demon, or some god,
Has chained you deathless to this earthly clod,
And death can't follow with your flowing blood—
I trust the gods above, and this good arm,
Will free your fettered spirit from the charm."

Then, bounding forth some paces in advance,
With whirlwind power he sent the weighty lance:
The spear (perhaps 'twas urged with too much force)
Glanced, like quick (12) lightning, from its destined course:
Grazing the chief, it plunged in Eli's breast,
Of all his friends, the bravest and the best:
Not erring thus, flew the Napthalian spear,
As, hissing on, it cleft the yielding air;
Below the Roman's shield, so forceful thrown,
The spear transfixed the thigh, and crushed the bone.
Staggering with pain, he doubles to the ground;
Shield, helm, and plumes lay scattered all around!
The groaning chief quick to the tower is borne,
And round his couch his friends and grieved attendants mourn;
While slow the victor joined his own array,
To wake anew the horrors of the day.

As when from heaven the fierce electric flash,
Midst thunder's roar, spreads the tall mountain ash;
The village school, vociferous on the plain,
Awed for some moments, from their sports refrain,

Then to their games return, with added yell;
So paused both armies, when Rome's hero fell:
So soon, both hosts, with more infuriate rage,
Rushed 'gainst each other, furious to engage;
Glory and triumph urged the Hebrews on,
And grief and vengeance fired the powers of Rome.
The Jewish ram-horns, which once tumbled down
The walls and ramparts of the accursed town,
Rang shrilly o'er the fields up to the sky:
The imperial clarion and loud trump reply:
Loud deafening shouts with their dread clamor join,
Fill wide the air and up the concave climb:
Then volleying flew, convulsing all the air,
The encountering storms of darts and glittering spear;
Sword-strokes on helmets and the brazen shields;
Discordant music brayed around the fields.
The Jews still charging in successive shocks—
The cohorts met them as a wall of rocks;
Beneath their shields conjoined, they still moved on
Unbroken, holding all the space they won.
O'er heaps of slain was each wild charge and rout,
While victory's scales hung trembling as in doubt
Above the bloody field!—As when a pine
On Taurus' top, or wooded Apennine,
Whose mighty trunk and branches upward rise,
Straight towards the zenith, towering to the skies;
Should woodmen the huge trunk with steel surround,
And on each side inflict an equal wound,
Long time the conic top, trembling on high,
Seems as uncertain in which vale to lie;
So wavered both the hosts, and victory's scale:
None yet was conquered—none could yet prevail:
Shrieks, shouts, and clarions rent the upper air;
Below, deep groans, and blood, and wild despair.

BOOK VII.

The Conflagration.

The conflict continues round the Temple—Judas slain by Cloanthus—His dying speech—The deeds of Phineas, Lysander, and others—Catonius's speech and descent from the burning portico—The last struggle before the door of the Temple—How it was set on fire—The acts of Salathiel, Lysander, and others—Lysander falls beside the altar—Salathiel, wounded, holds by the horns of the altar—Messiah manifests himself and forgives him—Titus stops the slaughter—The Temple in flames—The Romans retire to feast and rest—Titus gives directions to Ceralius—Must take John and Simon alive—Slay none but those who resist—Ceralius reports at noon—Has taken the two tyrants—The legions hail Titus as Imperator—The court and army feast at night—In the midst of the feast, Miriam and Hester fall before Cæsar's feet—Their several speeches, and replies of Titus—They finally obtain the bodies of the dead Salathiel and the wounded Lysander—Titus adds a delightful home on the Leontes.

Thus warred the nations—thus flashed spear and sword
O'er all the holy mountain of the Lord;
That sacred mount, where Shem fixed his abode—
That righteous king, priest of the most high God,
Who joined, as Media between God and men,
The mitre with a stainless diadem, (1)
Thence called Melchisedek—how changed the scene!
Now from slain thousands see the life's blood stream!
In wild despair and groans they yield their breath,
And wide and wasteful was the work of death.

At length the sun rolled down his western way,
And on the Temple poured its final day.
Mean time, as death the Roman cohorts thinned,
Fresh troops impatient poured from ranks behind;
Thus onward towards the sacred porch they pass,
A constant dying, undiminished mass.
Cerales now (the second in command)
Thus called around him a selected band.
"Romans," he said, "be what you 've been before,
Or let this great occasion make you more.
Yonder's their sanctum—to it now rush on!
Think of your fathers' glories and your own;
Strike down those robbers that obstruct your way,
And make their gold and glittering shrines your prey."

Salathiel saw, as in the front he stood,
The gathering storm, and raised his voice aloud:
"Hear, all ye sons of Israel—hear and come;
For lo! the heroes and the chiefs of Rome
Are rushing to God's Temple! Now 's the hour
To meet their fury with collected power.
Come, then, Lysander, Judeas, Nathan—come,
And save God's Temple—save your children's home!
Come, Simon Gorias—Simon from the hill
Whose gushing fountains marshy Merom fill;
Come, all ye Jewish patriots; with me dare
The weight and thunder of the coming war.
This sword and mountain spear still, still before
Shall gleam in front, all red with heathen gore!"
On this they charged. As when a southern cloud
Confronts one north, till peals of thunder loud
Burst their pent fury, so each adverse host,
On this appeal, was in fierce struggle lost.
Simon from Merom, far before the rest,

(With Joab's daring spirit full possessed,)
His weighty spear was not hurled o'er the field,
But firmly in both hands convulsive held:
Before his demon rage, at every thrust
Some warrior fell, and groaning grasped the dust.
Vain all defensive arms—with fourfold force,
It gored through all, resistless in its course:
Then Galba, then Lenteles groaning fell—
Syntaz and Nisus with them sank to hell!

Nor less Napthalia's warriors on the left—
There glanced their swords, and helms and heads were cleft:
Lysander and Judeas led the charge;
Their wasting swords made space and opening large;
One, by the great Asmonean's soul possessed,
While the famed Spartan ([2]) fired the other's breast.
Cloanthus marked them on their bloody road,
(A Dacian chief, filled with a heathen god.)
"Come on," he said, "you leaders of a band,
The shame and curse of this distracted land:
Both of you 'scape not—one ends his career!"
On this quick flew the strong, resistless spear:
Before its force defensive arms gave way,
And Judeas fell prone on the crimsoned clay!
Dying he cried, "Ye servants of our God,
Defend the Temple, and avenge my blood;
Die for fair freedom's cause, as now I die,
Or live victorious, crowned ([3]) with liberty!"
On this, as ebbed life's stream, passed his last breath,
And his eyes darkened with the glaze of death.

Salathiel, Jotham, Simon hear his words,
And answer gave with their avenging swords:

Resistless on the cohorts down they bore,
Their course wide marked with dead, and streams of gore:
Even Roman valor had at length to yield,
And slow receded from the ensanguined field.

But now new clamors and wild shouts arise,
With roaring flames and agonizing cries!
Silent, unseen, by secret ways and rough,
A cohort had attained the porch's roof—
A spacious structure, pillared high and wide,
Fronting along the Temple's northern side; ([4])
From this a storm of rocks and spears they pour,
The height still doubling the impulsive power:
With gathered force each javelin hissed below,
And death or wounds attended every blow.

Eliab saw, and instant gave command
To bring the oil, the pitch, and flaming brand:
"Apply the torch," he cries; and soon sharp flame
Twines, serpent-like, the pillars that sustain
The sacrifice aloft: their lambient tongues
Guard all descent, and round the cloister run:
No way remained to escape a burning death,
But plunging down upon the rocks beneath.
Titus and all the Roman host beheld,
With rage impotent—fierce the Hebrews yelled:
The pent-up victims, from the roof on high,
Sent forth a mixed, half-brave, half-wailing cry.
As when some peasant, at the evening hour,
To obtain the honey stored from many a flower,
Suspends above the match the waxen dome—
The bees' sweet earnings, and their hard-earned home—
With lessening buzz, the suffering insects drop,
In quick succession, from the smothering top;

So, from the porch's roof, driven by the flame,
The Romans drop successive to the plain,
Crippled and crushed; though some, by miracle,
That way escaped, (friends helping as they fell,)
While some remained above, midst smoke and heat,
Nor dared to take the wild, terrific leap.
Most horrible the sight! nor friend or foe,
Nor mortal power, could aid them from below!
Some, firm as martyrs, bore the smoke and fire;
Some plunged the centre, quicker to expire.
Close to the roof's west verge Catonius came;
(A western breeze rolled back the approaching flame:)
He raised his arm and cried, loud, calm, and clear,
"Hear, friends and foes! I want you all to hear.
O noble Titus, and ye sons of Rome,
Forbear your lamentations, tears, and moans;
I as a Roman hope to meet my fate,
And die a worthy member of the State;
But now I charge you, by these flames that rise
Round Romans burning, flaring to the skies,
That you this horrid sacrifice repay,
And with full vengeance sweep this race away!
As they delight in fire, let flames rage wide,
And sweep the accursed town from side to side!

"And now to you, ye savages, I turn,
Who joy to see your fellow-creatures burn;
Whose fell forefathers, in the days of old,
Destroyed whole nations, (as your books have told,)
Both man and beast—babes, mothers, by the sword,
And said it was commanded by heaven's Lord!
And now, whene'er we cease to shake your wall,
Do not your factions to fell murder fall?

Where 's Simon, with a devil in his breast,
And John, with fear and cruelty possessed?
Have they not through your city slaughter spread—
Snatched from the famished child the mother's bread?
Have they not trod all human feelings down,
And made you all the assassins of your town—
Each to be tyrant sole?—But by this flame,
Whose swift approach I can no more sustain;
By yon red sword, and all the signs in heaven,
I know full ruin, by God's vengeance driven,
Shall sweep your State—wrap it this night in flame,
And your proud Temple be no more a name!
Even while I tell you of your horrid sins,
See! in your sanctum—see, the work begins!
I now descend. My life, dear friends, you'll save,
Or to a soldier give a soldier's grave."
Then from the cornice swung. As thus he spoke,
A brother, as he fell, the impetus broke:
Both prostrate lay, and both were maimed for life—
No more to join in war's infuriate strife.

But not by guess his words. From his high stand,
He saw a Syrian leap in with a brand—
(Ignatius)—fired with Erastratus' soul,
(No window's height his fury could control,)
Another glorious Temple to destroy,
Urged on the demon with a frenzied joy.
While all eyes gazed upon the flaming porch,
Even in the Holiest he applied the torch:
Nor he alone; for Nausica, a dame [5]
For love and beauty of notorious fame,
Possessed by Thais' spirit—led by one
As mad as the world's king from Macedon—

Aided by him and some congenial friends,
The Roman courtesan at once ascends
The opposing window, and, with torch in hand,
Rivalled Ignatius and his flaming brand:
Her hand had sent towards heaven the Persian fane,
His Dian's Temple, on the Ephesian plain;
And having leave, fit mortals to inspire,
Each rushed to wrap the Judean fane in fire!

Titus perceived, and, to preserve the dome,
Or triumph with its relics, (6) entering Rome,
For a decisive charge the order gave
To force the Holies, and their treasures save;
But firm to guard the way Salathiel stood,
And with him many warriors stained with blood.
Most dreadful was the shock—deadly the war,
When valor met with courage and despair.
Salathiel and Lysander raged before
Their band, and back the Roman cohort bore
Beyond the altar: all the struggling way,
Midst curdling blood, the dead and dying lay!
Three times the Romans, with recruited power,
The charge renewed, to storm the sacred door;
Three times the Jews (though sinking wound on wound)
Repulsed the foe beyond the altar's bound;
Yet few could safely reach its hallowed side;
Most sank behind and swelled the crimson tide.
Lysander, foremost, still a moment stood
Near its south corner—then sank down in blood;
His fellow-warriors, though by crowds o'ercome,
Fought on till death—brave falling one by one,
And with them fell the State——the war was done!

Mean time, Salathiel, red with Roman blood,
Returned, and bending o'er Lysander stood:

And, "O my son!" he cried—"my dearest friend,
In this dread hour my arm shall still defend.
Some sign of life, some token, dear friend, give,
And then Salathiel will consent to live."
Then, stooping, grasped his hand, and hoped to hear,
But in his breast received Ventides spear:
The shaft broke short, but near the hero's heart
Deep fixed remained the barbed Roman dart.
Rising, pain-nerved, his last fell stroke was sped,
And down Ventides dropped amongst the dead:
The hero's sword, too, fell—long red with gore,
Doomed in the battle's rage to flash no more:
The altar's horn then grasped, he suffering stood,
While near his feet Lysander rolled in blood!

But now Messiah, to whose hands were given
All power on earth and this sublunary heaven,
His cloud-pavilion round (7) the altar spread,
Enclosed the chieftains and removed the dead:
Before Salathiel's face confessed he stood,
As when he bore the crucifixion wood;
The same his air and form as on the day
He moved, midst insults, down the dolorous way;
The same his placid smile, of sovereign grace,
As when the Mobarch spat upon his face;
As when the man before him, mad with zeal,
(Now weak and fainting,) spurned him with his heel;
When, in a few soft words, he spoke his doom—
"Unchanged and fixed, you'll tarry till I come!"

Salathiel by the altar stood amazed,
And on the great Calvarian sufferer gazed:
Trembling for his insults, he viewed that face,
So mournful, yet so bright, with heavenly grace:

To whom Messiah thus: "Your course is run:
Proud Zealot, you have tarried till I've come!
Yet fear not, poor weak mortal, but rejoice:
Thousands who then swelled high your murderous voice—
Thousands who then around Mount Calvary stood,
Wagging their heads, and glorying in my blood,
Bend down before my cross, and enter in
Love's kingdom, all redeemed from death and sin.
Even Saul of Tarsus, that fierce homicide,
Who havoc made of Christians far and wide;
Whose zeal, like yours, breathed forth, with every breath,
Threatenings and slaughter, tortures, chains, and death;
My gospel-banner now he bears unfurled,
And with great power proclaims it to the world.
Like him, through zeal, you sinned against high Heaven;
Like him you 've seen me (8)—like him, are forgiven.
As Israel's hero, I your soul dismiss,
And bid you rise with angels up to bliss."

These words benign the Saviour having said,
He smiled, and touched the deep-fixed javelin's head:
Instant the steel receded from the wound,
And gushed the imprisoned life's-blood to the ground:
The spirit, freed, rose up to heavenly day;
The body sank, a load of lifeless clay,
And stretched beside his loved Lysander lay!

To angels ministrant the Saviour said,
"Let both to Absalom's tomb be now conveyed:
With Heaven's embalming sound preserve the slain,
And mitigate the wounded sufferer's pain.
Then to their friends at Bethlehem relate
Their sad condition and impending fate;
Urge them to bend before the conqueror's feet,
And beg their bodies, and a calm retreat:

Their earthly destiny thus to fulfil
By miracle, is not my sovereign will.
To human feelings, nature's sympathies,
And deep heart-sorrow, bursting from the eyes,
I then commit. But through this work of love,
Safe guard you them, and obstacles remove:
To that sweet lonely vale, their destined home,
By natural means, it is my will they come.
Give them access, and then you 've done your part:
'Tis theirs to touch the youthful conqueror's heart."

Mean time, the legions, with increasing force,
Swept o'er the field, resistless in their course.
As when a foaming river, rising vast,
Pours 'gainst a mighty mound, deemed fixed and fast;
As mountain torrents raise it high, and higher,
To its foundations trembles all the pyre:
At length, o'ercome by the continued rise,
It crashing sinks, and deep in ruin lies,
While the freed flood sweeps fields in wild career,
And drowns the hopes and labors of the year;
So o'er the field the infuriate Romans spread,
Adding the flying to the slaughtered dead!
'Twas warfare now no more, but flight and fear;
Wild tumult, shrieks, and horror and despair!
Through every gate, with lamentation loud,
The Jewish relics faint and laboring crowd,
As from gaunt wolves the sheep wide trembling flies,
So fled the Jews, and so the hindmost dies!

And now upon the Temple Sol's last rays
Mixed with the Roman fires, in common blaze:
Night's canopy came down, and full displayed
The wide illumination, and its shade.

Titus, with the chief officers of Rome,
By flames were driven from the sacred dome,
With but small treasure. Round the holy fane,
In close embrace, circled the nimble flame,
Roaring—at length the structure seemed to rise,
A pyramid of flame, up to the skies!
Thousands of Zealots, rolling [9] on the ground,
With groans and shrieks, increased the awful sound;
Then, rushing furious, plunged the burning dome,
And in the Holiest gave their latest groan!

Meanwhile, through every street the Roman bands
Flashed their red swords, blood streaming to their hands,
Casting on every side the flaming brands.
Soon through this city, overwhelmed with woes,
In flames the palaces and spires arose;
Deserted houses, filled with putrid dead,
There piled by murder and the want of bread,
By foes were favored with a funeral-fire—
Their blazing corpses formed the mournful pyre!
As when that day shall come—that awful day—
When all sublunary things shall pass away;
As when the wheels of time their course have run,
And every planet flames forth [10] like the sun;
As then, wide blazing o'er the ethereal sphere,
To angelic eyes shall flaming worlds appear;
So to poor mortals in succession rise
Dome after dome, ascending to the skies,
And back returned Moriah's dreadful glare,
Great centre of destruction and despair,
Whence shrieks and groans conjoined, with gathering sound,
Rolled through the city to its utmost bound:
Jerusalem's dying dirge—the awful close
Of crimes stupendous, and stupendous woes!

From Scopas' heights, by his long lance upheld,
The conquering Titus the sad scene beheld:
Though deep incensed by their fanatic zeal,
His heart was human, and he could but feel.
Thousands, he knew, hemmed round by fire and sword,
Were slaves to tyrants whom their souls abhorred;
That famished mothers, with starved children crying
For bread, that moment were by poniards dying.
His heart was touched, and quick, with troubled haste,
He bade the trumpet sound the imperial blast,—
That signal sound which stops the work of death,
And turns back Roman swords into their sheath:
When heard, no Roman durst retreat decline,
More than if Heaven itself had given the sign.
The conquering cohorts back to camp return,
And slaughter, slumbering, waits the coming morn.

But still the flames burned bright; and Cæsar cries,
(Raising his right hand to the lurid skies,)
"I call to witness, all ye gods above,
Bellona, Mars, and high imperial Jove,
And thou, the only God these wretches own,
(Who scorn'st to sit on a divided throne,)
I call to witness all your heavenly powers,
This deep destruction is no crime of ours.
Long did we labor with sincere intent,
And strove with fate, this ruin to prevent—
To save this ancient city, and their shrine,
That glorious Temple, holy and divine;
But all my pleadings, all my offers failed—
A murderous frenzy triumphed and prevailed:
When told the fate we now behold would come,
They scoffed and blasphemed all the gods of Rome.

'To save your Temple,' this was their return:
'If God won't save it, let his Temple burn!' (11)
Hardened in blood and crime, their frenzied state
Proclaims that Heaven had sealed their final fate.
For, O ye gods, 'fore whom I now appear,
And mortals listening round, I this declare:
Had not the wrath of some offended God
Decreed this doom, Jerusalem still had stood:
Not the vast power of still all-conquering Rome
Could have their fury and these walls o'ercome.
So strong their bulwarks, fenced by nature round
With mountain ramparts and deep vales profound,
The powers e'en Rome itself could send so far
Might years on years have waged a hopeless war.
'Tis therefore God who has the vict'ry given—
Yon flaming Temple is the work of Heaven!
I am, in this vast ruin, but his rod—
A vial, to pour out the wrath of God.
Their murders and their social sins are great—
Enough, I know, to seal a nation's fate;
But still, some deeper crime, to me unknown,
Has moved high Heaven to pour such vengeance down;
Some sin which forced the bravest of mankind
To slay themselves, through party frenzy blind;
A rage intestine, deaf to reason's calls,
While Rome's imperial power was thundering at their walls!"

To whom Josephus thus: "Great, conquering prince,
Deep is the wisdom that your words evince:
Had they sent off their Paschal myriads home,
Their stores had lasted seven long years to come:
Had they united firm—like brothers stood,
To die for freedom and the laws of God,—

With that same noble, death-defying mind,
Salem had stood against the world combined:
Armies succeeding armies had in vain
Hung round her walls, till in succession slain;
But God in vengeance, as you 've justly said,
For hearts all guilt, took reason from their head.
But was it common crimes, you ask, brought down
God's signal vengeance on yon burning town?
Murder, rapine, and lust, the wide earth fill,
Was theirs transcendent, and more horrid still!
Great Cæsar, it is said, they 've done a deed
That does the sins of all the world exceed.
Jesus of Nazareth, that most wondrous man,
(If it be lawful still to call him man,)
Endowed with power all nature to control;
Noble in person, of a godlike soul;
With healing power replete, by touch or word,
All the diseased he instantly restored.
The dead his voice called from the bier or grave:
Illimitable seemed his power to save.
He claimed to be Messiah, sent of God,
To renovate and rule this mundane clod:
He, in deep night betrayed, the high-priests caught,
And bound to Pilate's bar, with insults brought.
To all expostulation, they replied,
'Away with him! let him be crucified!'
The clamorous mob at length a sentence wrung,
And instant on the cross the sufferer hung!
O mighty Cæsar, deem not that I am
A follower of this God, or wondrous man;
I only state facts known to reverend men,
And all the rulers of Jerusalem.
Hence, 'tis the murder of this Righteous One
I deem has poured God's vengeance from his throne;

For on the day of that stupendous crime,
Signs followed signs most awful and sublime:
As on Mount Calvary's top his cross they reared,
Sun, moon, and stars in darkness disappeared;
A midnight darkness wrapped the earth around,
While earthquakes murmured with convulsive sound;
The mountains trembled, and the solid rocks
Were rent and shivered with repeated shocks;
The strong-wove Temple-veil—that beauteous screen
Which veiled the holiest, lest it should be seen—
Was rent from top to bottom that dread hour,
So fraught with wonders and mysterious power;
Even graves were opened by his dying throes,
And sainted fathers from their tombs arose,
Into the holy city went, and saw
That scene, which shook the natural world with awe,
And there were seen of many, I am told,
Who then were young, but now are dead or old.
Still more: as he foretold, his followers say,
From death he rose triumphant the third day,
And in the sight of the far-famed eleven
(After seven weeks) ascended up to heaven!
If this be true, this sacrilegious crime
Is what brings down this punishment divine;
And you and Rome's great power and conquering sword
Are but mere agents of heaven's sovereign Lord,
Who has decreed (and his decrees are fate)
For this transcendent crime to end the Jewish state!"

Thus spoke Josephus, whose supreme delight
Was to prose on from morning ([12]) until night,
And then his long harangues still longer write.

To him the Roman conqueror answered brief:
"To do Heaven's will should be no cause of grief."

Then thus: "Now, warriors, go seek due repast;
Our struggle has been long, and long our fast:
This day's sore conflict for refection calls,
And rest—so yield to night and nature's calls."

He said, and, turning, with his freedman went
And sought refreshment in his inner tent;
Then on the pillow laid his thoughtful head,
And slept profoundly on a soldier's bed:
The war-worn legions also sought repose,
While Salem sobbed beneath her dying throes.
Pain, grief, and fear, made it dark, mental night,
While mountains round all gleamed with lurid light.
Moriah's Temple long superior shone
O'er every pinnacle and flaming dome;
At length, in one vast flash, it seemed to rise,
And burst like meteors in the upper skies!

Now over desolation, death, and woes,
From Sodom's Sea the sun resplendent rose;
The morning dew-drops, careless of man's ways,
Sparkled like twinkling diamonds in his rays.
But on Moriah's top in vain it streams:
No Temple spires reflected back his beams:
All was sad vacuum when the morning hours
Called from repose the conquering Roman powers.
Great Cæsar, as each legion filled its post,
Thus gave his orders to the assembled host:
"My valiant comrades, God at length has given
This town accurst, hateful to earth and Heaven,
Into our hands; yet much remains to do,
Which with strict orders I commit to you.
Let no more blood be shed—from that desist—
Except those cut-throats which shall dare resist:

Slay every Zealot who shall longer strive,
But take their leaders, if you can, alive—
Especially the tyrants, coward John, ([13])
And Simon, demon brave, who led them on.
Those two arch-fiends, the murderers of their race,
Whose hellish souls the human form disgrace,
Take them alive: their crimes so wide are known,
We must present them to the eyes of Rome:
Lead them in triumph, labelled, gagged, and bound,
While mocking multitudes their march surround,
Then let them (so Vespasian will require)
In lingering torments on the cross expire!
Make captives of the rest—let them be fed
With strengthening wine and soft restoring bread,
That when on sale our merchants them behold,
They may admit they 're fitting to be sold;
For as earth holds their vile, seditious dead,
So shall the living round the world be spread!
Plunder not now, but when the work is done,
You shall have license till the setting sun.
At noon, Cerales, we will hold our court,
And then we hope you 'll make a good report.
At fitting time, the buildings which remain,
Their walls and towers we 'll level with the plain:
So that the plough shall o'er Mount Zion pass,
And desolation call forth briers and grass!
But three great towers shall for Rome's glory stand,
Grand for their names, and for their structure grand:
Phasales, Mariamne, and Hippicus,
Shall tell the world the glory won by us;
Fame shall proclaim from those stupendous towers
Vespasian's glory, and Rome's conquering powers."

Now had soft, fleecy clouds the sky o'ercome,
And cooled the fervor of a zenith sun,

When on his tribunal the conqueror sate,
With guards, attendants, and the chiefs of state,
To hear Cerales, who had lately come,
To tell how he the task assigned had done.

"Great Cæsar," he began, "when to the crowd
Of flying wretches we proclaimed aloud
Life on submission, (as was your command,)
And for assurance stretched to them my hand,
The famished citizens with one accord
Gave thanks to Cæsar, praises to the Lord.
One hundred thousand, we are told, survive—
Poor famished creatures, scarcely yet alive,
Who, when they heard that order, (given as thine,)
That all should be sustained with food and wine,
Weak mothers looked toward heaven and murmured grace,
And tears ran down each sobbing mother's face;
Even the pale children, when they heard of bread,
With feeble shouts forsook their squalid bed!
Your name with praise to heaven sounds at this time,
For now they 're dealing out your bread and wine."

To whom thus Titus: "General, that was right:
We want no further sufferings in our sight;
But hope you did no higher promise give,
But only this, that they should eat and live:
From this strange land, which gives sedition birth,
They must be scattered over all the earth!
But where are John and Simon? tell us where:
Of those fell monsters now we wish to hear."

On this Cerales, with a Roman's pride,
Slow and submissive thus at length replied:
"The tyrants fled diverse, each with a band
Of those fierce Zealots, (curses of the land.)

Simon of Gorias was the first we found,
On Zion's hill, with his assassins round:
I sent a cohort round to bar his flight,
Then pressed down on him with superior might.
Instant surrender was my terms, or death;
'Twas answered by his sword flashed from its sheath.
Cæsar, that man—or fiend—is great in fight,
With soul all fearless, and an arm of might!
I saw, amazed, how high he held his shield,
With what a bound he rose above the field;
I bade even Romans from close fight forbear,
And gall the lion with the flying spear;
Yet not on him, but his, I bade them pour
Their storm of javelins in a ceaseless shower:
They fell like leaves before an autumn wind,
For death flew swift before them and behind.
I wished, as you commanded, to contrive
Some way to take the monster-man alive;
But, like a lion hemmed, he, with a bound,
Would dash and strike some Roman to the ground;
And I began to fear—and so all said—
We could not take him till we took him dead.
On this a Tartar from the Caspian shore
Said, if a proper cord I would procure,
He 'd cast it round the monster's neck, and then
He, monster-like, might be dragged from his den;
That all his life he through the wide Ukraine
Had chased wild horses o'er that boundless plain;
That in full flight he side by side would run,
Spring forth his coil, and then the work was done;
That he with others had pursued the trade,
And lived by captives in the forest made.
The cord was brought, and, wonderful to tell,
Round Simon's neck at his next bound it fell!

The noose, drawn tight, soon dragged him to the ground,
Where, midst wild ravings, he was gagged and bound.
But John, that fox for wiles and fawn for fear,
To a deep cavern fled, and hid him there.
Carolus, with his cohort, had been sent
To chase the tyrant, and escape prevent.
Though red with blood, now, their vile lives to save,
He and his crew plunged trembling to their cave;
When summoned to surrender, he replied
With curses, and our utmost power defied:
On this, combustibles and brands were brought,
And smoke and flames closed up their boasted vault.
A crippled Jew then to Carolus came,
Haggard and wild, and miserably lame;
'Roman,' he cried, 'behold me! look on one
Of many thousands crushed by tyrant John.
I had a beauteous wife—she caught his eye,
And he procured a sentence I should die.
All drowned in tears, she to his footstool came,
And begged my life: he answered, "Lovely dame,
Step to this room, and join in joys of love
With me, and then the sentence I'll remove:
On your sweet lips depends the fellow's fate:
If not, he dies a traitor to the state.
Come," he continued; "for your charms divine,
No man e'er felt a flame to equal mine:
Come, only spend with me one blissful night
In all the joys of mutual love's delight!
When in your arms I taste the joys of heaven,
Then all you ask shall to your wish be given."
To save my life alone, my wife had come,
But O! she felt the glossing serpent's tongue:
The poison touched her mind, then thrilled each vein,
Till blushing she confessed an answering flame!

Though of forbidding aspect, starched and sour,
'Mongst men, yet, O! how changed in lady's bower!
Each feature then would glow with kindling grace,
And smiles spread amorous glories o'er his face;
For he was great in love's lust, as of blood,
In Venus' orgies he unrivalled stood;
And as the snake's bright eye still closer draws
The fluttering bird down to his opening jaws,
So his sweet tones and soft seductive charms
Drew fluttering beauties to his opening arms.
Thus fell my wife! With a wild fancy fired,
Willing she to his sumptuous couch retired,
And spent a long, dark, sinful night with him,
In the vile raptures of forbidden sin!
This sealed her fate and mine—I was set free,
Only to see and know my misery.
Stripped of the earnings of an active life,
My father slain—a prostituted wife—
Raging for vengeance, I his steps pursued,
My frenzied soul all clamoring for his blood.
I thought in fancy—O! the thought how sweet!—
I felt his hot blood pouring on my feet.
At length I chose my time—rushed through his guard,
Struck at his heart—but fate the villain spared,
Or coward cunning—for beneath his cloak,
A vest of steel received my furious stroke.
I need not tell the tortures I've endured,
Or how at last my freedom was procured;
I've only said this much, that you may know,
I am the monster's most relentless foe.
Then hear, O General! south-side of the hill
Which opens on Gehenna, (type of hell,)
There is a trap-door, whence, from under ground,
He will escape, unless you it surround!'

"Carolus, on this warning, instant sent
A proper force his wiles to circumvent:
The crippled Jew went with them to make known,
As they came forth, which was the miscreant John.
The plan succeeded. Forthwith from the cave,
From flames and smothering smoke their lives to save,
The bandits rushed—and 'mongst the first, the one
We wished to seize, came forth the trembling John.
When caught, the coward no resistance made,
But for his life with panic fervor prayed.
He waits your will, bound with a needless chain—
The slightest prison would the wretch restrain.
The rest, as they burst forth, successive fell,
And from the cliff rolled to their type of hell!"

He ceased; and Titus, leaning from his throne,
Replied, "Brave Romans, you have nobly done:
'Tis this discipline, this heroic skill,
Which bends the world obedient to our will."

Mean time the legions, with triumphant shout,
Had brought their engines and broad banners out:
To them, as gods, in victory's hour arise
Their smoking incense, songs, and sacrifice!
All o'er Moriah's desolated mount,
By blazing altars, they their deeds recount;
Then round their general, on his audience-throne,
Crowded the legions and the chiefs of Rome,
And hailed him great Imperator! The sound
With acclamation filled the region round:
"Imperator!" filled mountains and the plain,
"Imperator!" they echoed back again.
Rome's victor legions in those later days
To some loved generals gave this highest praise.

Titus then rose, midst acclamations loud,
Bowed, and stretched forth his arm to still the crowd:
His plumèd helm he laid aside with grace,
And turned on all a proud yet grateful face.
"Romans, my countrymen and friends," he cried,
"Forgive me if this day I feel some pride:
I'm proud I am a Roman, and the son
Of great Vespasian, and Imperial Rome:
I'm proud I led on legions such as you,
In deepest dangers firm, undaunted, true:
I'm proud of our great victories—greater far
Than have been gained in any former war.
I know Rome boasts of many bloody fields,
Some lost, some won, beneath her brazen shields:
But what's a victory on an open plain,
Which valor in one furious charge may gain,
Compared to levelling those walls so high,
Guarded by furies sworn to win or die?
Nay, what are all the sieges Rome can boast,
Of cities taken at a mighty cost?
What's Syracuse and her Archimedes,
Compared with walls and Zealots such as these?
Metellus pillaged Corinth—rich indeed—
But what the hindrance that he should succeed?
Weak walls and vile degenerate Greeks alone
Were in that boasted conquest overthrown.
Rome's mighty rival on the Punic shore,
Whose fall young Scipio's name to glory bore,
Even a new name—'twas his historic birth—
(From Africa, the fourth part of the earth.)—
And what was Carthage?—a mercantile town,
Guarded by hireling soldiers, not her own:
Could her slight walls with Salem's tower compare,
Nor Hannibal, the soul of battles, there?

Nor fiery Zealots, mad with freedom's name,
To rush on death, and glory to be slain?
No! Romans, when those conquests are forgot,
And nations cease to ask; Where is the spot?
This dreadful victory, by your prowess won,—
Jerusalem taken, her proud walls o'erthrown,
Where corpses on the earth so deep were spread,
Flight and pursuit were over heaps of dead—
Where from Moriah's mount the streams of blood
Ran down and swelled dark Cedron's feeble flood—
These scenes terrific shall march on with time,
Their awful blazon never know decline:
Jerusalem's fall to time's last day shall sound,
And to late ages thrill the nations round:
Thus fame eternal to our arms is given,
Because our swords were but the sword of Heaven:
God's vengeance in her fall so plain appears,
'Twill bear our glory down through time's revolving years!
And now, brave Romans, who most glory won,
And who, in fact, have gathered less than none,
To-morrow may proclaim: then I'll bestow
A just reward on both the high and low:
The patriot hero and the coward knave
From this right hand shall ample justice have.
But now, ye conquering legions, turn to joy:
Let high triumphant feasts be our employ;
Let the fat flocks from Sharon late procured,
With kine of Bashan, smoke on every board;
There, as they carve the rich, the roast sirloin,
Fill high the goblets with Falernian wine;
Or with choice Chian victory's bowls fill up,
And to Rome's glory drain the flowing cup!
Soon Cesarea and her flowery plains
Shall gaze with wonder on our martial games;

For three long days, magnificent we'll hold
Those shows and martial games so famed of old;
Then, seated by the great Vespasian's side,
In triumph through Rome's splendid arches ride.
In a long gorgeous line shall march before
The spoils of nations, an exhaustless store;
While you, Rome's legions, glorious follow on,
Dragging in chains fierce Simon and mean John,
Till the wide Forum and the streets of Rome
Shall loud resound the wonders we have done!"

This said midst acclamations long and loud,
The Roman general left the applauding crowd;
His high pavilion sought. With him attends
A noble band of officers and friends;
There, round the festive board, (all chastely fine,)
So rich the viands and so choice the wine,
That great Lucullus' self, had he been there,
Had owned it with his luxuries might compare.
Round the rich banquet soon, with decent haste,
The chiefs reclined to share the genial feast;
A feast the Cæsar said each noble guest
Should hold with him till the late hour of rest.

Mean time with joy the legionary powers
In feasting high consumed the flying hours;
To Jove and Mars the unbounded sacrifice,
For countless tables, richest fare supplies:
From Hebron's vales all kinds of fruits procured,
Were piled in luscious plenty round each board;
Sweet Cyprian wine in flagons foamed around,
With Chian, soul of wit, whose gay rebound
Through every tent sent jest and laughter round!

Full bands of music, martial moving on,
In mounting tones proclaimed their victories won,
Vespasian's glory and his conquering son;
Till in the Western sea the sun sank down,
And shades of night, covering the fated town,
Called forth ten thousand lamps to gild the night,
And rival day with artificial light.
"JERUSALEM IS NOT!" the loud notes prolong:
Heaven's justice listened, and approved the song!

Now had calm Night, upon his ebon throne,
Near half his silent, soothing circuit run;
His soft dark mantle, (where no sin oppressed,)
Had wrapped the world in sweet restoring rest;
Even the gay party, midst their sparkling wine,
Round Cæsar's board began to think it time
From Roman news and festive joys to part,
Though wine and song had opened every heart.
Titus, though loth to break the party up,
With blandest smiles had named a parting-cup,
When, lo! two female forms, in mourning deep,
All bathed in tears, sank down before his feet!
The joyous circle gazed with mute surprise,
Scarce crediting the witness of their eyes;
And ere great Titus could pronounce a word,
The elder matron thus her prayer preferred:
"O conquering Cæsar! look down from thy throne
On us thy suppliants, wretched and undone!
In me behold the dead Salathiel's wife,
Slain in that last sad sanguinary strife.
Struggling with fate, he by the altar stood,
To guard a fallen friend, and there poured out his blood.
I own, alas! that Rome has suffered harm
From his fierce zeal and strong, untiring arm,

But my slain husband was an open foe—
The great Salathiel struck no dastard blow.
You then, great prince, who are yourself so brave,
Will to a warrior grant a warrior's grave;
Grant to his sorrowing wife the mournful doom,
To weep her life out on his honored tomb!
Nay, more, great chief, to whom the will of Heaven
The wide-spread empire of the world has given;
Know that Salathiel filled a fixed, bound state,
Doomed by the Christ (whose sovereign will is fate)
Changeless to live (as on that dreadful day
He spurned and drove him down the dolorous way)
Till he should come—and he in wrath has come—
And sweep Jerusalem with the fires of Rome!
Then grant, O Cæsar"—Here the hero broke
In on the suppliant's prayer, yet mildly spoke:
"Forbear, poor sorrowing dame, to urge me more:
Facts known to me your wishes will secure.
When, on that bloody crucifixion-day,
My troops before Napthalia's charge gave way,
As in the van I plunged the mountain's side,
To meet and tame their mighty chieftain's pride,
My noble courser floundered in the way,
Rolled on my sword-arm, and quiescent lay.
The prince had seen my furious advance,
And rushed to meet me with his high-poised lance:
Close by my side he reined his steed's career,
And o'er my breast held the suspended spear.
I deemed myself as dead—but, strange, not so:
'Cæsar,' he cried, 'I cannot strike the blow!
My country needs your death, but yet some God
Or honor says I must not shed your blood.
But when beside yon holy Temple's wall,
Or by her altar, pierced with wounds, I fall,

Remember then this day I spared your life,
And yield my body to my weeping wife.'
I had no time to promise, for my guard
Rushed with such fury, his escape was hard;
But mentally, while mounting, made a vow
To do his bidding—I'll perform it now.
But who is this that bends with you in prayer,
So sad, so pale, yet so divinely fair?
From whose soft eyes, tear, following tear, pursues,
As from fair lilies drop the morning dews?
Have you a boon to ask, say, weeping fair?
Nay, rise, you're feeble—take that vacant chair;
Make your request; and if it should be one
That stands with honor, you may deem it done."

"Great prince," she cried, "look down—behold in me
A helpless female, sunk in misery;
One who, though young in years, now feels the smart,
The desolation of a withering heart.
My friend, my love, my husband, mangled lies,
And I the cord that bound the sacrifice!
For O! through me he fell opposed to Rome.
To beg his mutilated form I've come,
To cleanse his festering wounds, his dear life save,
Or tend and soothe him to our mutual grave.
Then to my prayers my dying husband give—
Perhaps the sight of me may make him live:
My hovering o'er him may inspire new breath,
And strong affection bar the gates of death.
To you, great Cæsar, heir to earth's whole throne,
The power of heart-love may be all unknown;
But when the pure sweet thought fuses each heart,
They're one—nor can the strong the weak desert.

To us, then, by this spirit joined, O give
The blessed power to bid each other live!
With my dead father in a vacant tomb,
Lysander groans and waits his final doom."

"Lysander! did you say?" the chief replies,
While kindling fury darted from his eyes;
"What! that base, treacherous Greek, to me once known,
And fostered as a brother of my own?
In the late wars, when conquering by my side,
He shared with me the glory and the pride:
I held him as my friend—a second self—
And for his valor give him fame and wealth!
When great Vespasian, with a monarch's care,
Sent me to guide and end this Jewish war,
I sent for him with a small troop to come,
To strike once more for glory and for Rome:
Not that we needed aid; my only aim
Was to befriend and hand him up to fame.
Judge then my anger when I heard his sword
Was only second to Napthalia's lord;
That from that day they stormed Massada's towers,
Till Salem sunk beneath our conquering powers,
The traitor in sedition's ranks has shone,
A most redoubted, deadly foe to Rome!
I swore then—'twas in wrath, not to the gods—
(Though that, I think, should make but little odds,)—
That when a captive in my power he lay,
All former feelings I would rend away:
My friendship and my love, outraged, should turn
To vengeance, and all supplication spurn;
That crucifixion—death for vilest slave—
Should be his road to a dishonored grave!

Numbers of Romans, 'tis most likely, bled
From his sword blazing at the rebels' head,
Who else were living. Cease, then, cease to sue,
Poor mourning lady—I must mourn for you.
Treason is odious, both to earth and heaven:
For his, none gives excuse—none can be given."
On this a shriek, like that which anguish sends
From the rent heart, when we 've betrayed our friend,
Burst from the fair; nor followed swoon nor groan:
Grief energized she seemed, and grief alone.

"O noble Titus," eager she began,
"O hear my pleadings for this once loved man—
Once loved by you—intensely now by me—
In this his suffering, sad extremity.
That shriek burst from my heart, when keen you said,
'For him none makes excuse—none can be made.'
O hear me, Cæsar—that I should have done,
When first I bent before your august throne.
I 've that to say, which, if it cannot save
His mangled body from a felon's grave,
Will save his faith, preserve his honor bright,
Through life and death, even in Cæsar's sight;
For sure a nobler soul was never given:
A world of such would make this world a heaven!
I had gone down to sweet Tiberias' Lake,
To the warm springs, for health and pleasure's sake:
My escort small,—six men and a grave friend,
And on my steps two maidens to attend,—
When fifty robbers (Arabs, by their dress)
Seized us and fled for the East wilderness.
It seems they had perforce—or 'twas of God—
Some time to hold the main Damascus road.

One ruffian on my left, one on my right,
Rode by my rein, and urged our rapid flight;
When, lo! Lysander, with full twenty men,
Flashing in arms, (bound for Jerusalem,)
Wheeled from a gorge around the mountain's base,
And sudden met the bandits face to face.
I screamed for aid—regardless of the knife
The villain held, with threats to take my life.
Of the fierce charge, the combat and the rout,
The bandits' yelling and the victors' shout,
I may not speak; but while, to soothe my fear,
Lysander stooped, alas! an Arab's spear
Deep pierced his side—yet missed the vital part;
For deeper wounds fate kept his noble heart;
But flush his blood poured from the gaping wound,
As, it to staunch, they placed him on the ground.
I did not faint—Salathiel's spirit rose—
I could have rushed amidst a thousand foes!
The wounded hero said that he could ride:
He did, a friend attending at each side;
But when at length we gained my father's hall,
He fainting reeled, though friends withstood his fall.
Borne to his room, fever commenced its reign:
Nine days, delirious fancies ruled his brain.
Of you, then of myself, he'd talk for hours,
Till by excitement sunk his feeble powers.
'Come on, brave Titus,' he elate would say—
'One more fierce charge, and we have won the day!
See, see! their squadrons break, their masses fly!
Great Cæsar, what a glorious victory!'
Again at times he seemed to call to mind
That wounds and robbers held him still confined.
Again his war-horse armed he proud ascends,
And cries, 'Now Cæsar's camp, my gallant friends!'

At length the crisis came—the fever fled,
And left him passive as the slumbering dead.
Through all this time, O! how intense my care!
Prayers oft rose from me—oftener dropped the tear.
Alas, the consequence! He was undone—
Both hearts were fused by love—the two were one!
But when recovered, firm his faith he held,
Forthwith to join you on the tented field;
And yet he put it off from day to day—
Alas! how fatal was that sweet delay!
For Florus sent to bring my father, bound.
What happened, stunned the nations all around.
That sealed my dear lord's fate—the great, the good:
In my defence his sword drew Roman blood.
Till that dread night, his faith for Rome was true,
His praise, his friendship, centred all on you.
But now, called traitor, he all helpless lies,
To love and fate a piteous sacrifice.
O! grant him to my prayers—to ward off death,
Or mix my soul with his expiring breath!
Cæsar, we are not Jews, nor years have been,
But followers of the humble Nazarene,
The God of heavenly love! O Saviour, hear—"
Till then, all pale, she spoke without a tear:
Like beauteous woe deep-graved on marble-stone,
That she had life appeared by voice alone;
But as she named her Lord, the frost of fears
Dissolved, and she sunk down all bathed in tears.

"Mother," then Titus said, "to yon side tent
Your daughter lead—with hopes her death prevent.
By this old man that doth your steps attend,
Lysander's fate and my decrées I'll send."

Abihud then approached, and thus began:
"O Cæsar, I 'm an aged, God-fearing man:
One hundred years their course have nearly run
Since I my weary pilgrimage begun.
Your suppliant is my niece. The account she 's given
Is all as true as there 's a God in heaven.
We worship him who rules each earthly throne,
And called you to the mighty work you 've done.
Lysander's and Salathiel's vast estate,
Their acts to you or conquering Rome translate;
In mercy, then, grant us some lone retreat,
Where in our prayers your name we 'll still repeat;
And to his weeping wife, O Cæsar, give
Her husband's mangled form, and let him live,
If live he can—" Here Titus waved his hand.
The elder took it as a stern command,
And silent stood, bending his hoary head,
While the great victor thus resumed, and said:
"Not thousands, reverend elder, such as you,
Though a meek Christian or rebellious Jew,
Could have obtained the boon for which you sue;
But to that weeping fair—her sobs, her sighs,
Her pure affection and her streaming eyes—
Even I, a conqueror, must submit and bow:
To her I yield my rage and break my vow!
Tell her she 's conquered without spear or shield:
Her heart's pure power has made a warrior yield:
Say that Lysander fell by her and fate:
Great was his crime, and his excuse as great.
To them I give—it on Leontes lies—
The plain of Zed, a sheltered paradise.
There the white Syrian rose for ever blooms,
And fills the valley with its rich perfumes;

The village Zarah, too, their rule shall own,
With three miles each way from that central town.
I saw it once, and said, with half a sigh,
Were I not Titus, here I 'd live and die!
Here is a charter, sealed. Crito, you 'll fill
The blanks so as to meet our spoken will.
Give passports and a guard: let all be done,
To send them safely to their quiet home."

Then turned and said: "Elder, now glad depart:"
(Waving one hand, the other on his heart:)
"You, with your Christian friends, may dry your tears,
And pray for them who listened to your prayers."

And now the moral hero, smiling, said,
"My friends, our parting-cup has been delayed.
Pity has conquered anger in my breast—
Pleasing, I hope, to every honored guest,
For mercy is Heaven's opiate for rest.
Then fill up high the cups, till each o'erflows—
The pledge, Rome's glory and our good repose."

BOOK VIII.

The Vision.

The Jewish captives sold to merchants or slave-dealers—Family ties torn asunder—Some cannot be sold, because of sickness, age, and wounds—Left to die in distress—Abihud and his pilgrim family arrive at Zarah—Their reception there—Abihud stands on the Mount of Vision—Daniel descends and shows him the grand events to come, and the fate of the Church—Pagan persecution—The conversion of Constantine—The prosperity of the Church under him—The rise of the Papal power—The dreadful persecution of Christian Rome—The first wound given by Mohammed; the second by the art of printing; the third by Luther—Popish absurdities and Protestant divisions make many infidels—The Puritans and Free-thinkers vainly establish Democracy in the New World—The great body divided into three parts: Catholics, Protestants, and Free-thinkers—The immense march of science thereupon—Why the Pope will live till Christ comes—At the end of six thousand years, Christ descends, renovates the earth, and reigns a thousand years—Then comes the end—Daniel's Vision done, he ascends to heaven—Salathiel's obsequies—Abihud's speech on the occasion—The funeral-feast—The citizens of Zarah converted—A form of worship established, which changes the name of the lovely Leontes to Litany—The blissful greeting of the Christian pilgrims.

NATURE and time roll on, nor deign to show
A moment's pause at sights of human woe:
Heaven's orb of light rose with the same bright blaze
As when the Temple glittered in its rays;
(That errless time-piece Heaven holds down to man,
To show them daily their diminished span:)

Like a strong man, he rose to run his race;
But now his glories fell on empty space:
Beneath his beams, coals and black ashes spread
In mouldering heaps, with pale, unburied dead!
Famine, and fire, and sword, for miles around,
Had changed Jerusalem to a smoking mound:
Where domes and glittering spires and dwellings stood,
Lay half-burnt rubbish, covering streets of blood:
Great Herod's Tower alone was left to show
The power of those who struck the levelling blow.
Such Roman pride; while the great victory given
Came from a higher power—the power of Heaven!
Titus and Roman arms were but his rod:
Such full destruction showed the wrath of God.
Death's salt was sown, and aged men stood aghast,
As o'er Jerusalem the ploughshare passed,
When they beheld that prophecy fulfilled,
That Zion should be ploughed—ploughed as a field!

But houses, palaces, and temples burned,
And a vast city to a desert turned,
Is not such woe, so wounding to the heart,
As kindred ties by slavery torn apart,
When the hearth-circle from their homes are hurled
By conquest-power, and scattered round the world.
Such the keen pang, and such the crushing blow,
The bitter cup—the very dregs of woe—
Wrung to the remnant Jews; for, from afar,
Slave-merchants hovered round the Roman war:
Full ninety thousand souls to them were sold,
And no small part for trifling sums of gold.
Next came the parting scream, the mother's moan,
The husband's anguish, and the lover's groan;

The brother's madness, and the sister's sobs,
Enough to melt the hearts of men or gods:
But those who deal in flesh have hearts of steel—
Their trade has long forbidden them to feel.
So severed relatives, in mourning bands,
Passed through the different gates to different lands.
Northward the mother, with her infant load,
Is driven along the rough Damascus road;
The father is sent south to sultry climes,
To toil through life in the Egyptian mines.
At Cesarea, there the galleys wait,
To bear to Greece and Rome their human freight—
Virgins now brotherless, and maids who mourn
Their first heart's love, for ever from them torn.
A host to Parthia and to Elam goes—
More to Byzantium, where for ever flows
The grand Bosphorus—pointing to the wise,
Empire's true seat, and nature's paradise.
Thus through the Roman world was widely spread
Jerusalem's relics—envying of the dead!
Yet still more wretched, more to be deplored,
Were thousands who could not obtain a lord.
So maimed, so weak, so sick, so feebly old,
They could not labor, so could not be sold.
These, left to famish, houseless and alone,
Without a friend to hear their dying groan,
To yield to hunger their expiring breath,
And live a dying life, ending in death,
Was desolation's climax. Such the fate,
And such Heaven's judgment on the Jewish state.

Mean time, Abihud and the pilgrim train
Were journeying onward to Leontes' plain.

The slain Salathiel, by Christ's will embalmed,
Looked like Gennesaret's sea, when it was calmed
By his high word, "Be still!" Serene he lay,
Like Adam, ere God's breath inspired his clay.
The maimed Lysander, by the love and care,
The sweet appliances, the tender tear
Of Hester and her mother, quickly drew
Recovering breath, and convalescent grew.
Thus, in due time, the living and the dead
Reached the green plains and crystal streams of Zed—
A lovely stream, which, from Mount Lebanon,
Through flowers, to join Leontes murmured on,
Fringed with the oleander and woodbine,
Sweet honeysuckles, and the eglantine.
Through the gay gardens of the little town
(Dividing Zarah) the bright stream rolled down,
Fed by pure rills from the dissolving snows,
Trickling beneath the beauteous Syrian rose,
Which festooned every crag, and dell, and height,
With one vast sheet of waving, odorous white;
While, mingling at each bower, all brilliant glows
The scarlet crocus and rich damask-rose.
Each Lebanon in flowers sloped to the plain,
And all between each towering mountain chain,
Spread thick with fruits and flowers and waving grain,
A wilderness of sweets—a paradise,
Where Adam lived, ('tis said,) and buried lies.

But now Lenteles, deputy of Rome,
Commissioned to make Cæsar's pleasure known,
With Zarah's citizens, in form await
The weary pilgrims at the myrtle gate—
So named from a sweet grove of myrtles green,
Shading rich sward, with clumps of flowers between.

Here, after greetings, from a neighboring stand
Lenteles graceful waved around his hand,
And thus addressed the weary Judean band:

"Welcome, ye wanderers, driven from your home!
Welcome to one given by imperial Rome!
Hear, reverend elder; all around me, hear,
And may my words delight each listening ear!
The noble Titus, in his princely grace,
To you and yours donates this lovely place.
This quiet town is henceforth, from this hour,
With three miles round, subjected to your power:
The former Governor's house and farm are yours,
With all the furniture, and flocks, and stores.
A better place awaits him. Govern well;
Let peace and justice in your district dwell;
And for such service, let the taxes due,
Once paid to Cæsar, now be paid to you.
And should Lysander live, when you are dead,
Let him succeed, and be the district's head.
And more, the mighty Cæsar bade me say—
Whose will, east, west, and north, and south obey,
From the dark Euxine, onward, far, far west,
To where the great Atlantic heaves his breast;
From Dacia's shores to Afric's burning sands,
All yield obedience to his high commands—
He says, let all your band, in every prayer,
Remember great Vespasian and his heir;
Pray for the State and its imperial head,
And that their glories may for ever spread."

To this the Christian elder bowed and said:
"Tell princely Titus, he shall be obeyed;
That after Christ, my Saviour, King of kings,
Whose rule o'er worlds from God the Father springs,

There 's none we so much honor, love, and fear,
As conquering Cæsar, great Vespasian's heir.
Justice with mercy still shall be our law—
Good men protected, villains held in awe.
This happy vale, committed to my care,
Shall find I 'm neither careless nor severe.
While mighty Cæsar o'er the world extends
Woe to the wicked, blessings to his friends;
While barbarous nations, forced his laws to obey,
Are civilized beneath his clement sway;
While righteousness and peace beneath his hand
Shall spread diffusive over every land;
We hope, in this sweet village, kindly given,
To follow him, and do the work of Heaven.
And when the conquering Titus condescends
To ask our prayers, and treats us as his friends,
Doubt not, our prayers shall constantly arise
To Him who governs earth, and air, and skies,
That his just sway may spread o'er every clime,
And know no limit but the end of time.
That great Vespasian and his noble son
May long direct the destinies of Rome,
And that this wondrous man our Saviour chose
To end the Jewish state and crush our foes,
May from earth's glories as a Christian rise,
To brighter glory in redemption's skies;
That he may bow, and Calvary's sufferer own
As God's Messiah, heir of David's throne,
Shall be my prayer, and prayer of all my friends,
Both when yon sun arises and descends.
But should he not, by faith I now see one,
A great successor to the imperial throne,
Who, hemmed around with foes, shall see our sign
Blazoned through heaven, in characters divine—

"*By this you'll conquer!*" From that visioned hour,
The Cross he raises and moves on to power;
Beneath the Christian banner, thus unfurled,
He reigns sole sovereign o'er the Roman world.
But, noble deputy, with grateful breast
We now would seek our home, and food, and rest.
God willing, on to-morrow we intend
To inhume my brother and my dearest friend.
At noon the rites begin with solemn prayer;
And let us hope, my friends, you'll all be there.
Conspicuous was the dead to heaven and earth,
Great in his actions, great his noble birth;
Then let due honors to his dust be given,
Whose soul, we trust, is with the blest in heaven."
With gratulating cheers the assembly parts,
Each to their several homes, with joyful hearts.

Now had the sun, high over Lebanon's height,
Rolled down to the great sea, and brought on night:
On Anti-Lebanon his parting rays
Had Hermon's snow-capped top wrapped in a blaze;
From all his height, along his lengthened line,
Vast forests sloped in gold, and rills in silver shine;
While shadows at his feet umbraged the plain,
Set thick with flowers and undulating grain.
The pilgrim band had supped, and prayer and praise
Had closed this last of many weary days.
Lysander too, through Miriam's constant care
And Hester's love, could totter to his chair.
Such is love's mighty power—not that fierce glow
Which brutes and brutish men in common know;
But that concentered essence of the mind,
Distilled from passion—purified, refined—

Which stronger grows when dark misfortune lowers,
And warmer glows as freeze the sensual powers.
Such Hester's love: her pure heart, fused with his,
Was healing medicine; for it was bliss!

And now Abihud, with a solemn pace,
Pursued the Zed up to the mountain's base,
Where its two limpid streams, like arms, surround
A lovely convex plain, almost a mound.
Roses and oleanders fringed each stream,
With scattering oaks and myrtles spread between.
Upon the central point the elder stood,
And gazed upon the mountain, vale, and flood;
For now o'er Anti-Lebanon the moon
Rose, near full-orbed, to dissipate the gloom:
Down from his towering heights she poured her beams
O'er the broad valley and its glittering streams:
Libanus, from his base to topmost height,
Shone in a glorious flood of lunar light:
In bold relief the rocks to prospect rose:
Like stripes of silver every streamlet flows:
The swift Leontes glittered down the plain,
Through blooming orchards and rich fields of grain.
The old man worshipped at the glorious sight,
A paradise, o'erflowed with heavenly light.
"And here," he cried, "shall my dear brother lie,
Upon this mound, beneath this lovely sky."

Thus as he spoke, he cast an eye of love,
Mingled with awe, up to the heavens above;
When, lo! they opened, and a radiant form,
Eclipsing moon and stars, was downward borne!
Like him on Ulia's banks, the old man's power
Forsook him in that visionary hour.

Trembling, upon the ground, devoid of strength,
Before Heaven's messenger he sank at length!
But now (as Gabriel then) the vision said,
"O Christian elder, rise—be not afraid.
I come, as Gabriel once came down to me,
To lift the veil of dark futurity—
A messenger from the great God you serve,
And with this touch your palsied powers renerve,
To give your mental vision strength to gaze
On the great wonders of succeeding days.
Such is Messiah's will: from him I come,
To whom all Heaven says, 'Let thy will be done.'
And now, good brother, take this glass of heaven,
Aided by me—to it the virtues given,
To show you all the nations of the earth,
The death of empires and new empires' birth;
The sufferings of the weak, the guilt of power,
Fiendish oppression, and destruction's hour;
Virtue's great efforts, and the power of wrong,
With all time's wonders, as time rolls along.
"You know already how the apostles sped,
Their toils how vast—how wide the gospel spread;
How, bearing on Christ's banner, firm they stood,
Till called to attest his doctrine with their blood.
But 'twas by Jewish, zealous rage alone,
And savage mobs, they met their martyrdom:
The Roman powers of them took little heed,
Till Nero, to conceal his fiendish deed,
Charged them with firing Rome: then thousands fell
By that worst monster time has dropped to hell.
But every drop of blood—each human torch—
Sowed seed, and raised the glory of the Church.
The sympathizing crowds were inly moved
To believe a doctrine by such sufferings proved:

Each cruel death still more conviction gave,
And crowds of Christians sprang from every grave!
And now Vespasian and his greater son
Will through this century fill the imperial throne:
Beneath their righteous sway the Church has peace,
And great and glorious shall be her increase.
"But now, my brother, steady hold the glass,
And view the ages as they rolling pass:
See heathen altars half deserted stand,
Their Delphos dumb, their feasts forsake the land:
No victims bleed—no altars stream with blood;
A raging priesthood lack their daily food.
Hence, they besiege the throne with clamorous cries,
With vague assertions, and ten thousand lies.
Does Tiber, from the mountains, flood their land?
Does Nile's low flood (1) turn his rich fields to sand?
Does Antioch in earthquake ruins lie,
Or a dread hail-storm pour down from the sky?
They raise the clamor—'This vile Christian crew
Thus brings the vengeance of the gods on you.
Pass, pass the edicts! vindicate the laws!
To appease the gods, you must remove the cause.'
The priests prevail, and through the empire round
The flames arise, and shouts with groans resound.
Look, and behold! what new-invented pains!
Some burn on gridirons, some in unctuous flames;
Some hurled from towers, on crosses some raised high;
Some live through tortures; thousands, tortured, die.
See, see! that band of mothers, sisters, wives!
For Christ they freely now lay down their lives.
Will you look on? No; it would stop your breath:
Eyes can't behold, nor tongues describe, such death:
All decency outraged, and pains intense
Fixed in the organs of the acutest sense."

Here good Abihud with emotion strong,
Cried: "O my Master! O my God! how long?
O Daniel! highly favored brother, friend,
Say, when will this dire persecution end?
My soul no more such horrors can sustain."
"Then turn," the prophet said, "and look again:
You see a mighty warrior, stern, sedate,
In coming times called Constantine the Great.
O'ercome by numerous foes, he 's been at prayer
To all the gods, for help in his despair.
As he looks up to heaven, a cross of light—
The Christian symbol—looms intensely bright.
Deep graved upon its limbs, he reads these words:
'*By this you 'll conquer!* (2) and be Lord of lords.'
He takes the omen—has the sign unfurled,
And victory hails him sovereign of the world!
"And now behold, by his imperial word,
The Christian Church to all its rights restored!
Before his glance the persecuting fire
And fire-fiends down to dark disgrace retire,
Gone are the stake, the cross, the wheel, the groan;
And safely dwells the Church beneath his throne."
"Glory to God!" the joyful elder cries;
"Now may the Church in all its splendor rise;
Be perfected in love and doctrines pure,
And spread its triumphs on from shore to shore."

"Ah," said the prophet, ("though 'twill give you pain,)
"Here, take this visioned glass and look again."
He did; and straight before his eyes appears
The panorama of revolving years:
Beneath the imperial shield and golden shower,
Religion swells to form without the power;

The humble bishops, who in days of blood
Were satisfied with life and daily food,
Now strive for wealth and power, and emulate
The pomp and grandeur of the worldly great.
He sees their palaces, their grand attire,
Their lust, their pride, and wild ambitious fire;
A wrangling priesthood, to full discord given,
And all their flocks from light to darkness driven.
"From whence, O Prophet, brother, friend," he cried,
"This sad reverse—Heaven's blessings misapplied?"

To this the heavenly messenger replies:
"Paul told you how the Man of Sin should rise;
That he was then at work, but not revealed:
Some mighty hindering power kept him concealed.
That hindering power (3) was persecuting Rome.
Now he appears (since persecution 's done)
In all unrighteousness—all horrid crimes
Known to the present, past, or future times.
Yet so deceivable and dark his ways,
He draws no detestation, but high praise!
Mark how this Man of Sin, perdition's son,
Tranforms the Church to mystic Babylon:
See yon two priests, acute, swelled up with pride,
Through lust for power, the Christian world divide,
About dark questions neither understand!
Anathemas and edicts fill the land.
One, raging, makes Christ God—the great I AM;
The other makes him little more than man:
The blinded laity take different sides,
While a proud priesthood o'er the conflict rides.
Like billowy waves, the power imperial rolls
From side to side—now this, then that, controls.

Power Arius now, [4] now Athanasius gains,
As Constans or a Theodosius reigns.
Mean time the Man of Sin, that lawless *one*,
Grows to full power, and overtops the throne;
Sits in the Church (God's temple) as a God,
And kings and nations worship at his nod!
Son of Perdition, full revealed, he stands,
And chains and darkness overspread all lands.
A vile assassin, by him emperor made,
In turn proclaims him universal head
Of all the Church—him Gregory of Rome!
Putting all other competition down,
And placing on his head the triple crown.
"And now, enthroned, the Man of Sin proceeds—
What monstrous doctrines! what tyrannic deeds!
Behold! yon servile emperor, at his word,
Against his faithful subjects draws the sword,
To drive them into Church at his command;
And soon wide slaughter desolates the land.
All unconvinced, who cannot stoop to lie,
Meet sudden death, or else midst tortures die.
Because they still will serve their fathers' God,
The Pope decrees, and emperors shed their blood.
"Again: behold that servile, cruel king,
Chilled, standing barefoot, clad in garments thin,
Shivering three wintry days before the gate
Of that proud palace, where, [5] in princely state,
The holy pontiff toys with titled dames:
The sackcloth penitent unheard remains.
At length, half dead with sufferings and woe,
The tiara'd Father lets him kiss his toe!
Then lordly adds: 'I bid your penance cease:
You are forgiven: rise and go in peace.'

So great the power of Antichrist was grown,
The monarch stoops to this to save his throne!
"But view not only the pontific head:
See over Christendom a priesthood spread;
From the tiara down to meanest cowl,
All claim dominion over every soul.
Free from the tie of families or wives,
In catering to their lusts they pass their lives:
Their pard'ning power the virtuous fair subdues—
Few dare the anointed of the Lord refuse.
Thus highly fed, from flock to flock they rove,
And, as you see, take heavy tithes of love!
Whilst a priest-ridden laity look on,
Nor dare to think, or say, such things are done.
Even many deem they should the priests indulge
In gifts of love, since they cannot divulge."

Here the good elder, greatly moved, broke in:
"Yes, now I see the embodied Man of Sin.
And shall Christ's holy gospel turn to be
A fountain of such wide impurity?
In those dark days, alas! will none be seen
To rise, and strive against corruption's stream?
Some young Elijah, zealous to restore
The ancient gospel, and its rights secure—
Put down this priesthood, which the world deceives,
And save God's temple from a den of thieves?"

The prophet answered: "Some will strive, at least.
See the Paulicians, struggling in the East.
Beneath the towering Alps and Pyrenees,
Far in the West, behold the Waldenses:
Their testimony they, midst sufferings, bear
Against corruption and the papal chair,

Led on by Waldo, Claude, and Constantine: (6)
Their only weapon is the word divine;
Yet firm they stand, midst scenes of fire and blood,
Safe clothed in all the panoply of God,
Which shields from Satan's darts, but not man's wrath;
For see how blood still marks their Christian path!
To carnal power even Jesus bowed his head,
And lo! what myriads must his footsteps tread!
From the Bosphorus to the Atlantic's floods,
From Afric's sands to Asia's frozen woods,
This immolating power for centuries reigns—
Now fills the prisons, then lights up the flames:
It numbers slave and monarch with the dead,
And fills the world with tortures and with dread.
"We will not turn an eye on every scene
Of Christians martyred, with short rests between;
But all the persecutions Christians bore
From Jewish fury, while the Jews held power;
The streams of blood their bigot malice shed,
And all the thousands of their tortured dead,
If joined to all by fell barbarians done,
And all the beasts and flames of pagan Rome,
Could not compare, in suffering and crime,
With the soul-shaking horror of this time.
No! Christian Rome old pagan Rome transcends
In torturing Christians and Messiah's friends;
Fiercer the flames, wider the streams of blood,
Under pretence of serving Christ and God!
We will not turn heaven's glass on every scene,
From Constantine down to this hour between;
But gaze a moment at that blood-stained throne—
The awful climax of Perdition's son!
Behold yon Holy Office! Hear the cries
Of suffering martyrs from its cells arise!

See Dominic, with Servites at his side,
Assume his self-made throne with bigot pride.
Th' Inquisitorial Court they hold by night;
And midst those hours of gloom and dubious light,
Behold! what torturing engines rise to sight!
Here turns the wheel; and as it slow moves round,
Hear how the questioned victims' groans resound!
Yonder the pulleys rise—the arm-bound freight
Scream, agonized, from their suspended weight:
From screws and oil-dipped splinters hear arise
The short, sad sob, and pain's intensest cries:
Behold the iron boot! see hammers fall,
While quick, sharp shrieks sound dreadful through the hall!
"At length this mockery of justice ends,
And sentence on the whole in turn descends.
Some are released by gold—called innocent;
Coupled in chains, some to the galleys sent;
The maimed committed to the surgeon's care,
To wait for future tortures and despair;
The rest are doomed all to a fiery death
Before the world, as a great act of faith!
Then, grim and firm as Satan midst the fire,
The judges to their sensual joys retire.
"Behold the sun, how bright the following day
He looks on crowds decked in their court array.
There, high above Spain's mighty king and queen,
The great Inquisitorial Lords are seen.
They bid the anthem rise, and lo! a song
With Christ's name in it rolls through all the throng,
As to the stake they drag his friends along.
Aghast and pale, and dressed in painted flames,
The Christian martyrs move across the plains:
Myriads of papist fiends, with shouts and cries,
And cruel insults, bid the flames arise:

A Christian nation, nobles, king and queen,
Look joyful on, and loud applaud the scene.
Behold and hear, as shrieks burst from each flame,
The fiends sing glory to the Saviour's name,
To drown the victims' cries, (7) and voice of Heaven,
And that small inner voice to sinners given.
The flames subside; but heavy, gross, and slow,
Dark clouds of smoke spread o'er the plain of woe;
The fumes of burning flesh, slow billowy driven,
Taint all the atmosphere, and smell to heaven."

Till now, the elder gazed: then, with faint cries,
He on the prophet turned his weeping eyes:
"O sainted brother, Heaven-sent, I implore
I may behold such horrid scenes no more.
My faith stands trembling o'er the gulf of hell!
O Master, save, or I'm an infidel,
O! can the gospel I deemed heavenly love,
The basis of such hellish malice prove?
O Saviour, in this (8) Atheistic wave
I sink—I'm sinking! Stretch thy hand to save!"

To this the heavenly messenger replied:
"Brother, stand fast, and be not terrified.
Has not Paul told you that the lawless one
Must be revealed before the Lord shall come?
You've seen him, in God's temple, sit as God,
Claiming God's power, his sceptre, and his rod,
And urging on his claims with fire and blood;
But, as you fear your faith cannot abide
Such sight, heaven's telescope we'll lay aside,
While I events relate, as friend to friend,
Which must take place before earth's final end.
Grand events will roll on, be thou assured,
Before the glorious coming of the Lord:

I'll speak of men and things to thee unknown,
By names which they will bear in days to come.
"Know first the Man of Sin, the lawless one,
Perdition's father, called Perdition's son.
As slow his rise, his fall is also slow:
In Eastern climes first gleams the primal blow.
A warrior-hermit issues from his cell,
(Before whose voice his country's idols fell:)
I see him now, upon his Arab steed,
Of strength resistless, and of arrowy speed:
In his left hand a volume wide displayed;
His right grasps firm the keen Damascus blade.
In Revelation's land, where Abram stood,
And all the patriarchs [9] held discourse with God,
He stands, and cries to all the nations round,
And this the import of the imperious sound:
"There is no God but God! and know that I
His Prophet am—deputed from the sky!
Behold this book, which Gabriel brought from heaven!
Believe, receive this book, and be forgiven:
If not, this sword, now glittering in my hand,
Shall vile opposers sweep from every land!"
Thousands on thousands to his standard crowd,
And 'Allah!' 'Allah!' thunders far and loud!
From the Asphaltes to the Indian shore,
From Mecca to the environs of Balsore.
Arabia yields, [10] Bedouins and Fellahs rise,
And on their barbs to glorious conquest flies.
'Allah!' they cry. 'There is no God but God!
And Mahomed 's his Prophet and his Rod.'
Above this battle-cry their banner waves;
Whole nations tremble and become their slaves!
Victors where'er they move, they widely spread
Each battle-field with heaps of slaughtered dead:

O'er Euphrates and Tigris wave their swords—
Persia and Syria own their Moslem lords:
Parthia and Media vainly meet the war;
They fall beneath the Prophet's scimitar!
Next Egypt, Libya, and Numidia's sands,
Hear and obey the Saracen's commands.
When the great head Caliph or Sultan dies,
Instant his throne some fiercer chief supplies:
Armed with the book and holy Prophet's sword,
All Moslems own him as their sovereign lord;
And thus, for ages, conquering on they 'll go,
Till proud Byzantium 's levelled with a blow;
Before their arms the Eastern empire falls,
Till, conquering on, they reach Vienna's walls;
From thence the crescent its wide horns extends
To where the rapid Rhone through Gaul descends:
Here, like the ocean, its proud waves are stayed—
Two heroes rise, the sinking cross to aid:
Martel, of France, shivers its western limb; ([11])
The eastern, steeped in Moslem blood, turns dim.
The Polish hero all their power withstood
With his brave Poles, and turned their moon to blood.
Alas! for Poland—doomed to be enslaved
By kings and nations whom her valor saved!
But deep the Pontiff feels this primal stroke—
Half of his slaves bend to the Moslem yoke.
"More strange, more wonderful the second blow:
All nations feel it, though unseen and slow.
No fields of blood, by conquering warriors won,
Nor banded powers, will shake the Papal throne;
But a poor soldier ([12]) will a charm unfold,
By which, in time, all powers will be controlled.
A written book will, by this art, be whirled
At once to all parts of the reading world!

One page to millions his art multiplies,
And truths lie open to ten million eyes!
Light from the printing-press will glance around,
And deep inquiry more and more abound;
The slumbering nations science will awake,
And semi-infidels by millions make.
Then will bold Luther rise—a monk obscure,
And Papal power and priest-sold heavens abjure.
'Tis Tetzel's shops which license sell to sin
For sums of gold!—The contest will begin.
This will at first rouse the fierce German's wrath:
But wide, and wider still, will spread his path.
By threats incensed, he beards the Beast of Rome,
And hurls his thunders at the Papal throne.
Fired by his courage, myriads more will rise,
As through the world his daring doctrine flies:
Princes, long writhing 'neath the Pontiff's laws,
Will burst from bondage, and espouse his cause.
Half Germany protests,—and Britain's voice,
With Baltic kingdoms, in the light rejoice:
Holland and Prussia to their standards come,
And Reformation shakes the Papal throne.
But still the lawless one, through Gaul and Spain,
Austria and Italy, holds on his reign;
And as a wounded serpent fiercer fights,
Vibrates its rattles, and incessant strikes,
So will the Man of Sin rage and contend,
As rolling centuries slowly bring his end.
At length the wheel stands still—the fagot dies:
New worlds are found beneath the western skies.
Thither, on freedom's wings, slowly unfurled,
Will fly the sufferers of the olden world.
Patriots who vainly for man's rights had stood,
And toiled for years through miseries and blood,

With champions (13) of the ancient faith, will come
To this new world, fair freedom's destined home;
For Liberty's bright banner, wide displayed,
Soon calls enslavéd myriads to its shade.
A great self-governed nation will arise,
And throw its glories back on Eastern skies:
Philosophy and Science, in the van,
Form governments based on the rights of man:
A band of semi-atheists, made by Rome,
With pious bigots, (14) to the world make known
A constitution severing Church and State,
Leaving all creeds and dogmas to their fate:
Proclaim to all the world man's native right
To spurn all creeds, or with a creed unite;
That all religions only are a tie
Between man singly and his God on high.
This principle, in the new world secured,
Strikes from the Man of Sin his blood-stained sword:
His persecuting power before it flies,
His *acts of faith*, and human sacrifice,
Leaving him only (while his vengeance boils)
His deep deception and his fawning wiles:
By these his deadly wound is slightly healed,
For he must live till Christ shall stand revealed."

Abihud here broke in—"Ah! brother, friend,
I hoped the lawless one had met his end—
His power not paralyzed, but wholly dead,
And Christ's pure gospel o'er the nations spread.
What hinders, then, its glorious ushering in,
And the extinction of the Man of Sin?"

To this the envoy of the heavens replied:
"The Church of Christ, his persecuted Bride;

The Woman to the wilderness who fled
From Rome's fierce Dragon, (with the saints' blood red,)
Will be helped by the Earth in that dark hour,—
That is, by worldly, unbelieving power. ([15])
That power restrains the Dragon, less through hate
Than rage for liberty in Church and State;
To wrench all fetters from the human mind,
And legislators make of all mankind;
Unbounded license to man's mind to give,
And let faith live through reason, or not live.
This latitude to wild confusion tends,
And kills Religion, while it saves her friends;
For, from that grand, emancipating hour,
The demon of division shows his power:
Reforms on Reformation wide will spread,
Soon as the Papal burning power lies dead:
Thousands of would-be Luthers will arise,
Some pious, and some deists in disguise:
For reformation each will loudly plead—
For the pure gospel, (as each calls his creed.)
Thus subdivisions will divide the land,
And each clique form a weak and jarring band.
Protestantism will divide, protest,
Till each man for himself becomes a priest.
This kills the gospel. When Christ's seeming friends
His seamless robe with bigot fury rend;
When, heedless of his words, 'You must be one,
To prove that I have from the Father come,'
They spurn each other, and still disunite,
And hold such pictures up to worldlings' sight,—
Scoffers will cry, 'Behold! God is not there;
They all are wrong, as all of them declare.'
This makes more infidels, in days to come,
Than had been made by persecuting Rome.

"Mean time, deep science and mechanic skill
With new discoveries will all nations fill;
Sages will scan and probe the fount of day,
And all his planetary worlds survey;
With telescopes heaven's boundless space explore,
And show creation's sea without a shore!
Others the elements will search, and find
The wondrous powers that are to each consigned;
Will ransack deep the bowels of the earth,
And nature's hidden secrets bring to birth:
Fire, water, air, they 'll subject to their sway,
And make heaven's lightnings their behests obey:
From fire and water make the giant steam
Push loaded ships swift up the rapid stream,
Or cross vast oceans with so swift a flight,
'Twill leave the soaring eagle out of sight;
Or, harnessed to a car, sweep with its train
O'er continents as men now cross a plain!
This giant steam they 'll multiply at will,
Making some grind, like Samson, in the mill;
Some, rushing, drag the mountains' entrails down
To smoking factories or the shivering town.
Borne with the speed with which false rumor flies,
'Twill scatter round the nation rich supplies.
Nor stops the extended arm of science here:
'Twill seize the lightning in its swift career,
And send to nations, on its moment-wings,
The rise of prices and the fall of kings;
Bear tidings to the yearning mother's home,
From foreign lands, when she shall see her son;
Enable friends, whom fate may wide disperse
From distant firesides, at their ease converse. ([16])
"But art gives higher art—light greater light.
Soon through the air will mortals take their flight:

By gaseous globes borne in a pendent car,
They 'll rise and sail incumbent on the air:
Small vehicles will pioneer the way,
But followed soon by a more grand display.
Upborne by heated gas will ships arise,
And sail with whizzing wings along the skies:
To the wished point by their firm rudder held,
As oceans now, they 'll plough the aërial field;
Bear wealth or war high o'er the surging seas,
And lower down to the earth where'er they please.
Others, vast telescopes of wondrous size
Will form, and level them against the skies;
Bring down the planetary worlds, and scan
Each hill and dale, each varied race of man;
Gaze on each star as a broad, central sun,
Round which a train of rolling planets run;
Detect the natives at their sports or prayers,
Or red with blood, fierce raging from their wars.
"Mean time, steam-power its dreadful force will wield,
And heap with carnage every battle-field;
The rushing cars with their enormous trains
Of dire revolving cannon, sweep the plains;
Or, from commanding heights, the storm is hurled
Upon the crowded Londons of the world;
Till war, thus armed with elemental strength,
Dreadful becomes, and kills itself at length.
Nations from war, through terror, will refrain,
Nor monarchs dare to play the bloody game."

On this Abihud joyfully replies:
"Sure, then, Christ's kingdom will triumphant rise.
When liberty and science chain the Beast,
And war becomes so dreadful it has ceased,
Will not true Christian union then have birth,
And righteousness and peace spread o'er the earth?

Released from bloody wars and bloody Rome,
Christians will all unite, and be as one."

To whom the prophet: "These things but presage
The near conclusion of the gospel age.
For the great city then called Christendom
Will stand divided in three parts; ([17]) but none
Doomed long to stand. The one-third infidel,
(Made by the other two,) who mock at hell.
Shocked by the doctrines and the fires of Rome,
Their reasoning helped to shake the Papal throne:
Then Protestant divisions, strife and rage,
Increased their numbers on from age to age;
Clamorous for freedom and the unshackled mind,
They 'll push inquiries bold and unconfined;
They 'll probe God's works, and find, along that road,
God's works so wondrous, they will doubt of God;
Or bold deny the whole redemption-plan,
And that so great a God e'er spake to man.
"Another third, through wealth, will soon become
Such slaves to sin, they 're forced to fly to Rome.
Their long, luxurious feasts, and grand display,
Will give their passions an unbounded sway:
Their neighbors' beauteous wives each will admire,
And burn for them with love's unhallowed fire.
The tempting beauties, in soft luxury rolled,
Will catch the flame, and taste love uncontrolled!
Husbands, wrapped up, hasting to Room Eleven,
Will pass veiled wives late seen in Number Seven!
Murders ensue; and though five hundred slaves
From punishment the rich offender save,
Yet, midst the gospel having drawn their breath,
They dread those fires of hell which follow death;

Hence to the Church, which can absolve from sin,
Open heaven's gates, and bid them enter in—
In death's dark hour they to that Church will fly,
And buy with plundered gold a passport to the sky;
Hence will the papal power its wounds survive:
Its pardoning power will give it power to live!
"The other third—the great protesting third—
Will lose Christ's spirit, fighting o'er his word:
Divisions on divisions, widely spread,
Will strike the influence of the gospel dead: ([18])
Instead of the bright blaze of union's light,
Its thousand hissing sparks will end in night.
By separation they their saltness lose—
All power to save; and then the age will close.
The fulness of the Gentiles has come in—
All that the gospel could redeem from sin.
Two thousand years it will be amply tried—
Then, as an institution old, be laid aside.
Six thousand years from earth's creation-day,—
Three institutions having passed away,—
All mortal governments at once shall end:
The heavens will open, and the Lord descend.
Heaven's host in glory wide illumes his road
With the archangel's voice and trump of God:
Beneath his feet Mount Olivet divides,
And east and west a crystal river glides:
Down through Asphaltes (now Dead Sea no more)
The healing waters to the Red Sea pour.
"From the Euphrates, glittering on the east,
To Nile's long flood, its boundary on the west,
Shall Paradise, restored, be spread abroad,
As when it bloomed first from the hand of God.
Mountains shall sink, and the sunk vales arise
In undulating green, 'neath cloudless skies:

Translucent streams down each sloped mountain's side
Will flow in crystal currents, far and wide: (19)
Trees laden with commingled fruits and flowers,
With clustering vines and amaranthine bowers,
Shall widely spread o'er all this promised land,
As first it bloomed from God's creating hand.
Nor this land only: all the earth shall prove
Messiah's power and renovating love:
The primal curse his mandate takes away,
And all stands good as on creation's day.
The axis of the earth again will run
At angles with her orbit round the sun.
Hence equal days and nights throughout the year,
Will bless all parts of the revolving sphere;
Kill wintry frosts, cool summer heats, and bring
Round all the globe a mild, perpetual spring."

"O! glorious days!" the enraptured elder cries;
"A renovated earth and smiling skies!
But who'll enjoy them? Will the Lord again
Commit the earth to sinful, dying men?
Will not the resurrection then take place,
And earth be filled with an immortal race?"

"Yes," said the prophet; "as the Lord descends,
The trump of God the solid marble rends!
The dead in Christ shall then immortal rise—
The living, changed in a twinkle of the eyes,
Shall join with them; and all with joy prepare
To meet their Lord descending through the air,
And thus be ever with him, priests and kings,
And under him rule all terrestrial things.
His wondrous temple shall from God come down,
And with its glories New Jerusalem crown.

His lofty ensigns, from the walls unfurled,
Proclaim him God's Vicegerent o'er the world.
All nations own his power, and joyful bring
Rich gifts; and monarchs hail him, King of kings.
Then Israel's outcasts at his call shall come,
And willing nations bear his people home.
The promised land he 'll cause them to possess,
And they their God and righteous King shall bless.
High crowned on David's [20] throne, the Saviour then,
Instead of thorns, shall wear earth's diadem;
His resurrected saints will be sent forth,
Clothed with full power to judge and rule the earth.
All then shall know the Lord, and righteousness
Cover the earth, and the glad nations bless!
One thousand years his glorious reign shall last:
The other dead rise not till that is past.
Then judgment sits.
"But, brother, I have given
All that I know, or had in charge from Heaven.
O! highly favored of the Lord, return:
Bury your friend; but neither grieve nor mourn.
He saw the Saviour in his last distress,
Who pardoned him, and sent him up to bliss.
What I 've related of events to come,
Is only sent to you and yours alone,
The faithful inmates of your happy home.
Lead on the Church committed to your care,
And live, by faith, above all sin and fear;
That in death's hour you may, like dying Stephen,
See Jesus stand to take you up to heaven."

This said he, as a brilliant shooting star,
Or the great Tishbite in his fiery car,

Left earth and entered heaven, that clime of love,
And joined the songs of the redeemed above.
Abihud sought his home, though late the time,
Enfeebled by the colloquy sublime.

Now, when o'er Zed's sweet fields the sun arose,
And sent love's glances to each mountain rose,
Miriam and Hester, and Salathiel's son,
To morning prayers had, with Lysander, come:
Greetings of love had round the circle run,
When the maimed hero thus, with smiles, begun:

"Wife, mother, friends, blest be our sovereign Lord,
Who from my hand has struck the murderous sword.
My soul was bent on glory, wealth, and fame,
And bounding conqueror o'er the bloody plain;
My hopes were fixed on some great day to come,
When I should triumph through the streets of Rome.
Through thorny ways, and by afflictions deep,
Have I been brought to bow at Jesus' feet,
My power and station lost, my honor stained,
My body, in sore conflict, crushed and maimed.
For all I bless him, and now humbled come,
To join his people as a ransomed one.
Then, dear relations, built on Christ, the Rock,
Receive, and add me to his little flock.
He is a Saviour who can save indeed.
My soul not only is from bondage freed,
But, since I've owned him—blessed be his name—
Returning health seems glowing through my frame."

The circling friends, with sympathetic joy,
Sobbed with love's bliss—a bliss without alloy.
But more transported far above the rest,
His sister-wife hung weeping on his breast.

Abihud seized his hand, and cried: "My son,
Well have you lost the world, since Christ you 've won.
Paul, to win Christ, counted all things but dross,
Still glorying only in his Saviour's cross,
By which the world was crucified to him,
And he to it—Heaven's antidote for sin.
Let his example all our hearts inspire
With like submission, and devotion's fire,
And Christ be all the portion we desire."

And now went forth a solemn funeral-train,
Following the Temple's great defender, slain.
The mount's smooth flowery top at length is gained—
(Now by Abihud Mount of Vision named.)
Deep on the central point a grave was made,
And in earth's vault the strong, plain coffin laid.
No warrior's emblems, banners, shields, or spears,
But a red cross upon its lid appears.
The reverend elder slowly then arose;
His long white beard down to his girdle flows:
Solemn he stood, above the warrior's head;
First looked to heaven, then down upon the dead;
Then spake: "Great God! we own thy sentence just,
That man is dust, and shall return to dust.
Sin in our members warring while we 've breath,
Calls for the purifying pains of death.
The body dead, the spirit walks abroad,
Free from sin's chains, and lives again to God.
But thou, O Father, by thy Son hast said,
Death shall not hold dominion o'er the dead.
Friends, hear Christ's words while in this vale of strife:
'I am the resurrection and the life:
He that believes on me, though he were dead,
Shall rise and live with me, their living head;

And though entombed, as I, a while they lie,
Whoso believes on me shall never die.'
Believing this, as 'tis all mortals' doom,
We yield our brother to the silent tomb;
Assured of this, that he has gone above,
And sings, with Paul, his Saviour's dying love.
This, O my sister, daughter, brother, friends,
Heaven, to console us, by a vision sends.
He tarried, as Christ said, till Christ did come,
Saw Christ, was pardoned, and then taken home."

On this, loud shouts of joy and clapping hands
Spread o'er the mount through all the flowery lands.
Poor Miriam, with her ecstasy o'ercome,
And faint with joy, was carried to their home.

Then said Abihud: "Fills this honored grave
In death, a Christian always great and brave;
And know ye all, each brother and each friend,
In God's own time Christ will from heaven descend,
With the archangel's shout and trumpet's sound,
And wake the faithful sleeping under ground:
The dead in Christ all-glorious will arise,
With living saints to meet him in the skies.
Then will the proud, triumphant song begin,
'Where now, O conquering death, where is thy sting?
Where now thy victory, O boasting grave?
Even from the tomb our King has power to save!'
'All glory to the Lamb and God on high,'
Will sound on earth and warble round the sky!"
Then, looking up to heaven, with hands wide spread,
The pious elder slow and solemn said:
"Now to our God, invisible, unseen,
Who only is immortal and supreme,

The fount of life and wisdom, King of heaven,
To him and to his Christ be praises given
Through endless ages." (21)—And his full amen
Was loudly echoed round, Amen, amen.

Then to the town the concourse took their way,
Cheered with consoling hymns—nor sad, nor gay.
As governor, the good Abihud spread
Tables, with lambs and fowls, fruits, wine, and bread.
Each citizen was bidden as a guest,
To share with them the sad, sepulchral feast;
Many, of whom, upon the next Lord's day,
Confessed Christ's name, and washed their sins away.
A book of prayers and psalms was soon arranged,
And thus to Litany Leontes changed. (22)

Long did the Elder and Lysander reign
O'er favored Zillah and its lovely plain,
Still spreading happiness through all the glen,
Loved of their God, and loving all good men;
Still praising heaven for their Christian home,
But more for that eternal rest to come.

THE END.

NOTES.

BOOK I.

LINE 55.—The poet must have gone on tradition more than history, both as to the time and universality of the Decrees. But as an edict went forth before, "that all the world should be taxed," it is likely the decree for placing the emperor's statues in all the temples was equally comprehensive.—TRANS.

LINE 59, Notes 1, 2.—The poet and Josephus disagree as to the time when the golden eagle was affixed to the porch of the Temple. It is likely Ben-Asaph took some license, as is usual with poets in such cases.—EDITOR.

LINE 248, Note 3.—See Numb. xxv., where the history of the whole affair alluded to may be found. It may as well be noticed here, that Ben-Asaph must have been a close student of the Scriptures; as his allusions are so frequent, and almost literal in one place.

LINE 553, Note 4.—The expectation that Messiah would come and save them from the Romans, was common among the Jews, especially the Zealots; and the main cause of their obstinacy to the very last hour.

LINE 566, Note 5.—Or rather Capernaum, which was exalted to heaven, etc. See Matt. xi. 21–23.

LINE 590.—"The fiend then plucked his eyes: he saw no more." See 2 Kings xxv.

LINE 622, Note 6.—That the destruction of Jerusalem by the Romans was a judgment from God for the crucifixion of Christ, was a received opinion amongst the early Christians, and many of the Essenes; and that Christ, though invisible, was himself present wielding the Roman sword! Josephus says it was on account of the murder of James the Just. No doubt, one of his many mistakes. He should have said, JESUS the Just.—TRANS.

LINE 1093, Note 7.—This song of praise is a close imitation of many of David's Psalms; and his whole description of the feast shows that the poet was a Jew, and well acquainted with the Jewish ritual. Ben-Asaph's assertion, that Jerusalem is the oldest city known to history, is disputed by some in favor of Damascus. But that they both were famous cities in the days of Abraham, is certain.—See Gen. xv. 2; xiv. 18.

LINE 1128, Note 8.—"For all Moriah's Mount was hallowed ground." Solomon, at his great dedication sacrifice, finding the great brazen altar could not do all the service, hallowed or consecrated the whole hill. And indeed it would seem to be needed for his twenty thousand oxen, and hundred thousand sheep, etc. See 1 Kings viii. 63, 64.

LINE 1167, Note 9.—Some will think the poet was too sensuous in this place; but in those days men were not so fastidious as now. Deeds are now done by thousands who would rather die than name them. The deep depravity of the Jews at that time justified the poet. Herod, with his brother's wife, and no doubt rival daughter, dancing off John the Baptist's head, shows they were a people both sensual and devilish. See Mark vi.

BOOK II.

LINE 17.—"He said, and soon the deep-toned message flies," etc. Many poets have led their readers into heaven, and described the majesty of God, and the employment of the angels and glory of the place; but they all, in my opinion, (even Milton himself,) fall far short of the chastened and graphic sublimity of our poet on that subject.—ED.

LINE 73.—"O Branch! thou first-born of the primal seven," etc.—Here Ben-Asaph seems to give us a new theology as it relates to the powers of heaven. Instead of one "*Spirit of God*," he gives us seven—"The beginning of the Creation of God," and Christ the first of them. That the whole immensity of God's works are placed under their supervision, in separate vice-royalties; and that our globe, with many thousands of others, are under the government of Christ, or the BRANCH. This may be all true, and he has Rev. i. 4 to sustain him, in which they are mentioned, together with God, and as being before his throne, and no doubt were, according to his theory, the creators of all things within their several principalities. See also Zech. iv. 10.

The idea of "*the Spirit of God*," distinct from God *himself*, who is a Spirit, seems an absurdity in terms. Spirit of a spirit, is just as much a confusion of ideas, as body of a body. The Spirit of God, therefore, means only his *mind* or energy, seen or unseen. Hence, the creation of seven *spirits*, as his first act, to make and govern the universe under him, seems reasonable, and is inwoven in some form in man's faith, from the earliest ages down to the present day. Many gods, demi-gods, and sons of gods, formed the heathen mythology.

Jove took charge of the whole world—the lesser gods of particular nations, and the demi-gods of households and individuals. But when the Jews, Christians, and Moslems expelled Paganism, they substituted in their place angels, tutelary saints, and guardian angels: this as a consequence of the idea that God did every thing—even the locating of each flying particle of dust. Hence he must have a graduated scale of ministering spirits to attend to small matters, or they saw they would destroy their one lone God by attenuation, making him so extensively everywhere, that he could not be personally anywhere. Ben-Asaph's idea, then, of the Seven Spirits of God, is fully as good as any that preceded or has succeeded him.—ED.

LINE 101.—"Now, the first lesson wisdom could impart." Here the poet, I think, has given us juster views of God's dealings with mankind, than all the doctors of divinity from Paul to this day. The first lesson was, to teach them that they were brought into existence by a superior being, or God. The second, that God was a Spirit, invisible to mortal eyes, and that there was only one. The third, that man also was gifted with a spiritual nature, which, by being trained to pure morality, would be endowed by his Maker with eternal life.—ED.

LINE 440.—"An order to the conquering cohorts came," etc. Josephus says there was no reason for this strange retreat of Cestius: see Book ii., ch. 19, of his Jewish Wars: a very unlikely tale indeed! but like his accounts in many other places. Ben-Asaph's account of the transaction was no doubt from tradition, and far more correct. A Roman general to leave a city almost taken, without any cause, cannot be believed by any reasonable man. But if an army was marching to attack him in the rear, his retreat was, perhaps, the best thing he could do. Ben-Asaph certainly had read Josephus; but it is certain, also, that he relied very little on him; depending rather on myths and tradition than on history for many of his facts; and at times taking great license as it relates to times and places, as every poet has a right to do.—ED.

LINE 589.—"Bile-stirred," etc. The poet here alludes to a physical fact, that unusual heat acts on the biliary glands in such a way, as to make combatants more furious, and regardless of life.—ED.

LINE 845.—"God's wrath," etc. See Joshua x. 11.

LINE 862.—"Even those unwounded," etc. For the distress of the Romans on this occasion, see Josephus, Jewish Wars, Book 2, Chap. 19.—ED.

LINE 1155.—"All chance," etc. We may as well remark here, that Josephus makes no mention of such a chief as Salathiel. Ben-Asaph, therefore, must have gone on tradition, or some history of the siege that is lost; and the Rev. Mr. Croly must have done the same in his romance; for it is not probable that the novelist ever saw the Moriad. But that some Jew was doomed by the Saviour to remain in some situation till he came again, seems a myth, or tradition, from the earliest times of Christianity. *The Wandering Jew*, of Eugene Sue, Croly's *Salathiel*, and Ben-Asaph's *Moriad*, not to mention many other legends, are full proofs of this. But they all differ as to particulars. Ben-Asaph makes the second coming of Christ to be at the destruction of Jerusalem; Croly at the end of the world; and Sue in the eighteenth century. I will only add, that Dr. Thomas, and most theologians, agree with Ben-Asaph, that his coming was invisible.—ED.

BOOK III.

LINE 255.—"Thus spoke the King of kings," etc. The teachings of Christ in the first, and of God the Father in the third heavens, as to vindictive punishment, are quite new, and, as I think, perfectly correct. Our poet's theology is better than his poetry; at least under the disadvantages of my translation.—TRANS.

LINE 304.—"But now thou givest them blood," etc. See Rev. xvi. 5, 6. I will once for all here remark, how close our poet quotes the Scriptures he alludes to. His verse is almost a commentary.—ED.

LINE 334.—"'Twas Cannæ and Carræ," etc. The two bloodiest defeats the Romans had ever sustained.—ED.

LINE 384.—"The demagogues," etc. Read Paris instead of Nineveh, and the poet's illustration is a good picture of the Reign of Terror in France, at the Revolution.—ED.

LINE 539.—"When Pilate asked, Art thou King of the Jews," etc. The circumstances and wonders attending the crucifixion are very graphically described in this place by our poet, and in close accordance with the Evangelists.—TRANS.

LINE 642.—"Believing, were baptized," etc. See Acts ii. 38, 41.—ED.

LINE 719.—"And there lay dead," etc. See Luke vii. 12.—ED.

LINE 819.—"As when the vital powers," etc. The cause of ague and fever, physicians say, is a vitiated state of the bile, which causes a flow of blood from the extremities to the centre, leaving the limbs cold and shaking, which is the ague stage; but after the blood has accumulated round the heart, it is compelled to reflux, and rush to the extremities; and then comes on the fever hour, or hot stage of the disease.—ED.

LINE 1026.—"Haste, bring the brands," etc. Ben-Asaph, in his account of the burning of the Romans' Bank, and the fury of the Jews on that occasion, is sustained by Josephus. See Jewish Wars, Book v. Chap. 11.—ED.

BOOK IV.

LINE 28, Note 1.—"And at my prayer," etc. See 1 Kings xviii. 38. We may observe here, once for all, that our poet uses no magic-machinery, like

Tasso, or improbable ones, like Milton; but confines himself strictly to such miraculous interference as the Scripture allows, and is rendered probable by the Gospel history; such as being possessed by devils, the ghosts of dead men, and Christ wielding the powers of nature and the minds of mortals, as he did on earth before his ascension, when it was his will to do so.—TRANS.

LINE 215, Note 2.—"This fiendish den," etc. Here Josephus and Ben-Asaph agree in substance again. But that a wall could be built round Jerusalem high enough to imprison it, in three days, is a mighty fable for a historian, though well enough for a poet.—ED.

LINE 246, Note 3.—See Note 1, Book IV.

LINE 269, Note 4.—"Fear not the," etc. Here Ben-Asaph makes the possessed Zealot imitate the hyperbolical language of the Scripture prophets, while those of the milder kind are made to speak a very common hope and expectation of the Jewish nation at that time.—ED.

LINE 598, Note 10.—Salathiel seems to be a fatalist, as all the Pharisees were; and, in addition, that he could not die till he saw the Nazarene again.—ED.

LINE 666, Note 11.—It will appear in another part of the poem, that Lysander was on his way to join Titus, when he met a band of robbers carrying off Hester from the Tiberias springs, and falling in love with her, became a traitor, as Titus thought, to him and the Roman cause.—TRANS.

LINE 691, Note 11.—This is a very just epitome of the theology of the enlightened heathen. See Note 6, Book I.—ED.

LINE 727, Note 13.—The parting of Salathiel and Lysander from their wives I think very fine, and I have done my best to preserve the spirit of the original.—TRANS.

LINE 745, Note 14.—Josephus speaks of this wholesale crucifixion, but not exactly as the poet has done. He no doubt went much on tradition in this place, as in many others.—ED.

LINE 884, Note 15.—This the poet, it is likely, took from the narrow escape of Titus, mentioned by Josephus, in his Jewish Wars, Book 5, Chap. 2, and changed it, as Croly has done, to suit his purpose.—ED.

LINE 930, Note 16.—Croly mentions this circumstance in his romance, from some myth or tradition, the same, no doubt, that our poet relied on in this work.—ED.

LINE 973, Note 17.—The idea of a starving population shouting for a great victory is well expressed here.—ED.

BOOK V.

LINE 25 —See Levit. xxi. 26.

LINE 40.—See Matt. xxiv. 26, 27.

LINE 102.—Ben-Asaph and Josephus substantially agree as to the fact of a mother, who, through the stings of starvation, roasted her own child, ate part, and brought the residue out for a band of Zealots who had found it out by its odor, and threatened her with death if she did not bring that nice baked meat to them. See Josephus, Chap. 3, Book 6.—ED.

LINE 202.—Excepting as to the dates, the poet and Josephus harmonize very well as to this prophet, or insane man. See his Jewish Wars, Book 6, Chap. 5.—ED.

LINE 296.—Even from Josephus's own accounts, he figures but poorly as a General in his Galilee campaign; and no doubt all the war party thought him a traitor, for which his great favor with the Romans gave much color. See Jewish Wars, Book 3, Chap. 8.

LINE 325.—See Jewish Wars, Book 4, Chap. 2.—TRANS.

LINE 334.—See Exod xiv., the whole.—ED.

LINE 517.—In this episode our poet, no doubt, has gone on myths and tradition, though in substance he is supported by Josephus. (See his Jewish Antiquities, Book 18, Chap. 3.) Ben-Asaph has only changed time, place, and names, the better to suit his work, and for which he may plead a poet's license. Indeed, as to the *locus in quo*, there is no doubt he is the most correct of the two. For in the first place, the superstition that the gods sought commerce with women, and that women ought to yield to them, was not known at Rome; but common at Baalbec, and through all Syria and Phœnicia, especially, the Syrian damsels were devoted worshippers of Thamiz, (Adonis,) and candidates for his favor. This caused Milton to sing thus:

"Thamiz (Adonis) came next behind,
Whose annual wound in Lebanon allured
The Syrian damsels to lament his fate
In amorous ditties!"—[PAR. LOST, Book i., ver. 557, and onward.

Again, 2dly, Adonis (sometimes called Thamiz) was supremely beautiful: hence the proclivity of the Syrian beauties for his love; but Anubus, Josephus' god, to whom he makes the beautiful and chaste Paulina yield her charms, was one of the monster gods of Egypt, and is represented under the figure of a dog.

And in the last place, Josephus only writes from hearsay himself, in all which cases Ben-Asaph must be of vastly higher authority. Indeed, we should often take the advice said Rabbi gives his readers, when he states some things he can scarcely believe himself, not to rely on him, "but let every man think as he pleases on the matter, for I have only written as it was told me, or found in old writings." Hence, whenever our poet and the Jewish rabbi differ, we may expect the former comes nearest the truth; but where they agree, we may say, the fact is probable; which is enough for poetry.

LINE 565.—The Chian wine, from the Isle of Chios, in the Ægean Sea, was the most sprightly and delicious of all their wines, the champagne of the ancients. It does not rank so high now.—TRANS.

LINE 637.—Those cities were extremely licentious in those days; but perhaps not much more so than London, Paris, and New York are now.

LINE 714.—Prusias, one of the kings of Bithynia, made an inland sea, by throwing a dam across a river to take his aquatic sport in; but the dam gave way, and drowned an extensive district of country; on which the Roman Senate condemned him to pay the entire damage to the sufferers.

LINE 964.—See Ezekiel xxix., the whole of it.—ED.

LINE 1026.—The opal is said to give its light from the centre, and not from the surface.—ED.

BOOK VI.

LINE 11.—All authors, from Josephus down to Lieutenant Lynch, confirm the poet's description of the Dead Sea, that its water is extremely salt, heavy, sluggish, and contains no living thing.—ED.

LINE 46.—See Christ's prediction, Matt. xxiv. 2.—ED.

LINE 124.—This description of the upper Jordan agrees with Josephus, and all late writers on the subject.—ED.

LINE 147.—This is a disputed point; but geography seems to be with this poet; for the same range of mountains that encloses the basin of the Jordan, from Lake Tiberias to the Dead Sea, continues from its south end, on each side of the Ghor, down to the head of the Gulf of Elath, and at about the same distance from each other. This Ghor, or basin, is but little above the level of the Dead Sea, and it seems as if the river ran there as its natural outlet. Indeed, if we credit Moses, we cannot conclude otherwise; for he speaks of the plain as a fine country, "even as the garden of the Lord;" containing five cities, each a kingdom, and given to war. Now there is no other place on the Jordan where such a rich plain can be found. Of course it must now be the bed of the Dead Sea, if the account given by Moses be true. And supposing the substratum of that great plain to have been coal, sulphur, asphaltum, and other inflammable matter, and God ignited it by lightning, or other means, it would naturally sink down, and form the awful gulf in which the Dead Sea lies; a gulf extensive enough to hold all the waters of Palestine till they would evaporate; and thus the Scripture account of the destruction of the cities of the plain remains unimpugned.—Trans.

Line 208.—See Gen. xix., throughout.—Ed.

Line 280.—The fulfilment of Christ's prophecies while on earth, seems to be the main design of Providence in the destruction of Jerusalem, in order to give proof of his mission.—Ed.

Line 325.—That a maniac, or prophet, made this boding and continuous denunciation through and round the walls of Jerusalem for a long time before its destruction, is stated as a historical fact by Josephus. See his Jewish Wars.

Line 525.—So Josephus says. See Jewish Wars, Book 6, Chap. 4.—Ed.

Line 778.—The poet seems here to allude to Christ's enumeration of the signs that should attend the destruction of Jerusalem: "The seas and the waves roaring!" See Lev. xxi. 25.—Ed.

Line 795.—For this, see Josephus's Jewish Wars, Book 6, Chap. 5.

Line 840.—See Luke xvi. 6.—Ed.

Line 993.—The zigzag course of lightning, it is said, is produced by its velocity, so impinging on the air as to force it to glance aside.—Ed.

BOOK VII.

Line 6.—That Shem and Melchisedek are the same, is the opinion of many at this day; and it is possible; for Shem certainly lived till the days of Abraham.

Line 58.—"The famed Spartan." Leonidas, the hero of Thermopylæ.

Line 70.—One cannot but pity the Zealots, bloody as they were, for they fought for their temple, laws, and liberty, and believed to the very last that God would save them from the Romans. They differed from the deistical Jacobins in this—that they were really religious.

Line 84.—Josephus says this porch was on the west side of the temple.—Ed.

Line 167.—This possession of Ignatius and Nausica for the purpose of burning another temple by the demons or ghosts of Erostratus and Thais, is very fanciful. Josephus makes a Roman soldier do it.

Line 180.—Josephus says that Titus strove to save the Temple from pious motives; but Ben-Asaph, from a desire to seize its riches. The latter is, no doubt, correct in this.

Line 220.—The poet here (indeed, through the whole poem) assigns to Christ no greater power than what he exercised while as the *Son of Man* on earth.—Ed.

Line 251.—Paul saw Christ, and was forgiven. See Acts ix., the whole.

Line 307.—So says Josephus; but how any could be there after the dreadful slaughter made by the Romans, seems strange.—Ed.

Line 323.—This is a beautiful comparison.—Ed.

LINE 462.—Ben-Asaph seems, though generally an impartial poet, to have had a contemptuous opinion of Josephus.—ED.

LINE 592.—"Spring forth his coil, and then the work was done," etc. It would seem from this, that the *lasso* was not unknown to the Tartars. One thing is certain—they catch abundance of wild horses; and it is likely the South American lasso came from them.

LINE 662.—"Which opens on Gehenna," etc. The vale of Hinnom, on the south side of Jerusalem, where they burnt the impurities, dead carcasses, and offal of that city.

LINE 821.—"O conquering Cæsar!" etc. The pleadings of Miriam and Hester for their dead and wounded husbands are very fine, and more pathetic than any thing of the kind I have ever read, and place Titus, in the result, in a most glorious point of view; not only as a great conqueror, but as a good man, and real moral hero.—TRANS.

BOOK VIII.

LINE 24.—"That Zion should be ploughed," etc. This and the foregoing sale of the captives is very graphic, and suits our times and country.—ED.

LINE 87.—"Fed by pure rills," etc. The valley of Cœlo-Syria, through which Leontes (now Litany) runs, is one of unsurpassed beauty, and is not exaggerated by the poet.—TRANS.

LINE 231.—"When lo! they opened," etc. This, on the whole, I take to be a grander vision than any that has ever graced an epic poem, ancient or modern. Homer, Virgil, and Milton, are, I think, clearly outdone by Ben-Asaph in this respect.—ED.

LINE 270.—"And crowds," etc. This is literally a fact: the blood of the martyrs was the seed of the Church.

LINE 290.—By such clamors the pagan priests raised the persecutions against the Christians. Every calamity was imputed to them.—ED.

LINE 316.—This vision of Constantine's, and his subsequent victory, were the cause of his conversion to Christianity.—ED.

LINE 365.—The Emperors sided sometimes with the one, and then again with the other, of the wrangling Bishops, as they successively came to the throne.

LINE 390.—Such was the way the Pope treated that mean wretch, who butchered his Bohemian subjects to please him. See Church History.—ED.

LINE 432.—Not The Great, but a Reformer.—ED.

LINE 504.—Here the poet seems to intimate, that the most wicked feel the stings of conscience when engaged in their acts of cruelty. As for the scenes in the Inquisitors' Court, and the subsequent *auto da fe*, the reader is referred to general history on that subject.—ED.

LINE 518.—Many, in all ages, have been made Deists by the monstrous doctrines and cruelty of the Romish Church.—ED.

LINE 546.—It is remarkable that all the three great religions that hold the unity of God, are said to have been revealed from heaven in the land of Arabia, and at no great distance from the same spot where Abraham and Moses talked with God.—ED.

LINE 559.—For the rapid success of the Mohammedans, and their great conquests, see general history.—ED.

LINE 582.—Charles Martel, of France, fought the immense army of the Moslems three consecutive days, and gave them a signal defeat. Three hundred thousand, it is said, lay dead on the field. This saved the west of Europe from being overrun by the Saracens; while John Sobieski saved it on the east with his brave Poles, whose children are now enslaved by the nations they saved.—Ed.

Line 597.—It is said that the art of printing was first conceived by a lame soldier, and gunpowder by a monk. This may be true, or it may not.—Ed.

Line 635.—Refugees from political and religious persecution were the first settlers of the United States.—Ed.

Line 644.—There is no doubt the total severance of Church and State was the work of the deistical part of the Convention which framed our Constitution.—Ed.

Line 670.—"The woman," etc. The Christians who fled to the wilderness of America from Popish and Protestant persecution, were helped by deistical philosophers, such as Jefferson, men of this world. See Revelation xii., the whole.—Ed.

Line 732.—This is a fine description of Telegraphic power.—Ed.

Line 774.—This is a new idea. Instead of Rome papal, the poet makes Christendom the great city which is divided into three parts, to wit: Papists, Deists, and wrangling Protestants. See Rev. xvi. 19.—Ed.

Line 826.—A good description of Eden, which some say extended from Euphrates to the Nile.

Line 875.—That Christ shall descend and renovate the earth, and reign a thousand years, seems a Bible doctrine, and is expressly taught in many places. See Dr. John Thomas's Works, especially his Elpis Israel.—Ed.

Line 997.—This is a close paraphrase of Paul's Doxology.—See Romans xvi. 27.—Ed.

Line 1008.—That the stream that comes down through Cœlo-Syria, now called Litany, was formerly known as Leontes, is a fact, and it probably was changed, as Ben-Asaph says.—Trans.

ADVICE TO READERS.

Some of you may think the Moriad is not as old as the third century, and that it was not written by Ben-Asaph, because the original MS. is not produced. Now Homer's copy of the Iliad cannot be produced. Why then call for that of the Moriad, when you are told it is locked up in the bureau of a Turkish antiquary? But however this may be, I advise you all to read it as of that date, and as written by Ben-Asaph, or you will not do justice to the poem or yourselves. A poet or novelist, you know, has as much right to fix time, and place, and names, as any other incident in his work. But the merit of the Moriad, I should think, will convince most people it cannot be of modern growth.—Editor.

www.ingramcontent.com/pod-product-compliance
Lightning Source LLC
LaVergne TN
LVHW010222110826
845151LV00004B/1174
9781425526849